2020: THE ALCHEMISTS' AWAKENING

VOLUME ONE
JANUARY – JUNE 2020

JOSEPHINE SORCIERE

First published in Australia 2021

Ancient Future Publishing
Adelaide
South Australia
www.josephinesorciere.com

Paperback ISBN: 978-0-6451847-0-9
Hardback ISBN: 978-0-6451847-2-3

Printing process and paper contribute to
a sustainable environment

For Charlie and Harry,
my greatest creations of this lifetime.

For Anne, our Souls have met once again,
with The Work to do.

For all the Souls who hear my Tone of Truth,
I await your brilliance.

CONTENTS

URL REFERENCE LINKS

The Url links for the references made throughout this book which are shown as underlined may be found at https://josephinesorciere.com/taa-url/ or by scanning this QR code with your smart phone

PREFACE

The Age of the Golden Dawn 2.0 has arrived. For many, the New Age of Aquarius has been marked on the calendar since 2012. When in fact, it arrives in 2021.

Everything has been flipped. Polarity is reversing throughout the Universe. Including you. Your Alter Ego becomes the real you. There are no more heroines to be rescued, only heroes to be created.

Time and space have collapsed. We have crossed the threshold into the quantum realm, where there is no normal and nothing, yet everything, exists in this very moment. Accessible through your own virtual world.

A new playground across time, space, dimensions and realities, the dominions which have been my world for lifetimes. For when you master this, which can only follow having mastered yourself, your vehicle becomes Portalism. The ability to reclaim your prodigy through the portals of time. A continuous path of re-creation in every moment, change is what fuels you, the source of your aliveness. Return to your true nature.

For those who like 'normal', don't like change, love routine, stick to the same job or profession for years, this will indeed be a rocky road.

This memoir of insight is so not for them. It is for the few who are ravenous for the new. For what cutting edge consciousness really means. It can only be received at its fullest capacity by those Souls who have lived many, many lifetimes and know it is time, once again for a great Awakening.

The texts may not all land at a mental level, yet I know you will receive the essence of the energetics that come through from the page, embedded into the heart of the message. Trust your resonance, knowing when the time is right, all will be revealed in your own consciousness.

Humanity was ripped from its Truth three times before. The last time was at The Fall, 250,000 years ago. We have only glimpsed the tips of the icebergs of transformation since then. Each time we reach the water to dive deep into the truth of who we really are, the human powers-that-be rip us from the shoreline, for "our own safety", and drag us kicking and screaming back up the comforts of tribal consciousness. This time, The Fourth Awakening, we may just have woken up enough to tip the scales. The Alchemists have heard the alarm bells ringing and are ready to answer the call of their own Soul. This book provides the philosophies and awareness to be embodied, owned and authentically lived.

Chances are, you have never understood, let alone belonged to the human collective. For the spirit of who you are lies scattered across the multi-verses, which the mere mortals know nothing about.

You do though, and you know it is time to invite in your distant relatives to come and assist before humanity finally annihilates itself. It is such a humble privilege to be alive right now, you KNOW you have a deep calling to bring forward your innate wisdom, and once again, open the channels of communication and energy from beyond.

This is not a light and fluffy woo-woo book. It documents the events and decoding from January to December 2020. It winds together the aspects of my own life and work, what unfolds in the world, the astrology of the planetary influences, and what is changing in consciousness and frequencies.

The early months set the scene, get to know me. As the story rolls out, they become more entwined, merged, showing once again, everything is inextricably linked and woven by the very essence of the Universe, and beyond.

It will be written in two volumes as we journey through to establishment of foundations at the end of 2020. It will only be published when the Collective Consciousness has awoken sufficiently to be received at the depth in which it was written.

The new Human is being birthed at the end of 2020, and we will witness his journey through the first few months as joyous parents would hold their precious infant in their arms.

I may be guided to write throughout the next decade as the new cosmic consciousness finds its feet and takes flight in the world. Who knows? Well, the Ancient Ones do. For it was coded thousands of years ago, and the energetic engravings lay buried, hidden in the heart of life itself.

My role in this becomes clearer to me on a daily basis and will continue to evolve. It never ceases to astound me. I am utterly committed to my Soul Purpose, as a Key Keeper & Scribe of the Akashics, and as a Master Code Holder, Decipher and Encoder. Little did I know 17 years ago, when starting on my journey of awakening and self-discovery, the exhilarating path I would explore.

This morning (13 May 2020) I was told by Thoth I was a Cosmic Scribe, so I follow the guidance as always, and take to the keyboard. As a compulsive note taker, I have filled 5 journals this year with wisdom, learning and insights, channeled guidance and the journaling of my own story.

The Alchemists' Awakening serves to document the magical speed in which life can turn on its head, in an instant. Having been playing in the quantum for 6 years now, I have witnessed so many times in my clients the exponential shift which can occur when you leave the realms of time and space.

Now it is your turn to get a taste of what is coming, to be radically challenged with what you thought was possible. Yet it may just ignite an inner knowing and open the path for you to explore your role in all of this.

For you have been waiting to hear the call. Now you have. I called you. I am gathering the Souls who are running towards that shoreline, ready to dive in, with little idea of how to swim deep into the ocean of The Truth. The risk takers, the ones ready to dismantle all aspects of their human paradigm, to strip off the masks and learn to breathe underwater.

May you enjoy witnessing the journey as much as I am thrilled to be co-creating it. feel free to dip in and out as you feel called to. Skip the parts which may not resonate. To dive deep into higher consciousness teachings, find the chapters marked with an asterisk*.

Josephine Sorciere

NOTES ON ASTROLOGY CHAPTERS

All astrology notes were written up after the month had passed up until June 2020, when they were written in advance. All context is what was known at that time, apart from statements in italics, clearly defined as hindsight, where I added in additional references. Dates may vary by a day depending on your location in the world.

Whilst the astrology for the month is included towards the end of each month section, you may choose to read it earlier to get a feel for the landscape ahead. It is always fascinating to review in advance AND in hindsight to see how the charts played out.

I am not an astrologer or astronomer, at least not in this lifetime, and yet have religiously followed my own charts for 17 years. They absolutely provide the road map of planetary support or otherwise. It is a perfect source of synchronicities as the cycles of life play out time and time again.

I have only included a summary in mainly brief note form of the astrology for the month. So much more depth is available to those who seek it.

All astrological notes are taken from a combination of YouTube videos and subscriptions I have to various astrologers. The key sources are Anne McNaughton of Forecasters in NZ and Leo Knighton Tallarico – posts on Perspectives From The Sky.

JANUARY 2020

CHAPTER 1

KALI ARRIVES

The year had started off on such a high. I had just taken 48 women through a free online Challenge, "Claim Your Ultimate Desire", which finished on 31 December 2019. They were ALIVE again, energies of enthusiasm, clarity and power pulsing through their core.

I am utterly fulfilled when I witness profound transformation and reclaiming of who you are within another. It is what I do, what I am here for. I also have known for three years my work is far larger than working 1-1 personal upgrades. It is to fundamentally change the face of the planet, by encoding the Legacy Leaders and Change Agents to implement and facilitate a radical overhaul of the world as we know it.

This book, when it calls to you with its tone of truth and resonance of freedom, is the reminder of why you are here, right now, on the precipice of change. It was a deliberate choice before you came into this lifetime, to remember the depths of your abilities and unleash them into the 21st Century.

You are here to play full out in the game of life, it bores you completely to remain sitting on the sidelines, pretending to fit into "normal society" or even belong. It feels like a slow death to keep searching for what you are looking for amongst the regurgitated teachings, hoping to find a glimpse of the answers. The truth lies within you, the ultimate paradox of life itself.

2020 evoked a fundamental turning point for humanity – who will remain subject to their slave-self and who will claim their freedom from human conditioning once and for all. Mother Nature was getting tired of waiting and something radical had to occur.

I knew things were underway when the Goddess Kali swept in to tip the table of society over with greatest upheaval she could muster.

Not just in a quiet corner of some forgotten third world country where the western world could handily tuck out of the line of vision, not my problem.

No, Kali wanted the whole world to wake up this time.

"Enough is enough. You have slept in far too long this time. Get up, get out and start being responsible in your life!", like any stern mother would do, when she has had enough of gentle hints and persuasion, which hadn't worked.

It had been a year since I had published my first Kali Activation, the powerful encoded wisdom and energy transmissions, very loosely published (on podcasts and Insight Timer app) under the categories of 'meditation'. Though mine are far from the ideal tool to calm your mind..... I knew first-hand the personal destruction Kali could cause. Her and I were on first name terms after the devastation I experienced in my life over the years. A story for another day.

Many women discovered my work through these audio publications and knew how profoundly potent they were. Different to all other touchy feely, "let's make ourselves feel better", type of meditations. Which, frankly, make the unawakened run a mile and the dripping platitudes on offer by the spiritual crowd. No wonder they don't want a bar of it.

Whilst they recognised where Kali had come ploughing into their own world, many were taken aback with horror, she may deem to enter the world stage, in the guise of The Corona Virus.

The Crown. Chronos. Time. The virus to take down time. The Chrone Code. Wisdom will take down knowledge.

Back in January, the world was still firmly slumbering under the covers. Some were listening to the morning news, but it only affected China. Not to worry. Back to sleep. Let me have 10 minutes more....

It was the start of the Winter of Discontent. A time when seeds were planted in the dark womb of the earth, ready to come alive in Spring.

CHAPTER 2

BURNING TO THE GROUND

January is an interesting time here in Australia, made even more extreme with the devastating bush fires this year. "Black Summer", which started in June 2019, ravaged 46 million acres, killed 34 people and one billion animals died. More may be driven to extinction. 306m tonnes of carbon dioxide polluted the skies, even reaching Chile and Argentina.

It was like Mother Nature was burning everything down. She had had enough of humans raping and pillaging the land and sea with mining. The ancient energies of Uluru had been stirred awake and started ripping communities and forestland from the surface.

"You WILL listen to me!" she screams. "Nature has an essential role which will not be overtaken by man's greed". And so, society could do little but watch on, as temperatures soared in more ways than one.

In Australia's indigenous culture, Aboriginals have a very close relationship to the Earth as the Custodians of the land. Fire burning has been part of the maintenance for eons and is used to heal the land. After the fires, it was recognised that cultural fire regimes needed to be implemented across a wider expanse of land ownership.

"There's a huge interest in how Aboriginal people do fire burns and why", said the Local Land Service.

"Ah", I thought. "People are starting to return to the wisdom of the Ancient Ones. About time". So much knowledge of the land held by the Indigenous has been desecrated over the centuries by western culture.

What will it take for people to recognise how much more powerful nature is than man, and wisdom is more powerful than knowledge? It would take something like a pandemic to remind us. And so, it has.

* * *

Back at home, I was juggling school holidays with the days I was running Initiations for those who knew they had to work further with me, and finally understand the truth of why they are so stuck in their worlds.

Running parallel lives comes naturally to me. It is actually who I am. At a Soul level. I channel cutting edge consciousness one minute, and doing the school run the next. I operate under two names, Josephine Sorciere – my alter ego who is the true me, and my private name, which is, well, private.

For many, they leave their work life behind at the office, don the mask of parent or wife in the car on the way home, and arrive fully dressed as their other persona. They get changed into the various masks they keep in separate compartments of their lives.

It keeps them occupied rather than facing their true self, whose power and presence terrifies them. Who would they be if they did not conform and fit into society? What would they do if not living vicariously through the lives of their children?

They shudder with that thought almost as violently as I do when I think what I would do if I had to return to that life, one I had twenty years ago. Just. Not. Happening. Ever.

I adore the work I do. Well, I can hardly call it work when it is all merged because I live it. No matter what name I go by, or who I am with, my authenticity does not change. Like a sadistic mother who loves ripping off a bandage of their child's wound, I am fired up when I strip my clients of the illusions they carry so heavily around their bodies. So, they too, can have a glimpse of their own authenticity.

For some it is petrifying to see into themselves and the potency they hold. When I decode and reprogram the very core of their being to strip away what they have clung to so dearly for centuries, their vulnerability will be felt one of two ways.

They are left exposed, naked, raw and bewildered at what they are experiencing without their stories and masks. They quickly gather their clothes of victim and child stories, and run a mile, their minds trying to analyse and figure out what just happened.

Or others feel the breeze and joy of liberation, literally pulsing through their veins, as they realise the relief they have from not carrying that energetic baggage anymore. These are the ones asking where the shoreline is, so they can dive in deeper to retrieve their own truth, from the depths of their Soul.

They do not know how to navigate the treacherous waters of their minds or avoid the rocks of their wounds. Yet they know I will teach them to become Olympian swimmers in their own ocean, provided they commit to the training regime, often grueling and always liberating.

A few commit to going deeper, for they know it is time. Not only in their own life, also for a far deeper reason that was lying in wait just around the corner. For the whole world was about to be drawn into question and be faced with themselves.

Up until now, I had mainly worked with women who were ready to awaken and claim their own power and freedom. For it appeared to me they were more anxious to find themselves, ready and willing to do the work.

However, I was finding I was having more and more men who were curious about what it meant to be an empowered masculine and fascinated by my languaging and nature of who I am. For the last few months, I was meeting men who were open to stepping up and had the potential to.

Yet, as is often the case, the idea of committing to doing the work and being fully responsible for their life had them running. So many love the idea of being fixed, yet so few are willing and able to be responsible to undertake what is required. Men are fearful of being unmasked in front of a commanding woman. They often see vulnerability as a weakness, rather than the influential force it can be to upturn the current paradigms.

To reflect once again the nature of my businesses which I had run over 16 years, I trusted my instinct and went ahead of the game. Offering services that few others were. I have always been ahead of my time.... I now added the King's Initiation to my palette of offerings, ready for the men who ARE craving to claim their own authenticity. I can feel their collective curiosity that there is more to their current existence.

It is time more women offered transformation wisdom to men with recognition of how men work, and not the therapy room bedside chats which is the domain of the feminine. Coaching (urgh, that word…) is so often based on one solution fits all, certainly the path of awakening offered by the new age spiritual circles often requires the notion of the collective, and that we are all one.

This is a false myth, one I am on a path to shatter, as we need to wake up to the fact we are all from Source energy, yet FAR from being one and the same. Polarity within an individual and within relationships is essential. How women solve a problem is entirely different to the masculine approach, yet this is often overlooked in the psychotherapist's consulting room.

It matters not how far someone works with me to feel the effects on their own energy shift. For the magic lies in the unseen and held in the essence of the energetic frequencies in and all around us. When you are open to the change, the uplift in all aspects of you can be felt throughout your body and mind.

As I open the door for all individuals who come into my world, my coven, I also open the portals. These are the gateways for the energies to safely transcend within them for their highest good, to the level of capacity they are capable of holding in this moment.

For when people FEEL the energetic shifts, they begin to understand the intrinsic nature of energy itself. This is the very essence of consciousness – how far are we awake to be consciously aware of energy, to move it to higher and higher frequencies. This fundamental understanding is imperative as we transverse the realms of cosmic consciousness, or people will be left so perplexed and bewildered about where their old world went. Disappearing, more or less, overnight.

These are the new realms we are now playing in, the quantum realms. In January, the old world was taking its final dying breaths of pollution, and so were the people. In more ways than one.

It was time to bring the world back in alignment, and that starts with every individual. The new rising consciousness was calling for harmony and balance, the field had become so distorted, and off kilter. We required an injection of something so radically upending to expose just how precarious humanity is. The Force of Nature is the only energy mighty enough to sound the alarm bell louder and more viciously than ever before.

By the end of January 2020, Coronavirus had taken 213 lives, with 9776 infected cases. WHO declared the outbreak as a public health emergency of international concern.

Even so, many of the European countries and the US still regarded it as outside the scope of a problem they needed to be concerned about. It was the time of the year for the flu, how was this different?

CHAPTER 3

IT MUST BE WATCHED INTO EXISTENCE

The world as we knew it was dying, yet we did not know it yet. In hindsight, of course, it all makes sense. Which is the very nature of the quantum – the only thing that is predictable is its unpredictableness. It can only be analysed in hindsight, after the event, to be able to join the dots.

Quantum energy changes depending on whether it is being observed or not. We can see afterwards what happened. Yet before or around an event, an unfolding, all we can observe are the synchronicities that appear before us. Defined in the dictionary as "the simultaneous occurrence of events which appear significantly related but have no discernible causal connection" these are our reminders of not only how linked everything is even though we do not "see" it, as well as indicators of alignment.

For the process of observing the synchronicities allows us to decode the significance, placing it into reality, having observed it. It's like noticing the signposts, and marking them as such, to outline the path. Making them 'real', creating them in this reality, anchoring them.

Understanding these principles of how the quantum works and synchronicities becomes crucial as the story unfolds and the timelines start to break down. We will run on dual operating systems for a while, as any good tech team will tell you is essential when systems are being upgraded. Yet if we can start to understand the mechanics of the new system early on, it will save a lot of scrambling for the user manual when we do switch over, which of course, doesn't exist. Nothing Does.

Just like the quantum, this book may appear to jump all over the place, across timelines, and link seemingly unassociated events. Yet this is the very essence of how the new energies work. Chaotically, unpredictably, in flow, where we just surrender to what unfolds and look on with amazement how it all flows together so beautifully.

Where have you heard that before? For it perfectly describes the nature of the Feminine. Could it be we are moving out of linear time and structure, process and logic, control and mind – the nature of the Masculine, and into the essence of the feminine?

Yes. Exactly. This is the time the spiritual groupies have been talking about for eons. The feminine is rising. Moving towards love and light, we are all one.

Except we are not. This is Kali we are talking about. There are no white floaty dresses and Kumbaya singalongs to celebrate her arrival. This is the Descent of the dark, formidable, mysterious Feminine. One that has no desire to create Man in her image. There is little use for hordes of emasculated males which have been created by generations of "awakened females". Come, we know how to fix you, come, be like us, we will show you.

So, the men, tired of being outcast and unaccepted for who they are by the women, joined ranks and started holding hands in the circles to celebrate life. Completely forgetting about the fundamental requirement for polarity.

Those men who refused to have a bar of the namby-pamby, if you can't beat them, join them attitude, continued to work diligently in their ivory towers creating their empires.

A few remembered their true essence and evolved into an empowered Masculine. The Real Men. The ones who respect and adore the Goddesses, who are not trying to make the men like them. This is what the world needs, and I certainly know I will be working to assist this recreation process – to return to their innate nature.

However, most men continued to forget who they were, continuously DOING as this is the only place they are seen of value. For if they took time out, hid themselves away in their ug caves, with their papers or sport, the women grew tired of this. They were not allowed to BE or be different to women.

This is the crux of the matter. Men were no longer valued, a dying breed.

The very structures which held them together started crumbling with the arrival of the feminine. First in their households, with women domesticating them and insisting they talk about things to resolve the problems. What about respecting that men don't naturally do that?

Then in society, with the insistence of gender equality and political correctness, so no one feels left out. What happened to inclusion, but not making it on one group of people's terms – that of the "collective".

Whether it be government, schools, or families, the regard for individualism has left the building.

And now, the feminine energy is tearing apart the very fabric of society. The first few months of 2020 saw the economies plunder, unemployment soar and businesses torn apart.

To name but a few of the discarded remnants of society left in the wake of a force of nature. The prevalence of Kali energy, the destroyer. It was only Shiva that stopped her from a blood thirsty rampage killing everything off. For he knows the cycle of life is death, followed by resurrection and new life.

But we are not there yet, not by a long way. Return to the dying masculine. By that I mean individuals, AND the collective of society as we know it. The patriarchal domains of capitalism were not feeling well......

CHAPTER 4

THE ECONOMY IS DYING

In January, the economy was starting to show symptoms of its demise, although the decline was not a surprise. The predictive economists (I follow Harry Dent) had all shown graphs showing the cyclical nature of the economy over past 300 years. It also showed graphs & stats over a much longer period of time.

The world was coming into the winter of its economic cycle and had been since 2018. A time for hibernation, negative growth, waiting for spring again in 2023 or so. The economists know everything has a life cycle, just as nature does, and just as our planet does. This basic fact is long forgotten when talking about change.

So do not confuse the downfall of the economy was solely caused by CV-19. It just plummeted to the extremes far more quickly and to a greater extent that predicted. Yet, the US Financial Institutions had also taken previously unseen radical action in 2018/19 that was never predicted.

These are times of change indeed. Or rather time is being removed. Back to the quantum and improbability. Nothing drives an economist madder than statistics which do not fit their graphs and forecasts. Unprecedented indeed.

Who could have seen such death to all we held sacred coming? A few did. After all, it has been written in all the ancient texts, scriptures and religions for thousands of years. The Mayan prophecy of 2012. That was just a smoke screen for what is coming in 2021. Everything has been flipped. Including the numbers.

Yet Western culture pays little regard for the deep history. The mindset, based on science, is we only evolve forward in time (linear), therefore what was written thousands of years ago has no relevance on today. Basically, because it was not understood, it was dismissed.

Sure, much mystery is held around the construction of the pyramids. Historians have dated 'modern culture' based on ancient civilizations. Yet, even these dates move, as timelines expand, to be older. With the discovery of pyramids in Indonesia dated as 26,000BCE, the history books have to be re-written.

Just as the science books based on Newtonian theories were deemed kindergarten once Quantum Science emerged. Though it does not stop the theories from 300 years ago being the basis of our current education system….

To the masses, they had not really taken much notice of the symptoms. After all, it was in another country, on another continent. They were in denial.

CHAPTER 5*

GRIEVING: DENIAL

The first part of the grieving process is denial.

The symptoms had appeared. Deaths to a virus, economic downturn. The northern hemisphere was in the midst of their winter, hibernating away from the world, and its problems, outside. The Southern hemisphere were on their 6-week summer break, it was beach and barbie season. Not to worry about the new 'flu. She'll be right.

It is imperative to remember Coronavirus is just a representation of what is really going on. Just as the world was in denial of any real issue, 95% or more of the world's population were in denial about themselves.

About the state of their lives. About the qualities of their thoughts, beliefs, behaviours. About their disconnect from their bodies and health. Little consideration for the bigger picture – what exactly ARE they here for and what are they creating? Not in the remit of many.

The Awakeners – the ones on the path of personal growth – were still denying their inability to weave together their spiritual lives with reality. When they tried, the majority remained broke.

Denial of the state of their relationships. With themselves, with others, with their work, with the planet. Denial of their passions, purpose and potential.

ALL are in denial of their own power. It terrifies them. To own who you really are would put you so far outside the tribe of conformity required by human consciousness, it is not worth the pain.

The pain of responsibility. Very, very few are prepared to do what it takes to have their ultimate experience. How many make it to be an Olympian in their chosen arena of sport? How many rock stars fill the stadiums compared to the kids learning to strum their electric guitars in their bedrooms? How many home cooks end up running a chain of restaurants around the world, whose hobby is to collect Michelin stars?

Yes, there has to be natural talent. The precise science within your body waiting to be exploited to its fullest potential. Yes, many skills can be learnt and acquired along the way. Though, in truth, this is just awakening what was lying dormant in your very DNA. Which includes your Soul Contracts. What you came here to do. To master your psyche and return to your true nature. Realizing your own awakening.

Every. Single. One. Of. Us. Are here to master ourselves. We are built for it. We have every component required uniquely arranged in the orchestra of our mind, body and spirit held together with our energy imprints. All waiting for us to become the Artisan for our own lives. The unique expression of Source itself. The individuated spark of the All That Is if you want to get philosophical about it, the Godhead if you have a religious leaning.

What will it take to master ourselves? That will be revealed as the (never-ending) story unfolds.

For now, we are considering denial. It is a 'more pleasant' emotion than what would arise if you went into fear, which is what you are trying to avoid. Non-confrontation of the issue. Non-ownership. Not my problem. It's someone else's.

Someone else needs to fix this. Someone else needs to fix me. I don't know how to. It's not my fault. They did it to me. Who would I be without my victim story?

I'll tell you who you would be. You would be in charge of yourself and your stories. How you continue to be burdened by the baggage of memories and programming you carry around like a trophy.

If it's not someone else's fault, it's your body's fault. It's your mind's fault.

This conditioning is poisonous. Literally. It is killing us. Then again, natural culling is an essential part of life and one that is not accepted.

You only have to choose your life, your way. That is it. No one else's business.

When you deny the responsibility you have to your heart and Soul, to find your deep truth, you will forever remain operating through your own shadows of your mind.

Shadow, your fear, your illusions and control are the opposite of sovereignty, truth and innate energy. Do not confuse shadow with the dark. For the potent dark energy of the feminine is where the purest power lies, the eternal energy that exists at all time, everywhere.

Let's not get too ahead of ourselves.

The grieving process itself is all based on shadow. Who will I be without this person or thing in my life? It is not denying the emotional experience of that moment, which is important to feel. However, when that moment is passed, you have a brand-new opportunity to recreate. It starts over. To change up your thoughts, relationships. To get back into balance within yourself. For whenever you need someone else, or something, to fill you up, you are operating from shadow and human consciousness.

The ultimate liberation comes when you know, live and breathe a fundamental principle of Cosmic Consciousness.

No one and no thing has power over me.

CHAPTER 6

ASTROLOGY: JANUARY 2020

2020 started out with a bang, the Saturn / Pluto conjunction being the milestone. The first conjunction in Capricorn for 500 years. Little did we know the ramifications of these two giants coming together. The energy had been building since December 2017, we have had a long time to prepare for this. It would set the tone for the remainder of 2020.

The major conjunction is the astrological event of the millennium. Right in the midst of this we have a quadruple alignment, extremely rare, with not one but two occurring. The first being Mercury, Ceres, Pluto and Saturn, all aligning on 12th January. Two days later the Sun, Ceres, Pluto and Saturn were aligned in Capricorn as well.

Add to the mix the lunar eclipse on the 11th January shines the light, or rather the darkness, on the pileup of planets in Capricorn.

Let us hop back to the beginning of the month to start. Mars entered Sagittarius on January 3rd, supporting goal setting and motivation to achieve, though you could be scattered, and feel frustrated if over ambitious. Could be on a crusade, Mars is a warrior, stay focused.

Jupiter, the rule of Sagittarius meets up with the South Node, which is connected to the past and karma. It represents our beliefs, and we must let go of what no longer serves us, including judgement. Instead, tune into the higher frequencies to start resonating with what is coming.

11th January saw a lunar eclipse in Cancer. To make an important decision, or a trigger against the big planet players in opposition. Trying to shut out what is happening in the world, and we need to feel safe and secure. Neptune helps to escape and find support with your faith to decide what is important to you, by listening to your Soul.

Uranus went direct on 11th January, so all planets were in direct motion. Felt time was speeding up, all systems go. You may find there are shocks with sudden changes, to make sure we are paying attention to what needs to change. It is time to go off track and do things differently. Then we start a major transition period.

(Hindsight: impeachment was declared without any evidence at a trial; the breaking up of the EU. All occurred within days of the eclipse. Historical patterns of relationship tensions with Hong Kong, China and India playing out now too.

The much-loved Iranian leader Soleimani was assassinated by US troops on 3rd January. This is a last hurrah of the dinosaur generation, though it represents danger right now as he old religions of the world make revenge a good thing).

11/12th January starts a string of conjunctions.

What are we feeding our body and minds? A serious conversation is required about the planet and start speaking the Truth, start going deeply within. Five bodies coming with **Saturn and Pluto** meeting. It falls on the symbol of a soldier receiving medals for bravery in combat. This indicates we must be brave with our speech. What unfolds around this conjunction may set in motions things that will last for a much longer period of time.

When they travel together, their influence can bring about huge destructions of all structure of government, statehood, styles and customs. The destruction is then to be followed by a rebirth into the new. They seek to balance unjust conditions, circumstances and situations.

Look at the last time this happened when Saturn and Pluto conjoined in Capricorn between 1518 and 1520. This was the time of the start of Protestantism, when Martin Luther published the 95 Theses against the Roman Catholic Church, Papal supremacy, as well as indulgence of the high clergy's practices (mostly towards sex). Consider the similarities to the recent scandals in the Church.

The Conquistadors landed in Central America. They discovered the Mayan Civilization in February 1517 and Aztec civilization in May 1518. As we know, the Mayans had a great deal to say about the next coming of Age.

It has of course occurred at other times, just not in Capricorn. This conjunct is found on the ascendant of the Constitutional Chart of the USA of 1787. It is also found in the founding chart of Israel.

In 1914, the first World War began. 1947, mid Second World war with the worst snow fall in the UK. Dead Sea Scrolls were found. Saturn associates with history – secrets being unearthed. Roswell incident – the crashing of a UFO with alien bodies found on board.

Also, in 1947, the Doomsday clock came into being – the likelihood of a human made catastrophe. It was set at 7 minutes to midnight. In 2018 it was moved to 2 minutes to midnight. In 1982, when the Falklands War began, AIDS was identified, severe cold in the US as well as recession. It was the year ET was released.

This indicates a ticking clock when it comes to Pluto conjunct Saturn. It will begin the process of destruction of masked and shallow elements of our world and its institutions. It is essential we all start letting go, including the anger and guilt which keeps the old alive.

Note Saturn and Pluto were in opposition at the time of the World Trade Tower attacks of September 11, 2001.

When we look at films and music to be released, they give us clues to the planetary energies playing out. It is perfectly depicted in an upcoming movie, Godzilla v Kong. No time to Die, Black Widow, Ghostbusters, Antebellum = occurring before a particular war. Many references to war, hardship, stage occurrences, close to something that could be difficult.

The stock market is the US is being harshly triggered by this conjunction and the Lunar eclipse this month. A stock market correction was likely in January as its charts shows from 17 May 1792.

"Powerful denial" are the keywords for this conjunct. Those in power (Pluto) with authority (Saturn) don't want to listen because they stand to lose everything because Pluto is also wealth.

The failure of the economy means automatic failure of the administration's attempts to survive. Although with unprecedented events this year, previous forecasts may not play out. We will have to wait until the Election of November 2020 to see what unfolds. It will not be a clear-cut decision with the final result taking days to establish. Note the President will be elected with Saturn in Capricorn (structures, perhaps seen as patriarchy) and rule when Saturn comes into Aquarius. So many are ready to see the back of Donald Trump, yet I feel he could be the joker who reveals the Truth of what is happening, unknowingly or not.

We are being pushed to make change on a personal level, and collective issues will also come up, we need to pay attention. What we do now it will have a massive impact for future generations. Pluto has been in Capricorn since 2008, smashing the structures of Capricorn apart. Saturn came in December 2017 and has been trying to start some kind of reconstruction.

The darkness of the old world was about to get much darker and everyone needed to keep fear at a minimum, finding the Higher Self as the leader into a new way of life.

Pluto rules excretion, Saturn rules reality. The shit just got real, that is what this cycle is about. To clear out the crap from the old chapter of our lives. To start making room to commit to the new consciousness of the new chapter. Time to take a big dump.

Pluto rules Karma, Saturn rules death and resurrection. It indicates a deadline, indicating time is running out. This conjunction addresses the climate issues. It marks a point in history, it is a turning point to take responsibility for our rubbish, including rotting trade agreements and international relationships, tax avoidance, increased fascism and tyranny. Our shadow is showing. We must take responsibility for the collective shadow.

Time to get real and seeing it on the world stage. A time of harsh truths and essential to face them. Like the soldier who has faced war. To face our fears, we cannot cheat fate and try to outrun life. We must deal with our own personal shadow, and massive test of integrity and rite of passage. What is going on in the world reflects what is happening within.

(Hindsight: the US Military Complex was in dangerous confrontation with Iran. North Korea left negotiations with the USA)

We can step into our authenticity by dealing with our own personal stuff. This transformation of energy will ripple out. Phoenix and Flame moment of Pluto. If we show maturity and be honest with ourselves and take our time, we will come out stronger.

Looking at the transits, we get echoes of needing to be responsible (with Ceres). We feel something important is being stripped from us, we must guard against thinking in black and white, or extreme reactions. Do not react extremely or it will throw things out of balance. Personal transformation by seeing what is in our control, and to approach things maturely. Do not respond to the triggers like a child.

Mother Earth (Ceres) is integral to this conjunct in Capricorn. She was out of bounds in January meaning she wasn't going to play by the rules anymore. Instead, she was screaming at the top of her voice to listen. By January 10 we had 950 earthquakes. On 16th January David Attenborough warns of a climate crisis moment.

We must nurture ourselves through this process. It is an Initiation for us and for the collective. Venus moves into Pisces mid-January, to feel more empathy and unconditional love. Feel more charitable and be helpful, keep our hearts open. To recognise we are all in this together.

New moon in Aquarius on 24th January – associated with groups, network, society and politics. Also associated with higher intellect, away from the heavy earth energy. Gives a breath of fresh air. Be aware of where we need to create our own space and to identify your own unique skills and individuality. Now is the time for change, maybe a humanitarian effort together, for a revolutionary new start.

It could be a tense time, perhaps security is unstable, and important to change. An awakening comes at this time, and a potential for healing, to with Chiron and environmental issues. Figure out where we are resisting change. The conjunct with Saturn and Pluto will make you face it. It is an opportunity for healing.

Towards the end of the month it will be quite emotional with an outpouring to feel your way forwards with Venus. Sometimes feel overwhelmed and want to avoid, so start using your intuition throughout the month, especially if we feel the weariness. Keep tuning in. Focus on the things you love and you will find your direction.

INDIGENOUS ASTRONOMY

The First Nation cultures of Australia - Aboriginal and Torres Strait Islanders - stretch back over 65,000 years. This makes them the oldest astronomers and oldest continuing cultures in the world. They developed a number of practical ways to observe the sun, moon and stars and assign meaning and agency to astronomical phenomena, which informs Law (Tjukurpa) and social structure. It also serves as the foundations for narratives passed down the generations through song, dance and oral tradition of storytelling over tens of thousands of years.

Creation is believed to be the work of culture heroes who travelled across a formless land, creating sacred sites and significant places of interest in their travels. Songlines were established across Australia, which are the travelling trails of the Spirit Beings. Dreamtime is a term devised by early anthropologists to refer to a religio-cultural worldview attributed to Australian Aboriginal beliefs. Ut has various other names according to the collectives of the Indigenous across the land, who speak over 250 languages.

Aboriginal astrology saw 12th January, when Saturn conjunct Pluto, as a magical and eagerly anticipated union and believed a significant shift would take place. It was said a cosmic umbilical cord will unite heaven with earth.

The Anangu people (from Uluru) spoke of a great ritual at the sacred site which was disrupted and never completed at the end of original Creation Time (Dreamtime). It was said on this day in 2020 it was an ideal time to complete the ritual.

The ritual would see energy sent up and down the cosmic umbilicus and through the planet's leylines, connecting all the Earth Chakras together. There are two interconnected major energetic leylines, the Rainbow Serpent (feminine) and the Plumed Serpent (masculine). On a flat earth map, these two serpents form an infinity symbol according to legend. This connection will create heaven on earth, the Golden Age.

Uluru is the Planetary Solar Plexus Chakra, and the ideal spot at Uluru and Kata Tjuta to construct a solar cord from earth to the sun, to increase the higher frequencies of life. Uluru is a 300-million-year-old rock which rises form the red desert sands of Australia's heartland. It is half of the dual heritage listed site with Kata Tjuta, which scientist date the origins of the formations to at least 500 million years ago. They are a massive conductor of energy through the electromagnetic energy field.

An image of Kata Tjuta popped up as my screensaver the day after I wrote this and I realised I had never seen a picture of them before. I clicked through to this:

Kata Tjuta in Northern Territory, Australia

Scientists date the origins of the Kata Tjuta rock formations to at least 500 million years ago. The name translates to "many heads", a description given to the 36 rock domes by the region's native people, the Anangu – one of the oldest human societies on Earth. The towering rocks are mostly basalt, sandstone and granite, and the distinctive rust hue is due to a coating of iron oxide. The colour matches that of a close neighbour, the iconic Uluru, which rises from arid Outback plains 26 kilometres east of here. Both otherworldly rock formations are part of Uluru-Kata Tjuta National Park in Australia's Northern Territory. The lands in the park are sacred to the Anangu people, and both Uluru and Kata Tjuta are important religious and cultural sites.

The event on 12ᵗʰ January was an exact quadruple conjunction. It is also International Earth Chakra Day dedicated to raising awareness about Planetary Ascension and Cosmic Consciousness. It is celebrated at Ayers Rock Resort, Uluru annually.

Robert Coon was an expert on Earth Chakras and wrote a book of the same name. He said of the Magic Red Centre that "dimensions of space and time are now opening to reveal the true nature and essences of Australia." In October 2019 the climbing of Uluru was permanently closed and brought a newfound sense of peace to the sacred ground. Robert Coon believed by 2084 the whole earth will be experienced as sacred.

Some think these rock formations are artefacts left behind when the Pleiadians seeded the planet. The local Anangu believe the area was created at the beginning of time by ancestral beings. Uluru is regarded as physical evidence of the ancestor's activities during creation.

FEBRUARY 2020

CHAPTER 7*

CODED NUMBERS

My fascination for numbers has been in place for as long as I can remember. My requirement for symmetry and even numbers was paramount in all I did as a child, from arranging my teddies at night, to only allowing an even number of veggies on my dinner plate. To this day, I HAVE to round a tank of petrol to the nearest dollar, and will only buy an even number of pieces of fruit or veg. I feel completely lopsided if not. Bizarre habits, ones my boys have inherited without me saying a word.

You will see the importance of numbers as our story unfolds. I am sure you are familiar with the anecdotes of seeing 11, 22 and 33 in places – the Master numbers. Or you have your lucky numbers. We all have a relationship with numbers in some way or another. Your birthday helps to define some of your characteristics, whether it be the month or the day. The accuracy of a personal birth chart by a professional astrologist is invaluable to understand what the planets were doing at the date and time of your birth.

Western numerology long held my interest – until I stumbled across Chaldean Numerology. I invested in a reading with Joanne Justis and her book "Numbers - The Powerful Bridge Beyond". The resonance for me was astounding, to find a system based on the original root language of Sumerian and Chaldean.

The formulas for the number values of each letter are based on its vibration and can only be 1-8 in value. Nine is regarded a combination of all other frequencies, and therefore not individually allocated a letter in the formulas.

This is unlike the Western system where 1-5 etc was allocated to A-E. How could this possibly work when 4 extra letters were added to the alphabet after the Western system was (supposedly) designed by Pythagoras?

The other major differences are Y is always counted as a vowel, and W always as a consonant.

I had 2 past life flashbacks when I questioned whether I was part of Chaldean numerology creation, in a consult with my then spiritual mentor. I felt it through my heart, so strongly, so vividly, there was no doubt I had strong associations with the inception of the system itself.

No wonder I enjoyed my corporate career as a management accountant for 14 years, doing budgets and forecasts for Blue Chip companies – future planning and analysis of numbers.

When I started my first "Soul" business over 5 years ago, Chaldean numerology was one of the foundations I used to help people understand themselves at a personality and higher self-level. I still use this method of analysis with all my clients, and before any business decisions on names and date of registrations.

There is huge scope for synchronicities in numbers. To find the patterns, to see a recurring number could be regarded as a sign you are on track, or to verify something you have been considering.

It is imperative for me to have any business name or registration in alignment – in synch – with my existing numerical charts.

I analyse five numbers when doing Chaldean numerology. Your Soul purpose (based on the vowels), your personality (based on consonants), your life purpose (a combination of the two). Your date of birth provides insight into your life path and your life goal - what you come into in the second half of your life – combines your full name and date of birth.

Any change in name through marriage or Deed poll takes 9 years to imprint energetically into your system. You will always carry your birth name (as legally registered on your birth certificate). It is always worth looking at the numbers if you usually go by a different name, and certainly when you change your name.

When I took my new name of Josephine Sorciere, I reviewed the numbers to ensure I had alignment, after I had chosen (or rather, led to, my name). Every single one of the five numbers were the SAME as my married name, and ensured I picked a registration date to match the life path number.

Think about it. The chance of having the same Soul number is 1 in 9. To have the same personality number as well is 1/81. Same purpose number 1/729. Same Life path 1 in 6561. All five numbers matching, 1 in 59,049.

If I just analyse Sorciere, the numbers also match identically to my married name.

Three months previously, I had been shown the name Pregnancy Alchemy for my new business at that time. Once again, the numbers were an exact match to my married name. Not once, twice, but three times had the numbers come out the same. That's 1 in 4,782,969 (if my school maths has not failed me.)

I encourage you to be observant of numbers. Note when you see the same 'random' number two or three times in quick succession. It is an excellent way of helping you become more observant and present to life unfolding all around you.

The same applies to names, books or films. To anything really – it's just easier to identify those things with a label. Simply because humans have such an obsession with labelling everything. It helps them understand better and grow their knowledge base.

* * *

As individuals evolve, they begin to realise the irrelevance of labels. They can simply observe, without having to name, or judge, anything. It is a standard practice in meditation. When the mind can begin to conceive of the Isness of everything, It Just is, I Am, You Are as the yogis like to say, we can be in the space of acceptance and the energy – the frequency – of the situation or feeling.

Understanding everything is energy is fundamental to being able to grasp what is unfolding in the world, each and every day.

The energy field of humanity as a whole is called the Collective Consciousness. It is very much based on tribal consciousness, where fight or flight is the basis for awareness, decisions. Throughout time, the set point of this field of energy has raised its frequency; it only hit the tipping point of a positive frequency this century.

Simply put, consciousness is the measure of awareness people have about the truth of themselves. Are they disconnected from their core, their heart and living from a base of separation, and believe we have one life and one body? Or have they grown in awareness and re-membered with the innate knowing within they are part of a much larger picture?

We can feel the collective energy at a sports game or large rock concert, where the energy of the place is alive. The true definition of team spirit. How would the footie players feel in the first few games with no crowds, as happened here in Australia at the beginning of the season? A strange experience for all, without the energy of the crowds urging their team on.

Similarly, the Collective Consciousness could really be felt after word events such as 9/11, or the shock of Diana being killed in a car crash.

Humanity evolves at the speed in which consciousness rises. How much awareness each person has contributes to the overall energy frequency of the collective. It is like a wave of the ocean, ebbing and waning with the tides of how people feel. It is fundamental to how quickly, or how hindered we are, in moving forward as a human race.

CHAPTER 8*

CREATING YOUR LIFE AS ART

Back in my business, I continued to do Initiations and get well underway with the new clients who had committed to their own transformation and extend working with me for three months. I cannot begin to describe how much adore witnessing people Doing The Work, and utterly transforming how they show up in their life.

I was realising how the calibre of my clients was changing, which of course, was a reflection of my own personal growth and expansion over the years. The first month is always telling – how quickly will they learn to recognise, own and transmute their own shadow? For once they immerse into their own power, without the fears running the show, they step into the world of infinite potential.

I do not teach shadow management, the normal offerings from the spiritual Light Grid as I call it. I am an Alchemist and show others how to do the same. To finally dissolve those energetic patterns, thoughts and cellular memory held over eons of fear, doubt and false beliefs we have been conditioned for and programmed with. To unhook from all systems and structures which have not sprung from nature itself.

Once we have cleared a large portion of our shadow mind, we can then start regaining our own inner balance, between doing and being. The masculine and feminine energy that runs through each and every one of us. I call this your Inner Family. When you get to the point of having the most luscious, intimate relationship with yourself, you are then opened to have the most amazing relationships in your life.

For any upset, blame, arguments occurring in a partnership are always from shadow. Expecting the other person to operate from the same standards in the same way as you. It's how we ended up with generations of emasculated men, as women expected them to be as emotional and chatty as they were, or they weren't doing it right. They had little understanding the man's own personal evolvement, which looks so different to the feminine journey.

It is why women have been under the thumb of controlling, domineering, aggressive masculine energy for centuries, as men refused to accept women as they were, and different to them. Often disconnected from their bodies and feelings, only feeling valued in their Doing mode. Simply playing out their own fear of lack of control and immortality, often running on greed and corruption.

How would life be if all of us dropped both sides of these illusions? Within ourselves and with each other. Through governments and community. Through our relationship with earth and the environment.

Let us move from History to Mystery. His story to my story. The mystery of life, the wonderment and infinite possibilities. To move away from God programming, into the intrinsic essence of nature, of who we are.

Releasing from your slave-self is the ultimate freedom; as you increase your own conscious awareness, you liberate yourself from all the systems and technology of the matrix which lie behind the scenes. The energies which have been pulling the puppet strings of humanity for centuries are ready to be exposed. It is your job, your choice, to rip down the curtain and to see the Truth, cutting the cords from anything you feel subject to from an external force. Then you can return to your natural state of connection to Source.

For that is what we are all here to do. To realise the utter illusion we are living, to liberate from the shackles of the mind and to create our own lives, on our terms, our way – life as art. To be able to show up with the strongest of our characteristics, regardless of gender or sexual preference, and bring our own unique self-expression forward for the world to see. Regardless if they like it, accept it, value it, or not.

Your life as the ultimate work of art which gets created over and over is both worthless and priceless. There is no value on it, you simply create for you are a Creator. In whatever field, modality or canvas you chose to use.

When we start to treat life like this, we no longer place the definition of our own value in the hands of someone else, and what they are willing to pay for our service.

Consider the basics of work. Your first job if you earnt pocket money as a kid, was to do some chores, contribute to the household and get a weekly allowance. We were taught if we did, we got rewarded and recognition for it. A new approach is for kids to learn to cohabit and contribute simply because they want to, for the type of environment they chose to live in and with. The parents may or may not give them an allowance, or perhaps treat them to something when they ask.

Teaching kids they can have what they want, when they understand the criteria and boundaries, is an effective tool to help them co-create in future.

As you grew older, you may have got a part time job in a shop or café. You were paid by the hour, with a little extra for holidays, and tips if you were lucky. If your career progressed, you were paid higher amounts with the expectation you would work for whatever hours were needed.

Business owners face a different scenario. They have to believe in what they are offering is of value to others, take a risk, often without pay for months, even years, if they are simply driven to create and explore what they are here to do. Yes, it had to make economic sense to 'survive' within the climate of payment exchange in return for a product or service.

Within the home, the value proposition is somewhat different. The housekeeper, often the woman, was expected to keep the domestics in order whilst the man of the house went out to earn the money. As society changed, the women often got jobs, and still had to run the house. The partner may also help. There is an (often unspoken) expectation this is how life works together. Until one or both of them get resentful, often both are exhausted, and that's before we introduce kids into the equation which brings a whole new level of responsibility to the party.

Perhaps this is the reason the economy as we know it is starting to break down. Our sense of personal value has been removed and dictated by jobs and governments. Human evolution is starting to prepare for a whole new ethos of an economy, one that yet remains out of the scope of possibility for all but a few who have seen into the infinite potential.

CHAPTER 9*

THE FOURTH AWAKENING

An Awakening occurs when a new way of existence comes into being, a new order to break down the old structures and essence of society and life as we know it.

It is a profound unfolding which comes without warning unexpectedly to shake the world to the core. Whilst it had been predicted in Ancient texts and the date for the end of the precession is around now, no one knew exactly how Kali would sweep in.

The virus which would affect billions of people across the planet was not Covid. Whilst this infected many people, causing hundreds of thousands of deaths, it was not the main virus which would cause every single person to question their world. The real revolutionary virus was called TRUTH.

This Awakening is about exposing the truth of who really runs this world, the unseen adversaries with their own agendas, puppeteering the governments and military of the world. The corruption and capitalism so hugely distorted HAS to come back into balance, which will only ever be achieved by the People waking up and taking a stance for fundamental change.

The energy to support this runs through Collective Consciousness itself and it is these frequencies which are ready to be reopened to the higher dimensional vibrations. It is up to individuals to raise their own inner barometer to make a stand for their own purpose and potential as the game changers they came here to be.

Is there anything to be concerned about with awakenings? Apart from the possible annihilation of the human race as we know it, no. It is make or break time to progress the Collective or destroy themselves.

Let us consider the previous Awakenings. The **First Awakening** unfolded about 200,000 years ago when Home Sapiens emerged in East Africa. It took them 140,000 years to venture out of this area.

The Second Awakening was when spoken language emerged, around 50,000 years ago. This was the time when the great myths were told by the early shamans, passed down from generation to generation. The Aboriginal communities of Australia are an excellent example of this.

Humans were becoming more self-aware and realised they were different to nature whilst being part of it. They started to become aware of their own mortality and death became something to fear.

Complex rituals were begun to prepare them for the afterlife we hoped that existed, with a hungry search for immortality in any form.

The earliest cave paintings were recently found in Indonesia dating back almost 44,000 years. Across the world, modern man was depicting images similar to those in other parts of the world, which would only be discovered eons later. It was the first signs that man was deeply connected on both a spiritual and developmental level, none of whom knew the others existed.

Human development took a huge leap with the ending of the last great Ice Age. Just like all Awakenings, it was like something switched on for us inside. Man began to grasp the concept of time and planning, with concepts of the past and future. We started to plants crops and breed animals about fourteen thousand years ago. This led to larger fixed populations hubs, which would later grow into towns and cities. The population explosion began along with a series of cultural revolutions.

We had yet more examples of universal consciousness where people in random places around the world all independently went through their own Iron and Bronze Ages. Similarly, ship building, astrology and use of metals emerged at the same time in different locations.

It only took a few thousand years for man to move from being cave-dwellers to building city-states and great works of art and writing. Man understood whilst he could contribute to a culture that would outlast him, he felt he had a sense of immortality. To leave a mark on humanity's legacy for the future. Virtually all culture relates to this. Every single individual has a chance to leave their own stamp on the life experience.

About 3,000 years ago the Third Awakening began with the rise of modern religions and science. Between 800BC and 400BC there was an explosion in religions, events from the Old Testament occurred, giving rise to the Judeo-Christian beliefs. Taoism was followed by Confucianism in China, similarly Hinduism and Buddhism in India and later, Islam.

The balance tipped from religion to science about 500 years ago during the Renaissance period. Note this was exactly the time of the last Saturn-Pluto conjunct in Capricorn, the sign of structures and society, before January 2020.

Most people today live under secular governance, well established around 150 years ago with the explosion in knowledge of science. Up until then, the scientists had been concerned with proving there was a God, not to disprove it. As man evolved, he believed his knowledge was superior to wisdom, newfound facts preferable to the stories of old, the ego was the spur for capitalist development.

As writing and communication became more widespread, the reliance on historical texts became less important. Science was seen to create a higher form of immortality than religion.

The modern-day world has become an even tighter knit community separated by little, yet controlled by the similar mindsets. As the big ideas from the previous Awakening collapse, the new Awakening lays in wait, and is now tiptoeing in and destroying the very structures of society laid down over past 500 years. Science has had to retreat as both sides politicize environmental science for their own agenda, whilst space shuttles are no longer the remit of the governments.

As the Fourth Awakening dawns on the New Age, it will have the same thing in common as all the others: the evolvement of THOUGHT. It is time to move beyond symbols and thought and return to the essence of energy. To receive and transmit higher level frequencies from where we came – the planets and multi-Universes.

Many of us are discovering the immortality our predecessors have been searching 200,000 years for has always been a part of us all along. Are you ready to claim it?

* * *

How do people deal with the transition from one Awakening to the other? With all Awakenings, those with the most to lose will do anything, up to and including genocide, to maintain their wealth and force. Which is exactly what is being attempted in the world right now with the potential for enforced vaccinations, health passports and chipping.

Around each transition had swirled a great deal of violence. The powers-that-be clutch their last strands of control whilst the people stand up and take action through revolution.

Between the first and second Awakenings, the Neanderthals were wiped out. Some say they were replaced within a generation and a half. Back then a good age to live to was 30, so that makes the transition period 45 years. Exactly the same length of time I have predicted, starting in 1997, midpoint 2012, and moving into the last of the five cycles in 2021, before completion in 2030.

Between the second and third Awakening, first the Egyptian Empire fell and later the Roman Empire. The Dark Ages followed, where one emperor was replaced by more than a dozen kings and princes. The control was removed from an individual and dispersed.

Many saw the fall of Rome and Egypt as the death knell for education and literacy, sophisticated architecture, advanced economic interaction and the rule of written law. Life became nasty, brutish and short, with little written resources as guidelines. Specialised production and long-distance trade ceased for centuries after the demise.

However, others saw this as a necessity to destroy large-scale slavery and move towards a more equitable world. For a while, the battlefield replaced the bureau at the heart of elite life.

Could a comparison be drawn on the desire of a few to return to the Empire days and encapsulate humanity once more? Many believe this is the agenda.

The violent process of collapse occurred when the migrants forcibly stripped the central Roman state of the tax base with it had used to fund the armies. Landowners in the provinces survived by coming to terms with the immigrants.

As with all life, we move in cycles and patterns. If whole races and empires were wiped out in previous awakenings, is there a concern or a cause for celebration now?

Could we indeed wipe out the capitalist elite and return the power to the people with individual ownership and responsibility for our own welfare and happiness? This of course can only ever be achieved when humanity stands up for what they personally want and desire, without judgement or anger at others for wanting different things.

Or could this be the end of humanity as we know it, just as the Neanderthals were eliminated?

I believe aspects of all these scenarios are likely. The old 3D way of living on the Light Grid is fizzling out, both for the mainstream and spiritual crew alike. A brand-new territory awaits us. One that can be obtained in a much easier way if we all just grasped the magic of creativity and ownership waiting inside each and every one of us.

CHAPTER 10

DISAPPEARING ECONOMIES

Consider the possibility of having a society with NO FISCAL ECONOMY. How would this change our relationship to value? Would you still be doing the same job, business, domestics if we no longer had to earn our money to prove our worth?

Would you still determine your own value by how much service you gave to another? How would this liberate you if there was no price to pay or be paid, you simply did what you wanted, provided it helped you grow, expand, learn and master your gifts?

The future generations will not learn a subject and apply for jobs. They will create their own jobs on the culmination of their unique talents. Thought Leaders such as Roger James Hamilton are leading the way with this already, running Genius School as an alternative to current education systems. A world class entrepreneur education curriculum providing real alternatives to the outdated schooling paradigm currently provided.

Supposing we lived in a paradigm where your passions and talents were the key to your life. Forget the HOW it would operate. You would just know because it came naturally to you. Imagine if you will.

Obtaining finance is a 'matter' of understanding how energy works in the quantum. It does not exist until you observe it and create it as matter. There is no ability to stockpile or accumulate money beyond what you require it for, for your own self development or for the growth of others.

The extent to which you experience wealth is in direct proportion to your own self-worth and self-expression, and not based on anyone else's perception of your value for them to pay you.

The opportunity to embrace this new system is totally up to the individual and is a completely level playing field. There is no hierarchy dictating what you can or cannot do. It is up to each person to fully possess their own choices, of self-responsibility and their own creations. For you to decide what you wish to experience and create that moment.

It is not a system for freeloaders. The dense energies of shadow cannot exist in this frequency. Now is not the time to go into depth on the energies, I simply plant a seed of possibility.

I am sure many of you are saying this is an absolutely insane idea and concept, and I am off in la-la land. I have zero attachment to how this information is received, which is the approach I have to everything I share with anyone in my life.

However, just for a moment consider that if our world is about to go through such unprecedented change, and turn around so quickly, perhaps it is time for some out of this world radical solutions to show up?

Humans HAVE to move out of the belief that something is not possible. It is why the world is so fucked up right now. With scientists and economists dictating if they have not proved it, it does not exist. Or worse still, denying solutions do exist where it will not add to the bottom line, or to be able to control the population.

How have I come up with such a preposterous proposal seen by some as the Utopian dream? I do not think this stuff up. I channel, I write and I review with as much shock and amazement as you have.

The difference being is my thoughts are not limited to what I KNOW exists because I can already see it. I KNOW what could exist beyond my current belief system because the Universe is The Infinite Creator - Source -and is continually evolving what is possible.

It just needs human consciousness to catch up - to get out of the heavy density of fear and control and for people to start taking their power back. Was I the first person to download this information? Of course not, I received it as my energy was ready to be open to hear it.

The Ancient Ones from thousands of years ago held all this wisdom, and it has remained a mystery and a secret for centuries. It is time to open to what they know. To receive the frequencies so we can decipher this cosmic world of wondrous wisdom.

It is time to evolve, exponentially.

CHAPTER 11

NORMALITY LEAVES THE GLOBAL VILLAGE

In February 2020, the Collective Consciousness was starting to realise Coronavirus, renamed Covid-19 (CV19) on 11 February, was not going away any time soon, as countries around the world started to report their first cases. Watching what was unfolding in Wuhan, in China, where the first cases were reported at the end of 2019, for most of the world, it was still in peripheral vision.

The first death was reported in the US on 29th February, whilst Italy had over 1,000 cases by this time. By the end of February, it had spread to 49 countries, with 84k cases, of which 79k were within China. However, many countries were still in the phase of denial, and international travel was still going ahead.

People were beginning to consider what being part of a global village means. It was starting to become your business, something which could not be ignored as 'not in my part of the world, not bothered'.

The governments were trusted to make the best decisions for their country, many may have made different calls in hindsight, yet reflection is a wonderful thing. Whoever makes the decision must take full responsibility for it; that is being in leadership. This is not always apparent.

Governments are masters of the illusion they are in control. When in fact, there was nothing anyone can do, other than to limit liability, when it comes to a force of nature. If indeed, it IS a natural virus. Much debate has subsequently arisen as to the starting point of the virus, and I do not intend for this to become a political memoir other than essential facts to help explain the relevance to consciousness.

Control has become a more dominant word in many senses since February. If individuals, and the collective, were simply able to ALLOW rather than control, which is all fear based, the energies could move forward.

In February, we were still living "normal lives", yet unaware of what was around the corner, and we would never return to a level of status quo previously experienced.

Yet our normality was marked by unprecedented fires in Australia, where we lost 21% of forest. This was shortly followed by mass flooding as the rains finally came. The same was happening on the other side of the world, with the wettest February recorded in the UK since records began in 2010. Our weather patterns have long since been 'normal'.

None of this upheaval to the world's balance seemed to have much effect on individuals. Most are unable to join the dots between the extreme conditions in the world outside as a reflection of what was going on within themselves. A complete lack of balance.

So many people were living extremely busy lives, wearing so many masks as employee or business owner, partner, parent, friend. Juggling their life commitments between home, work, health, social, and responsibilities. All doing. Where was the Being?

How many of them were secretly wishing to just get off the treadmill for five minutes? So, they could catch their breath, re-energise and start doing things they loved again, rather than their obligations.

How long had it been since they had done anything creative, sat and read a good book, or had extended quality time with the family? Too long.

Be careful of what you wish for, it may just come true.

CHAPTER 12

ASTROLOGY: FEBRUARY 2020

Let us first consider some basic definitions in astrology.

Conjunctions (when two planets are aligned) and oppositions (when directly opposite each other) between planets are all pivot points. When they are at trine, they are 120 degrees apart and this is a friendly aspect when things flow smoothly for the planet and the areas of your chart they move through. A Square comes with pressure to take action, the push to do something. "trines make you lazy, but squares get things done'.

Eclipses occur when a new or full moon falls close to the lunar nodes. These nodes are the point where the Earth's orbit around the sun is intersected by the Moon's orbit around the Earth. They literally cast a shadow onto each other, creating an eclipse.

* * *

Already a ride, the year started with a bang, with the major alignments and conjunctions of the planets. We have the influence of Saturn, Pluto and Jupiter all year. Only for a couple of weeks in May will the conjunction not be in full effect. It still indicates we have serious issues to deal with.

The cosmic pile up of January would start to ease and the traffic of the planets become a little freer flowing. With so many planets in direct motion, January felt a little hair-raising like a car without the brakes.

At the beginning of February, we went into pre Mercury retrograde shadow. This acts as a handbrake to the crazy speed of things unfolding. These are times to be mindful that things are not as clear as we would like them. It then moves into Pisces; we need to be in touch with our intuition and allow it to lead in decisions. Mercury struggles in this sign, could feel a bit negative. Listen carefully and really hear what is going on in the world and quieten the mind.

Venus enters Aries on 7th February, a fast-moving fire sign. We may become more courageous and assertive to get what we want, at the same time, value your independence. Full moon in Leo accentuates creativity and playfulness. Claim your sovereignty and take risks, to get life moving again.

Mars went out of bounds on 9th February, beyond the path of the Sun, and don't follow the normal rules. It could either come up with genius solutions or have a criminal element to it. So, we may have a wild approach to achieving our goals. Until 2nd March.

Venus squares North and South node, we are moving towards a softer expression, away from structures, towards divine feminine. There is a missed step that needs to be done, know how to love ourselves, to become a family and love each other.

Uranus sextile - a long background run until May 2021; this is the 23rd series of 26 sextiles, it is containing an important message. In the sign of Taurus – stability and being the same, Uranus is saying things need to change. For example, move to veganism, change in farming.

Chiron in Aries says we need to heal through action. He is a big player in the environmental issues, the warrior element. We all need to make changes where we have been stuck for far too long. These energies support personal change.

Ceres as the planet of nurturing has returned to update needs and priorities. This is no coincidence with major planetary activity in the Aquarius ruled part of your chart over the coming months.

Mars moves into Capricorn on 16th and works well from this sign. On a global level, it will trigger the Saturn-Pluto conjunct. This could easily reference the tensions between Iraq and the US, where the threat of WWIII has been very close at times. It is a time for goal setting on a personal level which can be really constructive now and our confidence is high. Also, for personal fitness and feel committed.

Mercury in retrograde could be disorientating from 17th (*when CV19 was showing to be a real threat.*) Must feel our way forwards as the information may not be clear (*which was so true at this time for what we were being told about the pandemic*). Must find the mental peace to find the inner voice which knows the difference between fact and fiction, learn to discern and trust your feelings.

Sun into Pisces on 19th is a time for reflection in the last of the signs of the zodiac. Recharge in all areas of life. The first of 3 sextile Jupiter and Neptune.

Jupiter magnifies what it touches. Allow the increase in compassion and connection. An opportunity to build something that is truly meaningful, drawing upon our Soul connection that is visionary. Increase your own spiritual practice.

Mars trine Uranus motivates to liberate ourselves, just tempered by Chiron. Keen to move ahead then scared we may get hurt or triggered by what is going on around us. Use the triggers to look within at what needs addressing.

New moon in Pisces around 24th February, any new starts may be delayed until mercury retrograde finishes. Feels emotional, old material and unconscious is coming up, waves of feelings, maybe feel lost. Trust the tides will carry you to where you want to be and trust your feelings.

Mars will meet with South Node, we must stop doing doing, doing, we need to just BE. Question where you have let old conditions to control your life now. Mars activates old karma, always consequences of our actions. Let go of the old fights.

Illumination at this time, something will become clearer, but not all information coming forward. It is something we must pay attention to. When things don't end as we wanted, do not allow this to isolate us or effect our faith, keep focusing on the light.

Hindsight: the world was not yet that concerned about the virus, and lockdown not considered yet. We were still being given the directions of what was required up front.

MARCH 2020

CHAPTER 13

THE WORLD GOT CANCELLED

March was the month things started to get serious. We saw exponential rate in which the virus was spreading on a global scale. On 11th March, the WHO called it a Pandemic as the global death toll passed 4,000.

Governments had to think on their feet, and quickly. On 9th March, the F1 team arrived in Melbourne for the formula one Grand Prix. On 13th March, it was cancelled, after spectators gathered in large crowds to queue for entry. That day, it was announced all events with 500 participants in Australia would be cancelled from Monday. We still had the weekend activities booked to attend after all....

On 19th March 2700 passengers about the cruise ship Ruby Princess disembarked and travelled home to their own states. Within five weeks at least 662 passengers were tested positive to Covid-19 and 21 died. By the beginning of April, a criminal investigation was started into the debacle.

On 23rd March, all pubs, restaurants, gyms, libraries, cinemas and entertainment venues are also closed. Schools remained open and would quickly develop online education for its pupils. Shortly afterwards, the International travel ban was put in place.

Meanwhile, in the rest of the world, events and life as we knew it stopped almost straight away in mid-March, including travel bans. Border and state controls were put up in various countries.

And so, life as we knew it came to a grinding halt. We were beginning to realise it was the essential workers – the hospital staff, the shopworkers, the teachers – were our true heroes, not the folks sitting in their corporate offices, or rather, working from home.

The planet could start breathing again. The silence in the cities was stunning, as pollution levels plummeted, ozone holes were repaired, and rivers started running clear.

Mother Nature, along with much of the population, was having a break from the overworked capacity which had been expected of her for years.

We finally had time to catch our breath. This was the blessing in disguise the collective needed. The wake-up call to really consider what part of normal did they really WANT to return to?

However, the majority were still a long way off from even considering what life would be like after lockdown. They were so frozen in fear, fed by a media frenzy of doom and gloom. The mass hysteria generated from such easy access to information was so far removed from reality, it was not funny. The intoxicating collective energy was drowning us. Reflected in the physical symptoms of the virus itself – drowning in the lungs.

The inherent heaviness of government control and forced lockdown had the sheep scuttling inside for cover, addicted to the latest news and scrolling on media. The majority were just doing as they were told, soaking up the energies the domineering forces that we were insisting was right and proper to feel.

Through this time, there were also growing numbers of people willing to do their own research into the matter. To consider what natural health solutions would minimise the effects of Covid if they got it. To look into what was going on behind the scenes of the bureaucratic control. To really start questioning the long-term intentions of the governments, which appeared to be in unanimous agreement to keep us in lockdown until a vaccine was created, at least 18 months away.

This was getting a more ridiculous solution unwanted by many. The economy was taking a nosedive, unemployment rose to 4.4% in the US. There seemed to be little consideration for the effects on individuals outside the pandemic.

The long-term effects on suicide, domestic violence, mental health and wealth of the people would still be a long way off from being clear, though the stats were already pointing these figures would be far higher than any number of deaths due to CV-19.

What individuals could not yet see was this was the opportunity to awaken. To question their own lives. To question what was being told to them and discern if it was true for them or not. It was the wakeup call for self-responsibility, and few were willing to hear it.

CHAPTER 14

GRIEVING: BLAME

The second phase of grief is anger and blame. The world was in the thick of it. Blaming China, blaming their own governments for not shutting borders earlier. Blaming each other for catching it. People were seeing governments as taking their rights to freedom away and choice. With such an overwhelming attitude that it is someone's fault for how they feel, it was only natural, from the shadow perspective, for humans to put the responsibility outside themselves, so they could play victim once more to something they thought was bigger than them.

This is the sorry emotional state of the world. To live in such fear of a virus rather than having trust in the body's own innate ability to deal with a virus through the immune system. The irony is very few are talking about the personal responsibility for their own health and would they be in a natural state of wellness to deal with a virus as body's are designed to do?

With the current rates of sickness in the world, the majority are not. It is easier to blame the virus than to take the responsibility for their own health in the first place. No matter how you ended up in your current state of health (genetics, lifestyle, disease etc) there is still no valid reason to give your self-authority away in the form of fear to something that you may never get.

The only thing you can control at any time in your life is your attitude. When you stop being victim, blaming the circumstances or someone, you begin to reclaim sovereignty. The power is in this present moment, where you get to choose how you react and what you do with your life. It is a hundred times more beneficial to do what suits you right now, to keep yourself healthy, happy and occupied, rather than be frozen in terror at the what ifs. So many are cowering in the corners, waiting for Big Pharma to create some magical potion to "fix" the issue.

For that is how many choose to live. They want others to fix them, provide the solution, do the work for them, rather than be accountable for their health, wellbeing, happiness. The sheeple just want to stay in the herd, being guided along, being told what to do and not do.

This is NOT how humans evolve. This time is the key to unlocking self-realisation and empowerment to make different choices in their life, starting with the attitude they have towards the whole Covid-19 affair.

CHAPTER 15

OLD PATTERNS RETURNING

I was starting to recognise I was in fear of my old patterns coming back. The underlying buzz of anxiousness of losing control, and that others would start telling me what to do and how to live. I was playing the blame game.

I could see this was shadow of course, yet the daunting prospect of mandatory vaccines and microchips for travel control left me feeling sickened. For a short while, I bought into the impending doom of the world, watching all the alternative videos to discover the Truth behind all this.

I started watching the David Wilcock video updates, though his verbosity and length of delivery is somewhat trying, even at double speed. I had studied his theories extensively three years ago, when I spent 4 months watching and reading anything I could get my hands on the behind-the-scenes truth. Whether that be conspiracy theories of Deep State, the ancient wisdom hidden in the myths, or the practical aspects of quantum science and how it works.

All of that was laying a foundation of knowledge for me, and I spent a great deal of time channeling as well. I saw patterns no one else had documented. I could explain how my physical healing worked using quantum energies and redshift.

I channeled a solution of vaccine adjuvants, to make vaccines substantially safer. This is an area dear to my heart. I am not an anti-vaxxer, I am pro-choice, and an advocate for safer vaccine development.

I also channeled solutions for women who could not get pregnant. Little did I know within a couple of years, a high-level mentor, would say I was to help women get pregnant, and hence Pregnancy Alchemy was born.

In fact, in that Business Summoning Session at the beginning of April 2019, so much was unearthed about my path, or rather, reflected to me of what I already knew about myself yet was too afraid to own.

In that session I was called the Witch of Witches, and that I was so powerful, I could create a million-dollar business in whatever field I chose, though she recognised money is not my driver.

My issue, according to her, was I only stayed on the surface and dabbled, I never went deep with my clients, thinking I needed to meet them where they were at. I was Peter Pan, playing in the sand pit. If I didn't get out, I would end up killing myself.

This indeed was true when I worked in the Light Grid. Always staying safe, offering oodles of compassion and empathy, and never taking anyone out of their comfort zone because they "wouldn't get it".

I also knew she was right – I had sworn years ago I would fight until my dying breath and last cent in the bank, working out what my purpose was. If I failed, I would take myself out. A disease is not hard to manifest, and I could leave my children without guilt of suicide. Yep, I was playing Martyr to the Cause beautifully. I am sure it was not the first lifetime to do so.

* * *

It was one of the reasons I had a break from my healing business from end of 2017 to beginning of 2019. I really did not know what my direction was, how to truly discover what I was here for, and could not for the life of me figure out how to go deep with my work.

In July 2017, I "broke up" with my spiritual mentor, I will call her Katie, who I had been devoted to since 2013. I had put my complete faith in her for guidance. It was early in 2017 when I was writing and channeling and the wisdom I was bringing through was off the charts.

Katie and I went away for 3 days at the beginning of July 2017. Her physical body was in a sorry state of repair as it had been for decades, it baffled doctors how she was still alive. She had previously died, twice, and revived.

Having explained Quantum Healing to her, we did a couple of processes on her body, simply through my words and moving energy. Within 8 minutes, the continual pain she had had in her one remaining kidney was gone, for the first time in 30 years. Later I did a similar process on her spine, and she was pain free. She went to bed that night for the first time since being a child, without having to do her pain management protocol. She hardly knew herself.

The next day, the pain had returned, however, I knew this was a good start. We continued to map the dimensions, DNA, Soul realms and frequencies, unravelling the Truth of our very existence.

70

I was hugely excited and ready for what was going to unfold, with both of us working together.

Except Katie didn't really want to. She failed to be available for our next three scheduled meetings. A month passed. I was beside myself. It was dawning on me she was so attached to her drama, her body, her story and her shadow, she actually did not want to liberate herself from any of it.

I wrote her a long 16-page letter, outpouring how I felt, my anger, the possibilities, all I needed to express. I asked to get on board or tell me no. I hand delivered it to her letter box.

I never heard from her again, other than a note in messenger to say she missed me too and loved me, after I dropped her a line mid-August to see how she was.

I was devastated. I thought she was committed. I put the responsibility for my own development squarely on her shoulders, and who would I be without her?

I spent July – December 2017 in a desperate state. So lost, felt I had no direction. I kept myself going through a few wellness fairs, doing Akashic Record readings for $40 for 20 minutes and selling my Protect Your Energy products for EMF protection.

I was called to create some meditations and publish them on an app called Insight Timer that August, in time with the eclipse season that month. I enjoyed learning how to record and edit and get the feedback from people. They were such Light Grid recordings, and would remain so for some time, including a course called "setting intentions from your heart and Soul" which eventually got published in 2018 when the platform launched its course element.

In the second half of 2017, I returned to an oh so familiar pattern of feeling suicidal. I fantasised about how to end it all. I got my affairs in order, wrote up my will, sorted policies and paperwork. I would call Lifeline in the middle of the night, desperate for someone to talk to, as there was no way this was going on public display.

I had no close friends I would share this with, and who was I to admit my bi-polar traits were getting the better of me? After all, I had created a course in 2016 called "28 days to radiant living" and I was meant to be an expert on how to hold your shit together.

At this point, I had been out of my marriage 3 years, living as a single mother with zero income, and zero government support, a temporary resident of Australia, unable to get permanent residency. They took Medicare from me after 5 years of being here. The only money I had coming in was $18k child support. My rent was $25k per year. The only thing I had mastered was accumulating business tax losses over 13 years. I continued to live off my savings, though at this point I could not see my future at all. At the same time, I did not feel victim to any of this, I knew I was fully responsible for the whole experience, it was what I had chosen.

A friend of mine recommended I go to see a healer up in the hills. So off I went to the most bizarre and confronting "healing session" I have ever had.

"You will not like what I have to say, and you probably won't agree with it. I may tell you that you will never be able to do your work again.

So, you have a choice, you can leave now, or hear what I have to say", he started off with.

"I have nothing to lose, there is nothing to hold on to. I will stay". It was my honest response.

He worked in a very strange way; I really was not convinced though went along with it. He said at one point, "you are working with Shiva, he is a hugely powerful energy, though I do not know why you are working with him".

Still feeling very lost, I went back to him a couple times more, with pages of notes with all the options of what I was considering creating, who I would work with, and through kinesiology he would say yes or no. Once again, I was relying on other people to decipher for me what it was I was meant to do.

After the first session, I went online to see if I could buy a picture of Shiva which would resonate for me. I came across this.

I immediately bought a canvas of this and pinned it on my bedroom wall. It spoke to my heart; I adored the energy and the power of it.

In December 2017, I came across a video from Adam Hudson talking about Amazon products. He had been the creator of one of the first business products I had got involved with and set up a business with my husband in 2005 in New Zealand where we lived at the time, called Wealth Essentials.

Maybe that is what I needed to do. Get out of the healing and coaching game, or at least have a break from it.

I went out for a walk and asked to be shown what was it I could create that meant something to me, and I could sell online. I immediately saw a triangular wrap, two sided, in silk, with my Shiva Shakti image on.

I was sold.

Hence, Prasamana was conceived and birthed in 2018, with the delivery arriving on 8th December, $36k later. It had been an incredibly challenging year dealing with Chinese suppliers, though mid-year I was blessed with the most amazing designer, Saerah.

I had known I was not going to create just one wrap, but a series of designs. I would channel the designs and sketch them out, and she would graphically recreate them. She was astounding at understanding my requirement to build in the energetic layering in the dimensions of the images.

Saerah also recreated the Shiva Shakti image, using the canvas as a basis and we put our own energy layers and details into it. This is her modelling the design.

Note how he is now looking at her on the front, and on the back, she looks at him. The reverse side are massive angel wings – like the wings of Isis.

I created a range of silk and wool wraps, 15 in all. Sorted the Trademarks and went into production. I adored the process of creating a luxury product and brand, which could be used in conjunction with my healing work and as a meditation/activation creator. I even included a 9-day Activation series on the Inner Family, which I channeled at the beginning of 2019, as a giveaway with each wrap and scarf.

Listings went up on Etsy, my own website went up, www.prasamana.com. And nothing, well not much. I could not bring myself to learn the antics of Amazon, there was something that really deterred me from that path. I had never bought a single thing, other than a book, from Amazon and just could not go into a platform my market was not shopping on. I also have a massive problem with the ethos of Amazon. How does a multi-billion dollar global company pay no tax in the US exactly??

By the start of 2019, my linen cupboard, every empty cupboard, my en-suite shower was filled with Prasamana boxes. Saerah had gone AWOL mid-December and dropped me an email at the beginning of January saying she could no longer work for me. No explanation. And I had zero interest in it. I loved the creativity and the joy of bringing something to life. Now what?

I put out there I needed a mentor to help me bring Prasamana and Your Universal Self (my healing and coaching business) together.

At the beginning of February 2019, someone left me a comment on an old Mintaka video I did. I ended up talking with her, and she led me to the mentor with whom I did my business summoning session and discovered Shadow Alchemy work.

Around the same time in April of 2019, I also came across an associate with whom I did a huge amount of rebranding work with. In my identity reading, Amanda called me "The High Priestess of the Coven". This totally fitted with being named a Witch the week before.

Hence Josephine Sorciere was birthed over the following few months, and I had a naming ceremony on the first day of my 50th year, my birthday on 21st July. The rest, as they say, is history.

* * *

Let me jump back to March 2020. I had put myself outside my comfort zone and done a Burlesque Fringe show the first weekend in March. I had loved being back on stage (my home as a kid), and dancing again. However, the high quickly turned to a low, before the second show even started. Being around 300 women and sharing an under-stage, claustrophobic dressing room with 60 of them for hours on end was a test on my patience and nerves. My ability for small talk had waned long ago.

I was feeling edgy. I addition, my health had not been on top of the world. A trip to the naturopath a couple of days after had me realizing I had stopped taking my adrenal tablets mid last year when things were evolving quickly and my body didn't need them.

My monthly health checks with a holistic practitioner were showing it was not emotional response and just a chemical imbalance. It took six months to join the dots and recalibrate with the health support my body needs.

I drop this in, as not all currents of underlying anxiety are emotional based, and I highly recommend a good naturopath who does iridology and live blood samples to recommend exactly what your body requires.

I also love the book, The Hormone Cure, by Sarah Gottfried to get you up to speed on what your body is really doing.

So back on track with health, I could once again regroup and be far more objective about what I was reading and watching in the world.

The minute you buy into and believe that the Government is about to take your independence away with no freedom of choice, you are back in shadow.

Just because you cannot see a solution does not mean one does not exist. What if the solutions were so out of this world, literally, no-one could see them coming?

It's why I started watching Wilcock again. To get up to speed on what has been revealed. Whilst he is very much Light Grid, and operates through fear of his own life, he is dedicated to bringing forward all versions of possibilities. I ordered a copy of his book, The Synchronicity Key, it was about time I read it.

Once I had got my chemical balance sorted, I could feel into the collective energies far more precisely. I was being reminded to trust the process – allow the experience to unfold to take us all to the next level. To process all the fear I was picking up on from the collective and alchemize it. It was not mine.

I have never bought into a concept of not being strong enough to escape this virus. I put complete trust in my body's immunity system to deal with it if I were to get it. However, the world was really buying into the fear of it all, and media was focusing on the death toll, without highlighting the 95% recovery rate (it is 98% by May).

I knew I had to refocus on what I taught: self-responsibility, balance, alchemizing all fear and trusting. All done though the process of continuous transformation, creativity and expanded awareness. Keep upping the frequencies.

It was exactly these areas I focused on for the Claim My Desire Masterclass. I could hardly believe it was only three months since I had run the challenge. My life, consciousness and the world around me had so radically changed.

I was realigning with Who I Am, as a catalyst for change. The collective energies had shifted, and people were starting to question and discern the truth. They were beginning to move out of frozen fear and into ownership, though the majority still want someone else to fix them rather than be self-responsible.

When I work with clients, my job is to show them the map they have been searching lifetimes for, clear the path & reprogram (energy encoding) and hand over the keys of ownership.

This is not something I have learnt in this incarnation. It is an accumulation of eons of wisdom, brought forward from the planetary systems and Universes I originally evolved from.

It has taken 16 years on my own path of self-discovery, and I know I have found the radical short cuts to help others find their own Genius too.

By the end of March, I knew I wanted to work with high end clients who would have an influence over the masses. I adored working with the influential corporate women, open to disruptive innovation. To create radical change in the world, and so Dark Disruptors was registered on 24th March 2020. This was a matter of hours after the vernal equinox, when the conception of the Golden Age took place. I only realise this now.

I felt it was time the world had been waiting for. The Crone Code was here to revolutionise the world. I needed to step up as the leader of Legacy Leaders to reawaken the dormant codes and energise the portals of transformation once more.

The Equinox was a turning point for the world, for consciousness. The energies started to move exponentially in a matter of hours, sometimes a couple of days.

The implants from other Collectives and Sleepers were now beginning to be activated. The alarm clock was being rung by the Great Central Sun for all systems across the multi-verse to wake up.

For it is time to assist the evolvement of humanity and create the contemporary human, one who can transcend the fight or flight mentality and programming. One who is ready to return to the Truth of Who We Really Are.

Spiritual Beings having a human experience.

CHAPTER 16

ASTROLOGY: MARCH 2020

March will help us move out of the black hole, the vortex, we have been stuck in. When we have conjuncts it can take days, weeks, months up to a year to feel the full effect of them. Events have to 'catch up' as it were. It is less about the virus, more about the government imposing institutional control and national emergencies.

When Saturn moved into Capricorn in December 2017, he only had one job to do until he leaves Capricorn and that was to meet the Lord of the Underworld, Pluto (Greek word for Hades, meaning Hell).

Jupiter, Saturn and Pluto were setting in for the long game when along comes Mars, the planet of passion and warrior planet of the cosmos returning to Capricorn. He was here to remind one and all that if the three Big Guys were meeting just this once in Capricorn in our lifetime, we needed to exploit the potential now. This is a time to bring into being the potential for radical change and shake up the year began with *(and didn't it just)*.

On March 4th Venus moves into Taurus, the energy of enjoyment of the home comforts. She will encounter Uranus here and gets excited about new things, you may feel a little agitated if not keen on change.

By March 8th, Sun is moving through Pisces where transformation happens through imagination. This is the place of illusions which may be the basis for us to build our dreams on.

(Hindsight: if people could see the opportunity opening up rather than suppression of impending lockdown, seeds of dreams could be planted).

When Sun is close to Neptune 7-9th March there will be real stuff going on. The full moon in Virgo on March 9th is incredibly potent where fact and fantasy come head-to-head. We must feel into it and desire useful facts. Be able to see things from opposite sides of the same coin. We may feel destabilised, however this could give us the solutions we would not have otherwise considered, new ideas. *(Started working from home was a new concept that wobbled people yet gave a great solution for many. Countries had not yet decided if lockdown and restrictions were necessary).*

On 9th March at same time of full moon Mercury turns direct. This is pushing us into a dark void – we do not know where we are going. Venus square Saturn has to pull back and do things differently, may feel isolated within your relationships.

It would only be the final nine days from 22nd March where we would really see the power and potential of the Big Guns in Capricorn. Saturn was off for a few months in Aquarius before returning here until December. He will then not return for another three decades. As he moves on, he will change the shape of this year. He is the taskmaster to put in the work and take responsibility, whilst taking slow and careful steps.

As Saturn stepped aside like a camper van out of the fast lane, Mars, Jupiter and Pluto could move full steam ahead. A massive difference from the previous period. Up until then, Saturn is testing all the structures of society, whereas Pluto is about death, rebirth and transformation. Jupiter is about opportunity and growth, Mars about direction and energy.

This is the time for the planets of luck, war and revolution coming together as Saturn moves out of the way, creating a game changing acceleration in the latter part of March and into April that will be felt globally.

Saturn in Aquarius is less about the structures more about the collective ideals, we will start to have inklings of the future. Saturn will turn retrograde and move back into Capricorn on July 1 and return to Aquarius on December 16th. In March 2023 will move into Pisces.

At the Spring Equinox we have a clean ending before the Sun moving into Aries, closely followed by Mars & Jupiter. This is an enthusiastic pairing, which may play out with exciting events, "good or bad".

New Moon on March 24th in Aries, the fire sign working with his intuition, to bring new things in spontaneously. This is the real new beginning of the Equinox. These few days are for great creation. It also opens our wounds with Chiron in play.

(N.B. mid-March to mid-May was the entire period of serious lockdown. Some restrictions easing in June for various countries. Still far from all aspects of society back in operation. Ties in with Saturn moving to Aquarius and returning to Capricorn from July 1 in time for "the new normal".)

INTERLUDE

I have set the scene in the first few months of the year. What was unfolding in my business & background, world events and how consciousness was entrenched in fear.

The turning point of events and speed at which energies were shifting happened at the March Equinox. I see that as the Conception Point for the New Age.

It will take nine months gestation period, with a due date around Solstice in December Just like morning sickness, the world felt unwell for the first Trimester. By end of June, colour returns to the cheeks of The Great Mother as we shift to life in the "new normal".

It is a period of the most profound channeled messages, synchronicity spirals and wormholes, which unfurl and expand like never before, especially from Easter onwards. The remainder of the book will open your awareness to the infinite possibilities never before conceived.

You will discover the path to the Portals which were a large focus in the second half of the year, as the doorways were opened once again for the Cosmic energies and the Ancient Ones to emerge and merge.

APRIL 2020

CHAPTER 17

PORTALISM IS DEFINED

I published my Kali 2.0 Activation on Insight Timer on 1st April. It stood out a mile amongst the Light Grid meditations of how to cope with fear, stress and death.

I always create for the joy of it, rather than being attached to outcome. However, it does make my heart smile to read the reviews of it being the single most powerful message they had received about the world stage.

When you deliver in your fullest authenticity and continually develop your wisdom, power and abilities, you will stand head and shoulders above the rest. Competition is not a word in your vocabulary, and you develop your very own dark brand.

I was taught this philosophy by the Dark Luxury genius Amanda Cromer, who I had worked with extensively last year to morph who I am into Josephine.

In the best of divine timing and synchronicity, Amanda started to offer sessions to update marketing tactics. She was able to hone in on my market and message in their language, and over a couple of weeks and sessions, I developed my new website www.darkdisruptors.com

She also suggested it was time I had my own -Ism. What phrase could I coin as my own to explain my work. At the end of our second session, something was mentioned and I blurted out PORTALISM.

For that is what I do – work across the portals of time and rewrite the Akashic records. As the site developed, definitions and refinements got tighter. I sum it up as "unearthing your prodigy through the portals of time".

I knew it was time to start streaming my work. I would still assist individuals ready for their fullest transformation under "Unleash the Alchemist" .

I was also ready to work with my high-level Corporates and Entrepreneurs who I would take to the next level to immerse the masses with a new framework of operation and radical solutions.

These are the people with the drive, determination and backing to get the job done. They are ready to bulldoze through the barricades to their Truth, absolutely driven to finally find their inner Prodigy.

They would have lived as Leaders over many lifetimes, and Soul contracts to work with me would have been established eons ago. The Dark Disruptors are the ones to pull back the curtains for the masses to see the truth of evolving consciousness and allow the next layer of people to move on up in their own personal empowerment and truth.

My job is to ignite their codes once again once their shadow mind has been slayed, so their Cosmic Genius can stream through as a catalyst of radical transformation.

The Dark Disruptors do not have to go down the long path of befriending their intuition and listening for the hints and whispers as to what to do. It is already ingrained in them, they are programmed for their gifts and knowing. There is nothing to learn.

The Light Gridders LOVE to be told what to do from intuition, angels and a myriad of guidance from outside themselves. It means they do not have to be fully responsible for making the decisions and trusting themselves.

The hardest path to take is for a Darkworker to stumble through the Light Grid doing their best to feel they belong, to keep their mouths shut on the truth they see in another for fear of upsetting them. So much has to be unlearnt when you come home to the Truth. That you already are wired to access your prodigy, it's simply clearing the debris of density first.

Then both the Alchemists and the Prodigies can have their codes reactivated to access the higher frequencies and depth of truth behind their Soul – their cosmic counterparts. Which is what I do. It is time.

* * *

Before developing the new site, I took a quick look at Pregnancy Alchemy, and discovered the site had been hacked 6 weeks earlier and left me with a Hello World post. Hosting backup only goes back a month.

At some level, I knew I had sabotaged that as well as by someone who really has nothing better to do than destroy sites. It had been an arena I was told to work in, rather than choosing it myself. Whilst I am fully confident in opening the Conception Codes in women once they have

91

claimed their own abilities as a witch, it never lit my heart to be my only line of clients.

When practical issues like that arise, it is always time to review what part did I played. I do not buy into victim hood at any level.

I also realized it was time to withdraw my political standpoint in my shares from Josephine. It is not my job to get involved on this front - many others have this role. Whilst I continued to share informative and alternative videos and articles on my personal page, I had to walk away from getting involved.

Always know your battleground, your arena of play and who you are targeting. Anything outside of this remit must be left alone.

CHAPTER 18*

REBELLION IS REQUIRED

The first few weeks of April had me more concerned than at any other point of the progress. Consciousness seemed to be at a standstill, having done what they were told, programmed by the Governments.

Many sat at home, now unemployed, wallowing in the doom and gloom. This was not the time for self-pity, rather, step up and question what they were doing with their life.

The world agenda was nudging each individual to discern their own truth. Was mass media giving them the whole picture? It never ceases to amaze me the ignorance with how media is tied in with the big business. Even Kevin Rudd, a former Australian Prime Minister, got on board recently with an interview of how distorted the ownership of media is here with the Murdoch empire ruling the roost. We will only be told one line, one directive, with no avenue for freedom of speech.

So much unawareness how the large media companies are so deeply entrenched with Big Pharma and the financial institutions. I often shake my head at the world's ignorance.

It was always going to take an event like this to give people an opportunity to wake up, smell the coffee, or BS in this case, and work out what is real and what's not.

For them to see the long-term agenda of population control and tracking for all individuals, led by Bill Gates. I will not use this book as an outlet for my distain of what he has done and intends to implement, other than to say, if you still want freedom of choice, you need to wake up.

Without the general public becoming aware of what is going on and standing up for radical change, the human race is on track for self-destruction.

It is make or break time for the survival of humanity.

The only way for the Collective Consciousness to rise above this dense, fear mongering, fight or flight survival mentality and energy is to rebel against the enforcement.

At this stage, it was not about taking to the streets in protest (though that will be on the cards if things do not progress and open quickly). It was for individuals to step up and choose what to believe. To move away from other people having control, or at least the illusion that comes with it.

This enhances the collective energy, the fundamental determinant to what happens to civilization. The frequency and vibration of the collective had to change from the level we "should be" according to mass media. In fear, shut away inside.

The shift required FROM THE PEOPLE and not from the governments, medical or military is the determinant for moving forward, and the breakthrough required.

At the end of March, they were still not seeing this.

* * *

What IS required to help lift the energy of the collective?

The Light Workers were nowhere to be found. They simply could not hold the collective energies, their prowess for empathy had got the better of them and were simply overwhelmed with the waves of despair ebbing and flowing from the populous.

Illusional empathy is martyrdom.

"I'll take on the burdens of the world, it will make me feel valuable, and as a vessel of love and light, that's my job". Bless those Mintakans. They really were letting the stormwaters in to blow their own light out.

This was their backbone of servitude, of martyrdom; it was just too heavy to carry. They had to get out of ego, become present and dissolve the illusions of being in control.

The Lightworkers could not feel the new energy because they could not see it. The dark cannot be seen in the light. Their third eyes were not working and could not tap into the resources they usually relied on.

The Light Grid was fizzling out and they were really losing their bearings. Playing victim to the fear, then trying to rescue everyone with myriads of meditation to deal with terror. How to pet it like a dog, just as they always do. It's why my Kali meditation stood out a mile on

Insight Timer – it told the Truth and stopped pandering to the global energy.

We are ready to call in the assistance and frequencies from other realms.

It is time for the cosmic energies to be reopened through the portals and uplift the frequencies at which humanity operates. However, it must be done at a rate which can be sustained by the Collective, or it will freak them out, or fry their toxicity of fear within them. Or both.

The Aliens are coming. Some are already here.

It is the Ancient Ones calling their long-lost relatives.

"It is time you came to visit. The current houseguests are about to get kicked out."

Sounds cheesy, something out of a movie. Yet evolution depends on planets like Earth to expand consciousness through a living being. Humans have been extremely slow on this take up. Yet it is essential for civilization to grasp what they are actually here for or face wipeout.

Do not think for one minute the governments, media, big pharma and military do not know about this.

They are doing everything in their power right now to "protect humanity" from these higher frequencies so that we can remain forever the human race that we have known up until now. Slave selves.

Patriarchy developed as an absolute fear of loss of control and death. Hence being in such full force now, as they know it could be the final years of civilization as we know it.

It is the elite at the top who feel they would like to play God for a while and unite in a force called "Deep State", the Cabal, or the Illuminati.

They are simply terrified what would happen to their empires if people woke up and realised how powerful they are.

This is the very reason YOU are reading this book.

There are two frequencies fighting for the same dominance over humanity. On one hand, we have the control of patriarchy and ancient human protection mechanisms – the Collective Consciousness. The Matrix. On the other is the collective of all other planet frequencies and the Ancient Ones ready to assist.

Without which, humankind will annihilate.

Rebellion is required to transcend the energy. To turn the cog in the clockwork of time, moving us into the next frequency. This must be observed to take hold.

The dynamics of dominating control and manipulation must change. If this continues, it is game over.

Instead, we must shift to co-operation and consensual collaboration. Dropping in personal creativity and self-expression. The new way.

This book for the chosen few who can see through the BS spurted from the lips of the Idols, and witness with horror, how the sheeple react in obeyance to their rules.

You are reading this because you know there an alternative way to be, which requires a huge influx of other energy to facilitate radical transformation on this planet.

It is also reopening your contracts with the Ancient Ones. We are boarding the vessel of Portalism to play with time & space and create a new reality.

Your Soul contract has you enlisted to play an essential role in this upgrade of consciousness itself. To be part of the "Cosmic Rollout Plan". You could have one or more roles to play over the next few years. Welcome to the ultimate Virtual Reality Game of Life.

The objectives of the next dimensional energies will remain unknown to us for at least another three months, taking us to July. We must prepare.

We have Gatekeepers. The Deciphers of the Codes. The Facilitators. The Dark Disruptors. The Encoders. The Translators. The Transitioners. With many, many more roles to be developed and defined as we unfold into a new operating system.

Where to begin?

CHAPTER 19

BEGIN WITH CHANGE WITHIN

If you are reading this, you know exactly what is required to regain your sovereignty. You recall how your life dramatically changed when you started to own who you really are.

This is not the case for the majority and as Change Agents, it is part of our role to influence the choices the collective makes. To nurture and inspire society.

First and foremost, it is your own high frequency that must be maintained. You cannot dip into the level of Collective Consciousness because you have any requirement to feed your old programming of empathy.

It can be observed, and your finger dipped in to test the temperatures of the water. Yet if you decide to immerse in the depths of the despair of the majority, it is a long haul to swim to the shoreline.

Besides which, now you continually wear your lifejacket of your own making, it is increasingly difficult to sink into the quagmire. It is only your shadow that punctures holes in your life raft. And it is only your mind which allows with glee for those holes to be made.

Just as individuals need to find their own power, so do countries. Think about an international sports match when the anthems are sung. I cry every time, regardless of the teams. I bawl if it's England, New Zealand or Australia, the three countries I have lived in.

I feel the loyalty, the power, the heartfelt emotion at the dedication of the players and the fans to that country in that moment.

We are required to regain a balance between the global marketplace and our own countries. To maintain our cultural mind identity, the points of difference. Where have we sold out to other nations and given away our bargaining power?

The planet has become a disposable plastic factory, despite the efforts of recycling. Recognition of what we have on our doorstep is paramount.

The talent, the produce, the land, the people. How can we be self-supportive and only export our excess beyond our people's needs? If you took out the profiteers, this would be simple.

It is part of the paradigm that is being ripped apart; it is the start of the downfall of global economies, as discussed before.

The decisions about the economy, who we trade with and what we trade must be taken out of the hands of the Capitalists. It can only be done by the people themselves taking a stand and supporting their own economy and land first, whilst giving credence and support to other countries.

It boils down to self-responsibility, a message which appears time and time again in this text. Accountability for self and the choices we make, followed by those of our families, our community, country and planet.

The needs, not wants, of which must be made in all purchasing and sales decisions by everyone.

This will naturally cull the greed of the nations, the requirement to hang on other coat tails to enjoy a free ride and look after the best interests of the people first.

The real shift in energies will only become apparent when we reach the tipping point of ownership.

Assistance comes to those ready to help themselves. With the attitude of "it's someone else's responsibility to fix me/ my job/ the economy/ the health system / my body", no wonder we are floundering as a race.

When will that tipping point arrive?

In the Northern hemisphere, spring was only just emerging in April. It was quite happy in a way to hibernate away in self isolation.

It was time to come out of the cave. Though we were not allowed.

CHAPTER 20*

GRIEVING: BARGAINING

The third stage of grief is bargaining.

"If I stay at home for 4-6 weeks, I would have done my bit, followed instructions, and so you will make everything right, ok?"

The world will not be fully let out of lockdown (or rather, in and out of lockdown for 18 months or more) until one of two things happen.

First option: The sheeple are good and do what they are told, cower in the corner with fear, having no faith in their body's immunity system to get over a virus as we are designed to do. They will wait patiently until a vaccine is created and then they can buy into the illusion that they are safe. They will have been good children and be rewarded with a concoction of gene therapy and a donut. Thanks Krispy Kreme for your contribution to society.

Second Option: people stop putting blame on the circumstances and go deep within to restate their own attitude towards what has happened. They are present to their options and gain the unbiased information they require to make their own informed decisions.

I am ALWAYS about pro-choice. To empower others to make decisions that are right for themselves and their family, not simply because they are told to believe it.

This stage of grief in the bargaining is quickly passed through when you let go of the battle, the blame, the fear.

April was the start of the golden ticket to create a new life. To consider what part of normal did they really want to return to, and what will they not go back to.

It was an opportunity to get resourceful, creative, innovative. The very nature of who we are, powerful creators who can utilise our gifts to the fullest for the deepest sense of fulfillment ever imagined. Discovering, honing and evolving your craft.

So many had been given the gift of time in which to experience this yet not all were taking the bait. Many were still floundering on the sidelines of this new pool we were swimming in, feeling no support from the armbands of society and Collective Consciousness to keep them buoyant. Still so scared that they could not swim in this new current.

For those who have awakened and receiving the new energies, it is imperative to create the network of grids to the new frequencies and place on top of the collective energy, like a weighted soothing blanket.

April energies needed calming, and this will always continue long beyond the cross over to the new operating system of self-liberation. The more people who take the stance of self-empowerment, freedom of choice and excited anticipation of a brand-new world, the quicker and easier the transition of energies will be.

It is imperative the Collective Consciousness reaches a sustainable higher frequency than we have ever had. It is the only way the new energies will be able to anchor here.

To move them out of sedation into active life once more. This period of quarantine was essential in April for us all to have the time out of society, to observe with a questioning eye what we were being told by mass media.

The enforced shutdown was imperative on so many levels. Yet so many were terrified about coming out of lockdown and facing the new world, however that would look like. There was still no sense of perspective about the whole situation, no realization that every single person had a choice about their own attitude towards it all.

The cosmic powers that be are waiting to determine the outcome of consciousness v corruption, which can only be established by humanity.

CHAPTER 21

SAFE VACCINATIONS – DO
THEY EXIST?

I have studied so much on the effects of vaccinations over the past 12 years and beyond and I chose not to vaccinate my children through the medical route. Instead, they are homoeopathically immunized which I initiated a few years ago.

I am an avid supporter of the work of Robert F Kennedy Jr, reading all his findings every week. He presents clear evidence to enable the individual to make informed vaccination decisions.

In 2017 when I spent many months immersed in the ancient teachings and channelling my own wisdom, I downloaded a solution for vaccines. This chapter provides my findings from then as well as current date insight.

The following is channel from June 2017.

"Silica it is proven to work as alternative beneficial adjuvant instead of aluminium. It cannot be sourced from Earth; it must be mined from one of the planets or the moon. This will contain higher energetic frequencies and be free of contamination and pollution.

Once it is established and its functionality it can then be scientifically replicated. All materials can be re-frequenced in the energetic patterns changed to affect the outcomes. Again, once science sees the process it will create recalibration equipment to do the same.

The planetary silica can be used in vaccine safety with no adverse effects. It will take 20 years to be fully integrated into the mainstream. In the meantime, vaccination damage and other diseases can be dissipated through re-frequency programs. Using the principles of Bio-resonance, the AI's can be matched and programmed.

I am able to re-frequence substances and materials which are consumed by the body. Any upgrade through re-frequencing must be delivered in conjunction with a healthy diet and exercise plan including oils and homeopathy. Alternative frequencies can be facilitated through the DNA to override the body's disfunction.

Use of medicinal drugs during the healing process slows down the re-frequency process. Medications can also be energetically re-frequenced and must be taken for at least three weeks prior and post the work.

Silica allows structures to return to their natural geometry. Understanding the geometric pattern formation will provide the correct construct for vaccinations.

Aluminium and other toxic ingredients destruct to dissolve the DNA formations especially once crossing the brain membrane. It destroys the natural formation, hence damaging the body.

Aluminium attaches to the DNA in telomeres. It is blocking the ability to receive the electric current through them. Instead, it reflects within the brain which causes seizures and neural programming disorders. The brain is not wired up properly because aluminium is blocking the free flow of the energies between all particles.

It is only frequencies beyond this time and reality which can transmit the aluminium throughout the brain and the body. The circuits can be rewired and rebuilt properly in conjunction with proper nutrition and holistic care.

It must be brought into the recipient's awareness through to be effective (the quantum law of observation). If the individual denies the effects of vaccinations, pharmaceutical treatments and disassociation of the issue, it cannot be resolved within the body. The recipient needs to be willing and open to give his own body and Source permission to reverse it.

Mercury also expands and contracts in the presence of the torsion field. So, when administered to an infant so much pure light is running as a torsion field, it affects the natural functioning of the brain and body cells. The reactions to the chemical compounds vary in the presence of torsion fields. Metals reflect torsion fields which are essential to our health.

Science showed some stars caused deflection of torsion fields. If the Soul has originated and spent time in that star system and aluminium is introduced to the body, it overrides much absorption / deflection of the base material.

Many are ready to receive the light connection to reawaken DNA. DNA naturally evolves as we move forward in the solar system. If strands are not open, they cannot survive. The majority of negative based people able unable to receive this reprogramming.

The biggest killer to DNA structures was when the Draco interbred with us and it dissolved the strands. I am not from this bloodline, I am from alien blood. I am part of the 7% (O- type blood). It is not infected by Draco.

Sacred fractal geometry can also be used to heal DNA as it is reconnected with the original cell patterns and distortions of lost. Geometric patterns can be produced for the frequency of each DNA strand. This provides top up calibration.

There are sectors of people, autistic, ADHD, who are more attuned to receiving programming and re-frequencing because it is a wiring issue. Once neural pathways realigned, they can comfortably live in 4D and move towards 5D, just challenged in 3D.

People with these issues are largely Parallels and are choosing to have a different life experience here. Their frequencies cannot adapt to those of Earth, they are out of tune.

When their frequencies can be reprogrammed to the original six Solfeggio frequencies, this activates DNA strands in the body so they can receive the ID (?) frequency. They will know it is safe and good to do so and their behaviours will change.

Certain frequencies activate the wiring in our brain and activate DMT – neurotransmitters. These are wired up to the DNA and hence open the bodies abilities at a cellular level and DNA structure level to receive & experience consciousness.

We are moving from 6 to 7 Carbons in our biology, the foundational block for survival. Science has shown silicon would be much better suited as a biochemical base for life than carbon on other planets. We are moving from quartz based cellular level to silica, so we can receive more light away from the density."

There is not a shadow of doubt in my mind that vaccinations affect our DNA. With Bill Gates supposedly leading the world on vaccine solutions, and the main funder of WHO, we need to see what his plans are. Never mind he has zero medical qualifications, just deep pockets.

The following quote is taken from his blog 30 April.

<u>Bill Gates Blog</u>

"I'm particularly excited by two new approaches that some of the candidates are taking: **RNA and DNA vaccines**.

Here's how an RNA vaccine works: rather than injecting a pathogen's antigen into your body, you instead give the body the genetic code needed to produce that antigen itself. When the antigens appear on the outside of your cells, your immune system attacks them—and learns how to defeat future intruders in the process. You essentially turn your body into its own vaccine manufacturing unit.

Because RNA vaccines let your body do most of the work, they don't require much material. That makes them much faster to manufacture. There's a catch, though: we don't know for sure yet if RNA is a viable platform for vaccines. Since COVID would be the first RNA vaccine out of the gate, we have to prove both that the platform itself works and that it creates immunity. It's a bit like building your computer system and your first piece of software at the same time.

A small—but not insignificant—number developed more serious reactions (from the smallpox vaccine). (It) was far from perfect, but it got the job done. The COVID-19 vaccine might be similar.

If we were designing the perfect vaccine, we'd want it to be completely safe and 100 percent effective. It should be a single dose that gives you lifelong protection, and it should be easy to store and transport. I hope the COVID-19 vaccine has all of those qualities, but given the timeline we're on, it may not.

The two priorities, as I mentioned earlier, are **safety** and **efficacy**. Since we might not have time to do multi-year studies, we will have to conduct robust phase 1 safety trials and make sure we have good real-world evidence that the vaccine is completely safe to use.

We have a bit more wiggle room with efficacy. I suspect a vaccine that is at least 70 percent effective will be enough to stop the outbreak. A 60 percent effective vaccine is useable, but we might still see some localized outbreaks. Anything under 60 percent is unlikely to create enough herd immunity to stop the virus.

The big challenge will be making sure the vaccine works well in older people. The older you are, the less effective vaccines are. Your immune system—like the rest of your body—ages and is slower to recognize and attack invaders. That's a big issue for a COVID-19 vaccine, since older people are the most vulnerable. We need to make sure they're protected.

Once we have a vaccine, though, we still have huge problems to solve. That's because...

We need to manufacture and distribute at least 7 billion doses of the vaccine.

In order to stop the pandemic, we need to make the vaccine available to almost every person on the planet. We've never delivered something to every corner of the world before. "

DNA technology is actually gene therapy. Genes are injected into the body and they permanently alter the genetic makeup of the recipient in unknown ways.

RNA vaccines would carry the danger of triggering autoimmune reactions, meaning the body goes to war against itself.

It is crucial that humanity wakes up to the possibility that DNA could be ever altered from a vaccine. Whatever they devise, it will not stop future viruses.

Another interesting fact about Gates - he is not leaving his financial legacy to his kids, it all goes to charity. He is ensuring karma is not carried forward. Bill Gates' agenda will be uncovered, it is only a matter of time. He is protecting his children from being accountable for his actions.

* * *

Pursuing silica as a potential solution has been on my mind for the past three years. Rather than actively pursuing development and implementation, at this point I am energetically "putting it out there" for it to be considered an opening the door with alternative solutions.

At the beginning of April, I came across Dr. Shiva, who is running for US Senate in Boston. He is huge advocate natural immunity, to "Create the Future for Truth, Freedom, Health" as his slogan goes.

It dawned on me that THIS was the Shiva I was meant to be working with. I felt a deep soul connection and moved to tears when I realised this. I know he is open to alternatives and he has considered silica (when I tune in) though he has not pursued it.

I am aware it is more than metals that create vaccine injury. However, removing them would make them 83% safer (tested through kinesiology). We are all absorbing metals from the earth through foods, more than we have ever done.

It was most disappointing to find himself selling out to the political diatribe and slating RF Kennedy in public, stating he is in collusion with the Clintons etc. He succumbed to the egocentric slanging matches of politicians, behaving like a child having a tantrum because he felt left out. His Soul sold out. He annihilated himself, lost sight of the greater good.

Whilst I now know I will not be pursuing Shiva with the potential to develop solutions, I know the new frequencies will bring forward alternate ways for disease prevention. I also know I would love to discuss options with Robert F Kennedy, Jnr.

As I bring forward this new body of writing on consciousness, I have been challenged on a few perspectives I have held rigidly in my belief system. Vaccines were no exception.

It has been clear to me that those with autism and ADHD are already programmed to receive higher frequencies, to tap into their genius and bring forward their unique creativity and potentiality. I have known that for a long time.

I had never joined the dots that **"vaccine injury" was actually contributing to the opening of neural pathways ready to receive the higher frequencies.** Their bodies cannot handle the density on the Light Grid; they needed metal to anchor because of their planetary energy.

Humans (3D) do not, hence the majority do not experience "injury". Those who are programmed differently to "being normal" are on the fast track to claiming who they really are. They simply need to remove themselves from societal norms and find a way to express their brilliance.

Humanity needed a higher level of Souls programmed ready to receive the cosmic coding. This increases the number of people who can maintain the frequencies as they arrive. It also reduces the number of people who feel it is essential go through spiritual awakening on the Light Grid.

The biggest danger for new age thinking is that you must eliminate your abilities to obtain knowledge and find acceptance by your tribe. You were sold into the myth of being a victim to life itself and not seeing the power within already exists. For those already coded, this is doing shadow work on your genius.

There are a few purebloods; who have not had vaccinations, not autistic, though highly likely to have been diagnosed with some kind of neurological disorder in their life. These people, such you and I, hold the cosmic codes already.

I was pleased to hear when I tuned in that even if vaccines become mandatory, it will not undo the cosmic work to move us further forward. Sufficient energies are already coming through to make it work. The cosmic opportunities not been lost.

It is imperative people are aware the cover-ups the health organisations have made to meet their agenda of mass vaccinations. Big Pharma's profits are always come before the health of the population.

Over the last five years more people are being exposed to the truth through films such as Vaxxed in 2016.

Experts, whistle-blowers and parents came forward to share their side of the story.

Specialists such as Dr Suzanne Humphries, pictured here with me in August 2017, have been talking about the myths of herd immunity for some time.

Suzanne Humphries – Herd Immunity

We need more scientists, doctors and parents to come forward and speak from a place of experience.

Then other parents can be informed and consider the choices. I know most children and adults alike will never experience the adverse effects of vaccines. All I ask is for parents have the free choice to decide for themselves to follow their innate wisdom what is best for their child.

Perhaps it is time for the world to revert to solutions which have been in place for thousands of years. The indigenous people around the world immunize children with the herbs and trees of the earth.

Holistic health is the way to deny vaccines. Whilst I cannot say a soak in a mud bath is the entire solution, when used alongside homeopathy and bio resonance, it could provide a safe and alternative solution.

Herbal practioners have been persecuted for years for their understanding of the relationship between humans and nature. It cannot be explained by the scientists, therefore made wrong and ineffective, simply because it cannot be proved.

It is an essential part of returning to the essence of our nature, as custodians of the land. To work in harmony and balance, not against what we were provided with. Bodies capable of miracles.

There is no body that cannot return to its optimum state of wellness when given what it innately wants.

That state may not be defined as "Normal" by societal labels yet it is what that individual chose before this incarnation. The sooner humans stopped labelling them as broken or faulty, the sooner they can find the courage and confidence to live through their unique characteristics and abilities.

CHAPTER 22

THE END OF REFLECTION

Time for a recap on the Grids and consciousness.

About half the population are asleep, happy in their dream world of separation, one life, petrified of death, and likely to remain that way for this incarnation.

Out of the remainder, there are a percentage that are Cosmic Beings, not of this Earth, and have little grasp on the reality of human life.

Some are live wires, achievers, driven visionaries who lack any interest for the New Age diatribe from the bits they have heard.

These New Agers are firmly keeping the Light Grid in place. Operating through tribal consciousness, oozing empathy from every pore, saying "there, there" to all the victims in each of us. Moving towards the light, with little regard for the shadow behind them, patting it like a good dog and giving it some attention when it starts barking.

Their whole life is based around reflection, seeing themselves as mirrors of others, and their purpose is to be of value to humanity.

When you get to the place of making a different choice, enough of living through fear, knowing it is not your true nature, then the lure of the dark, feminine energy beckons to you.

When dedicated, you go through the often excruciating and drawn-out process of dying the death to your human construct. The moment of stillness, where there nothing left but the bones of dark light.

It is only at this point, when you know how to alchemise your fears are you able to enter the vessel of Portalism, to claim your Prodigy, lying dormant in the dark. All it requires are your Cosmic Codes to be ignited to start feeling your way into the dark unknown, the purest lightest light.

Up until recently, we had to hold and store the frequencies within our DNA and ascend them upwards. Now, with the structures gone, we can tap into the frequencies of consciousness from all around us, once you have dispensed of the illusions telling you otherwise. We can access all dimensions, there is no longer a structure determining a linear approach to move up or down through the dimensions or frequencies.

The Inner Guidance System of Abraham Hicks is well and truly obsolete. You align with the frequency you wish to experience and absorb it through your access codes. We are synchronising the frequencies – becoming "frequenters of energy". This allows the potentially of cosmic connection to ALL, which is our new reality.

Cosmic awareness comes through vibration, pulling the frequencies into our bodies, into this reality. This is the job of the Encoders – to ignite the abilities to receive the new energies. As always, it is the individual's responsibility to awaken to themselves, and no 'fixing' through entitlement can be done.

Whilst many may glimpse and experience these frequencies, it is only through commitment to ownership and authenticity may they be continually accessed. From that space, you can operate from the remit of continual creation in every experience.

When people realise the truth held in the codes is already within them, their innate power, they see they don't have to give up anything. It was the fear which the spirituals created has us believing that.

We have no idea what the dark looks like, it is a new playground to explore, led by our dark hearts of gold, and not our minds.

What we do know is the structures of light do not exist here. The Grids have gone. We are entering the chaotic world of the Feminine. It is up to us, the Cosmic Leaders, to find the way, the codes, the new currency in which to morph and extract our deepest genius.

Dark energy is where the Cosmic Codes and frequencies reside. They have not been able to drop into the Collective Consciousness before now in any sustainable manner as the density was too thick for them to be received and experienced.

For a few of us who have been dedicated to processing the density over several years, we have glimpsed it, then learnt to harness it within us, so it becomes stabilized.

We know how to do this because we have been doing it for lifetimes. Our DNA was already open to receive ignition of the codes. It was in our blood to drive forward in search of the Truth of Who We Are.

Only a handful have this innate ability and wisdom, who can utilise it for the essence of human evolvement and facilitate the new energies landing as a new field of consciousness.

There are many who think they can, have learnt some skills, yet have no emotional attachment to what they are getting involved in. There is no deep comprehension of the frequencies themselves, and what is required to bring forward even higher frequencies from the planetary systems from whence we came.

They have a weak emotional bond to the elements of the planets themselves. Their own inner balance is off kilter, with their Feminine and Masculine swinging wildly from other to another for periods of time, with no middle ground for operation.

I have witnessed brilliant Illusionists, masterful marketers and excellent puppeteers who has people eating out of their hands. Some claim they have invented the magic pill, or provide the wisdom that NO ONE else can see, to fix them. With no mention of frequencies in sight.

People seek these self-called Gurus as a reflection of where they would like to be, with zero connection, feeling or believing they have the ability. No concept of The Truth.

To increase your frequency - your awareness and consciousness - you must have consistency and connection. When you align with the higher frequencies, ego dies its death, and all judgement is removed. There is no fear, it is what is.

You cannot jump in and out, like flicking a light switch on and off. That was half the issue for the Light Gridders – felt great in the frequency of meditation and lost the connection when it comes to reality. No idea how to integrate it, live it, breathe it.

If there is no connection, and you remain in a state of nothingness, you cannot transcend anything, because there is no frequency. False idols will fall.

Which is exactly what is required on the remnants of the Light Grid. The Deep State Idols and their agendas have to be exposed. I digress....

I have no doubt many have the ability to read and decipher energy. However, if it is not encoded and ignited in your DNA and blood with you have no capacity for connection to it, no amount of theory making will actually shift and sustain the new frequencies within.

I have seen the synchronicities between the higher wisdom of consciousness I have brought through and what is being described by others as "the only channel on this planet who can decipher the new myth of consciousness." Er, no, there are a few of us witnessing what is unfolding in the energetic fields upon this earth.

The synchronicity which made me smile was I saw a post promoting a particular company as "the leaders of a new family of betrayers – the dark disruptors".

Synchronicity indeed. I left a comment saying I had created a new brand called exactly that, a month ago. You know, just setting the record straight.

When choosing who to work with, be aware of these Illusionists who feed on the power of their ego. Most often, driven by money and wealth accumulation. They are unable to create an authentic and sustainable heart-felt connection to the frequencies calling them home. Which is what you truly desire to be reunited with.

Many of the Dark Disruptors coming forward will not have attempted Light Grid mastery. They had no taste for the New Agers, though probably dabbled with spirituality at times, but their circuitry felt it was too restrictive. They have gifts they are aware of, yet no avenue for them to be explored in their "reality". So, they locked them away for safekeeping, until they realized they were their ultimate gifts.

There was no requirement for them to explore deeply. They did not develop intuition to know their path. It is already ingrained within them; they are already programmed for it.

That is not to say Dark Disruptors cannot have gone down the spiritual path to begin with, to awaken. It just means there is more to unlearn and decode.

It is the new frequencies arriving that is setting off the alarm bells in their core. They know they have a part to play in this unfolding and have no idea what it looks like.

The reason the Light Grid must collapse is to dispel the myth that time is essential. We were betrayed that time was relevant to us. It was a grand illusion created eons ago to help man structure their existence.

By taking the masses out of their normal routine, they were starting to lose their sense of time, of normality. Consciousness was laying the foundations for what is to come. For us to return to the timeless infinity, back to the multi dimensions. Hence time was starting to split out.

How will this play out?

Welcome to the realm of the Quantum.

CHAPTER 23*

REALITY NO LONGER EXISTS

There is one other person I would like to introduce you to. Anne, my energy rebounder and silent partner. A Sage who is an Encoder and Decipher as I am. Her Soul realms include Blueprint Originator, Sirian, Polarian, and Parallel.

I am Blueprint Originator, small part Hadarian, large part Parallel and a percentage in a Numerical realm, which has only just been made aware to me and still discovering.

We both have 8 aspects of Soul in other multi-dimensions, and our contracts go way back on many levels. Her expertise is reading the frequencies precisely, and sound, mine is numbers, and we both do colours. These are the three aspects of code interpretation and why we work so well together.

My work with Anne has morphed immensely over the past few months. I would channel and discuss with her, whilst she filled me in with the nuggets from the cosmic energy side. Our meetings have now developed into streams of consciousness, both deciphering what is being shown.

We both understand consciousness must be spoken, and written, into existence. We are both bringing the ancient wisdom back to life, rewritten for the current cosmic climate, and I am the Scribe, just as I was the first times around.

Anne is an Encoder, just as I am yours. She does not decipher with anyone else. We all have different contracts with different people. Anne knows I have work to do with the masses. We are all here to help land the cosmic consciousness efficiently and as smoothly as possible, so it's all hands-on deck, whilst leaving our egos back in the Light Grid.

Geniuses and prodigies have no concept of competition. They are here to create from way beyond their human capacity as the individuated aspects of Source they are, ready to play in the dark space of the cosmos.

I had a personal astrology reading on Venus wisdom at the end of last year. With Capricorn in my 8th house of Collaboration, it would be a huge year in 2020, running throughout. I denied I would be working with anyone else; it did not resonate with me at all. Now I see once again the stars do not lie.

When we considered our synchronicities, it was quite uncanny. I am originally from the UK, she from Guernsey. I first moved to New Zealand when I left England and married a man from Christchurch where she lives. Anne is part of my first legal name. Anne always knew that Adelaide (where I live) had a strong draw for her and put it down to her Grandmother's name being Adelaide Anne. Anne's maiden name is an alternative spelling of her married name. The Universe gives us all the hints, only ever seen in hindsight.

* * *

On 28th April I channelled 9 long pages of hand-written notes, weaving in and out of consciousness, quantum, masculine and feminine. I downloaded how synchronicities worked in relation to personal frequency. I was shown how consciousness was playing out in the global field, and what the Game of Life really means.

Come and peak into my download, I have distilled the essence for you.

I had woken from a dream at 3am hearing "end the eternal quest and step through the portals of time to claim it". I knew this was as much for me, as it was my clients. I spent the next 3.5 hours downloading.

"Time wraps and freezes in a holographic box, where all networks of realities of all times feed through the energy circuits. With new consciousness programming through encoding, the patternings are wiped out in a nano second and updated to the new operating system. This runs on much higher frequencies, power and capabilities.

What is required is the intrinsic balance of masculine & feminine within - the ultimate love with no judgement. All the programming is from within – clear the shadow mind through time to access. Igniting the light codes in the DNA to wrap around the dark bones of the feminine eternal.

The density of the body must be removed so the frequencies can be received.

On the Light Grid, the system through which you have operated up until now, had sunlight above – the masculine energy, radiating on the feminine earth below. We refer to the frequencies here, as the planet in the solar system moves through a 'passage of time'.

As the poles begin to reverse, the dark energy of the eternal feminine is all around, creating chaos with no structure, the void of stillness. This holds the highest frequencies – dark matter -where the power is.

Within the structures, the dark is the core, light is the matter coded to receive and communicate with the dark codes. As matter is observed, it changes. This is the Law of Quantum Physics – particle wave duality, where you can only predict probabilities, nothing is certain. Atoms can be in two places at once by adding together waves. This is called superposition. (N.B. the definitions are textbook, not channelled).

It is only through the activation of the light body can the dark be experienced. So, light requires removal of shadow density (fear & illusions) to increase the frequencies, hence allowing the dark codes of cosmic consciousness to be experienced.

The integration of the dark matter (the purest lightest light which cannot be seen on the Light Grid, it is off the spectrum) into the light body raises the frequency of consciousness itself to be experienced.

It is only in the experience of the dark matter – the observation – can it be turned into matter.

NOTHING MATTERS.

Dark matter is consciousness itself. The higher the frequency of light in the structure, the more the dark frequencies can be observed. It has to be in balance in the quantum equation – the dark and light, the masculine and feminine. This activates in the bones, the structure of the being.

Collective Consciousness must raise its set point in vibration to gain its first glimpse of this field of higher frequencies and must raise further still for it to be accessible and sustainable. The higher the level of light within structures, the more time and space can dissolve and transmute, back to nothingness and the dark. i.e. back to the dark feminine.

*Without the structures, in the chaos, the random events can occur — **the** **synchronicities.** These can occur across time because the illusion of time no longer exists.*

If you run in a powerful position in one lifetime and took the constructs of time and space away, you would always be running that power, that frequency. It is the shadow you accumulated in the lifetimes without being in your fullest power has you running at less than full wattage.

Without the structures, there is nothing, and nothing matters — ie. comes into reality through observation because you are now operating in the quantum field.

In meditation, you leave the light and go into the stillness of the mind — the nothingness. This is where the power is, in the unstructured energy systems.

You came through various star systems — your Soul Realms held in dimensions and Universes of higher frequencies first. The game of life is to see if you choose to return to that higher-level frequency when dumped in the swamp and density of humanity.

How does all this relate to what is unfolding in the world?

The Light Grid structures have enforced rigid structures and controls, taking away freedom and rights — or so the human mind perceives.

When consciousness awakens, it is for each individual to realise their external circumstance have NO BEARING — i.e. no weight — on your own internal freedom. You put your perceived restrictions outside yourself. They are not real in terms of your own power and choice.

So as the world wakes up claiming their own power, freedom and choice WITHIN, only then can it show up in the world externally. You have to claim it first before the external liberation occurs.

So, when Collective Consciousness reaches a tipping point of wanting their own freedom (of their minds and personal limitations) the external structures have to break down. This comes through exposing the truth and revealing the corruption and incestual companies & interests holding society together.

This is Universal Law. The dam will break, when the ocean (of people) has enough force of the true power of nature (of feminine, of freedom) to breakthrough.

The New Agers have a great deal of incorrect myths around the frequencies of light. They have been built upon texts which were amended by the western world, long after the original ancient texts were decimated or "lost in time".

They confuse shadow with the dark, it is misunderstood, and is held in a place that terrifies them. This is the true dark goddess energy, the overbearing power of Kali and her cohorts from the underworld.

The new programming of the dark where genius can be unleashed, means you have accessed the higher frequencies of consciousness, not previously known to mankind. Their abilities are therefore also unknown. Just as AI is being developed, it is the forerunner of true human potential.

It is exactly these abilities which are required to work in/ for / through the Cosmos, to exponentially change the human paradigm and experience. "

CHAPTER 24*

AWAKENING CODES IN OTHERS

It was not just me who was starting to have a profound awareness of the cosmic consciousness entering our phase. One of my Dark Disruptor clients, Deena, had been working more deeply with the Galactic Council since her Initiation and sessions.

Deena had been given a clear message from them to share with me, about her.

"I'm chosen to lead into the new age and facilitate the relationship between the Cosmos and Earth, over the next 10 years. It will be revealed to Earth, and the relationship and collaboration between the aliens and Earthers. When we have had a huge shift in consciousness, you will be key in supporting the collaboration. You help support the integration of aliens into society. They are extremely different and will be a shock to humanity (in the way they look – and that they are here). All part of the of the New Age Revelation."

As an HR Manager for a global conglomerate, Deena's role was always going to be about relationship between humans, and beyond.

In our tune in during session, we opened the parallel portal for her, and she landed in the new realm. She described vividly what she could see, which as always, I was also witness to. I assisted her to morph the energies into a more tangible form to connect, and she soon met with her Arcturian guide, her equivalent facilitator within the cosmic realms.

Between them, they are to work out how to translate the frequency of the vibration to a form for integration on Earth. There will be a middle ground as a basis for translation.

The Arcturians know they must find the individuals to be the bridges between the realms. Most are stuck in their five senses and this requires a new level of understanding.

Previously they had tried to connect into the human energies in the 1960's and were not ready back then. This time the energies will come through the workplace and economies.

They are calling on people who have credibility and standards, and who can express this. For me to hear this, it was a massive reiteration of why I had been guided to create Dark Disruptors within the last month, to work with the individuals who had an influence over a large audience or work force.

I knew Deena was the first Dark Disruptor to come on board with this integrative work. She will be one of the founding members of "The Cosmic Rollout Plan" which will unfold over the next 11 years.

In our next session Deena shared how she had been meeting with her Arcturians, who had introduced her to their way of communicating and reproducing through energy frequencies.

She has received clear directives as to her role and knows her abilities to facilitate this will unfold as she continues to evolve, expand and encode.

I explained the importance of synchronicities and to be aware of them. I mentioned I had recently watched Indiana Jones and the Crystal Skull with my kids, and it had very much reminded me of how Deena had described the Arcturians. Deena had watched the same movie in the last two weeks and thought the same!

I also referred to Egypt and know one of our Soul contracts was from that time. I went on to explain the latest revelations in consciousness and what I was bringing through. I mapped her Soul realms to the dimensions and knew which ones required opening.

During tune in, we opened the Egyptian coding in the Akashics, and guided Deena back to her past life with Isis. They met in the middle pyramid, and Deena versed what Isis shared in terms of their Soul Contract. It was profound and powerful. There is no going back once you have received direct transmissions about your Contracts from Isis. Deena was moved to tears of joy and happiness, for finally realizing her true purpose.

In later sessions I downloaded for her what the HR and recruitment industry would look like outside corporate structure. Deena already had a vision for changing the philosophy to human potential, people driven focus, not using them as assets.

Imagine a space where jobs were filled based on the frequency of the role and that of the individual. No more hiding behind qualifications and false promises of abilities. It could be a system of energetic matching were the ideal people found and placed into roles without any necessity of being physically present, for the world is becoming a virtual playground.

This would allow people to work solely to their passions and capabilities with no criteria they must be this, that or the other. The notion of equality becomes irrelevant as it is based on frequency of the creation required and the person ideally suited for that role.

Part of the system will include indicators for people who no longer met the frequency and had free will to move on to a more suitable role. Employment is created by the person seeking the work rather than the employer who does not know the benefits which can be obtained by having a particular person in that role.

Deena is already disrupting the HR industry and with visions such as these she will be on the leading-edge catalyst of change. The true Dark Disruptor.

I look forward to working with Deena over the next three months and way beyond. It is the Souls like this who heard the call and are committed to playing their part in the Cosmic Rollout.

* * *

One of my other clients, Ali, is a chiropractor. She had been questioning if that is what she is really here to do, or what the bigger picture is for her. I was blown away when I received insight for her.

The Baroness (her alter ego name) will work with the Bones of the Dark, the ones who are coming, the aliens. Some are already here and will find her. All cosmic beings work on energy and will align with her codes to find her. All she needs to do is redefine her exacting standards and maintain her connection to the frequencies of the higher light.

She will adjust their bodies to be functional on the Light Grid, and innately know how their bodies work, different to human bodies, and how best to treat them. They have a far more flexible bone structure than us, they do not require the same structure (for anything). There is nothing to learn, it is about trusting what you are guided to and who to work with.

It will not be long before she is offering remote healing on other humans, using her abilities as medical intuitive to adjust bodies and prescribe herbal remedies and exercises for the individual to maximise the body functionality. She is finally getting to use her witchy skills which laid dormant for centuries, fully owning her abilities because she simply got out of her own way.

This is obviously a great deal to comprehend, and it would be easy to slip back into old habits and fears when the mind cannot grasp the concept. This is when the deepest alchemy is required, of breaking down the illusions you need to know the how.

The facilitation of this new work is determined by the degree to which you are committed to being a dark worker. If you chose to slip back into human consciousness, they will not pick up on your frequency codes required to be activated in your awareness. This goes for any dark worker, and their ability to sustain the frequencies required.

It was not long into writing this book when I was called to invite a group of women including some of my clients to witness the texts into being and to form part of the weaving together of the story. Hence The Alchemists' Coven was birthed. I know the Coven will also help to ignite the cosmic codes within the individuals present to the space.

To be clear, it does not replace the requirement for alchemy and magick which I teach and facilitate. Nor does it ignite specific codes individuals are destined to access.

The Coven provides the cauldron for the new frequencies to be harnessed through the access points of the participants. It is up to them to embody and embrace the new resonance. As each steps up into responsibility and ownership for these hidden abilities and gets out of their own way, their life experience will never be the same again.

CHAPTER 25

ASTROLOGY: APRIL 2020

Astrology is not a prediction tool, it can merely help to pinpoint the energies at play at any given time. Seeing as energy is everything, it is imperative we are familiar with the energy mapping of the ethers and apply it to the situation at the present moment. It also assists us to navigate our way through the unprecedented times.

It is a little like the Tower Tarot card, the structures and realities we thought were set in stone are now crumbling. The whole world is experiencing this all at once, a huge opportunity to come together and recognise we all share the foundational energy.

Saturn and Mars are now in Aquarius for the first time since 1994. We have been given the discipline and motivation to embrace this. Saturn is the sign of social networking, togetherness and teamwork. It also rules the internet, inventions and is future focused. The world crisis is like the birthing contractions, speeding up the process of delivering a brand-new way of being, with new solutions. I have already referred to the gestation period of the New Age and in April we still didn't know the world was pregnant with a new consciousness.

Innovations are especially noticeable in the field of technology, it is this advancement which facilitated so many of us to work from home. It provides the platform for us to connect to one another, face to face virtually, anywhere in the world.

The other aspect of Aquarius called upon at this time is the energy of kindness. To support the essential workers, to watch on as world events emerge. All practicing social isolation, all sharing the same experience. It is truly a prevailing time of Aquarian energy.

We began April with Jupiter conjunction Pluto at 24 degrees Capricorn. Last time they were both here was in 2008, another time of financial crisis. They meet every 12-13 years. It was also conjunct at the time of the Spanish Flu in 1918 and in 1981 when the first HIV case hit the US.

Jupiter expands everything it touches and it seemed to be doing a great job of setting the world in fear, assisted by mass media. Pluto is linked to survival and global events. It was suggested there could be fundamental transformation (Pluto) and change in Laws (Jupiter) both of which absolutely played out over the month as the world went into lockdown under tight government control. It is about bringing the higher and lower energies together – as above, so below. It could be seen as paving the way for heaven on earth and will always be a matter of balancing ego with higher self.

Mercury conjuncts Neptune in 4ᵗʰ April, the Sabian Symbol for 19 degrees Pisces is "a table set for an evening meal". So many around the world were contemplating potential food shortages as so many shelves were laid bare for weeks at the supermarket. Even the bizarre shortage of toilet paper was a reflection people were concerned about their basic, root needs.

The full moon in the Air sign of Libra on 7/8th April also helps to balance relationships and we can feel the additional cosmic support. We would feel the opposition keenly between self (Aries sun) and others (Libra moon). It was also a supermoon meaning she will be closest to Earth for 2020, pulling on tides and tectonic plates as well as our emotions.

This was also the day of Jupiter-Pluto conjunction becoming exact, magnifying the underlying energy, bringing up profound psychological material from the shadows. People had been in lockdown for about three weeks now, so the novelty value was wearing off and the dawn of realisation they simply did not know for how long this would continue. Being in close proximity with your immediate family with no respite could be extremely challenging for many.

Also, on 7 April a Mars-Uranus square carried a potential of a sudden breakthrough or breakdown. Uranus was here to finish the job off which started in 1778, when the American Revolution was on hold by that winter. It has no respect for big egos and ready to take them down. The combination of Uranian and Aquarian energy gives a surge of "I want to be free" in some area of our lives.

Chiron was involved in the full moon around 9-10 April. This opens the avenue for ideas and actions which can be taken to lead the way in improved circumstances. It is important to prioritise your own health at this time, including your mental wellbeing.

One April 15-16 the sun forms dynamic squares to Pluto and Jupiter to agitate the pot even further. It is the same energy to give the fire in your belly the momentum to push back. I see this as pushing against mass media and questioning all we were being told, to seek out the truth and discern for ourselves.

The sun moved into Taurus on 20 April followed by a stable new moon on 23 April. The energy of home comforts and to provide us with an opportunity to take stock and set realistic goals. The following days could see you challenged to delve deeper for answers, start thinking big. This energy is enhanced by Mercury squaring Pluto and Jupiter on April 25-26. This of course is the push for individual responsibility to seek the Truth, not just go along with what we are spoon fed.

Sun-Uranus-Mercury conjunct in Taurus at the end of the month provided an excellent backdrop to brainstorm some innovative solutions to the global issues. New ideas and methods come to light and enthusiasm is peaking. The world awaits the outcomes of this brilliance from individuals and companies, for it was not being seen on the political or corporate front in any way.

MAY 2020

CHAPTER 26

THE WRITTEN WORDS & NUMBERS

My focus at the beginning of May was very much on the Dark Disruptors. With the new website complete, I was keen to glean the ideas of how best to reach my audience. So hungry to find the big players, ready to bring chaos to their niche, embracing new technology and power, whilst rewriting the script for the structures of society.

I once again turned to Cromer and after coming up with a range of ideas said that I was to write a Dark Disruptors Manual. This was something that had never crossed my mind, yet once the seed was planted, I got an instant download on the style and message of the book.

I read The Future is Faster Than you think by Peter Diamandis, a favourite author for insight on the incredible potential for breakthrough solutions for an innovative world. Someone who I have followed for eight years and is on the pulse of new technology. The book provided an overview of all sectors of life and I felt so excited to be calling in more dark disruptors to work alongside some of the brilliant minds of today.

There's an excellent short video explaining why we need to embrace disruption by Jason Silva as part of his channel Shots of Awe. Other videos on his site give a great insight on technologies just emerging which he created 6-7 years ago. An excellent way of hindsight and how far we have come.

I watched a couple of interviews with Elon Musk, the billionaire who created Tesla Cars and the SpaceX program. It was a moment in history when the first private space company sent astronauts to the ISS in June 2020, one month after his son X AE A-12 was born. Musk is the very definition of a Dark Disruptor, a complete alien. Notes from both interviews may be found in Appendix I.

I started writing the book, the ideas pour so easily when you are absolutely clear on your client. Four days later, I heard from my guides / higher self I was a Cosmic Scribe, to leave the current project for now and to start documenting what was unfolding.

The introduction to volume one set the scene, there is little that comes from my head in these texts that I must consider or think about. The writing simply flows with what needs to be shared.

I know I have been a Cosmic Scribe in several lifetimes before. I hold an innate wisdom and connection to consciousness and have continually feel the truth of it. I read Ancient texts which are oh so familiar. I recognise myself as a Master Key Holder and Scribe for the Akashic, the energy which weaves all aspects of time and dimensions together. Hence my definition of Portalism, it is simply what I do and have done for lifetimes.

When Anne and I peered into the past lives, we could see I was the right-hand man to Thoth who wrote the Emerald Tablets. I know I was part of the Egyptian scribing for Osiris and Isis.

What also was coming to light was the dark. This New Age was not about rewriting something I had done eons ago. It was brand new cosmic consciousness being created which had never been experienced before. A documenter of the new energies and frequencies, writing up The Blueprint v2.0.

With this revelation of responsibility and new awareness, I wanted to check in my Soul realms for I felt they had changed. Or rather our awareness of the energies awakens the codes to access different realms and dimensions. It must also correlate with our capabilities, responsibility and ownership.

I re-read my own Akashic records as 27% Blueprint Originator, 15% Hadarian, 75% Parallel. Whilst checking in with Anne, she also saw another realm I was part of, a numerical realm held in the 9th dimension. This resonated strongly, my connection with numbers had always been paramount.

I was guided to consider what percentages of people are associated with the original Blueprint and Master Code Holders. Anne and I verified these numbers together.

Master Code Holders (MCH) and Blueprint Originators mean the Souls have a small percentage of these abilities within them. No Soul will have a large amount simply for the protection of the codes and the individual.

Population as of 13 May 2020		7,784,096,862
Population will never be open	47%	3,658,525,525
Population awakening though cannot sustain the frequency	18%	1,401,137,435
Cosmic Beings	14%	1,089,773,651
Master Code Holders (MCH) – Blueprint Originators	3%	233,522,906
Awakened to being MCH:1.5% of that 3%		3,502,844
MCH, Deciphers and Encoders 0.325% of that 1.5%		11,384
Of those, 0.21% are Deciphers		7,356
Of those 0.35% 0.115% are Deciphers & Encoders		4028
Scribes and Encoders of the New Consciousness who work between the dimensions, preprogramed for this		37

* * *

I also feel your Soul realm patterning is coded into your Chaldean numerology. My life path is 18/9.

I have eight other Soul fragments in the multiverse which all have a pairing. Me in this reality plus eight in other realities make the nine. In total there is 18 aspects of my Soul, some in this Universe's realms, some in multi-verses, all with different frequencies. By opening the portals to these other realms, the frequencies can merge and be accessed through my conscious awareness.

Energetically, 18 and 108 hold the same frequency.

The number 108 is considered sacred by the Dharmic religions. In Hindu tradition there are 108 attendants of Shiva and hence Shaiva religions use Malas of 108 beads for prayer and meditation, as do Buddhists. All gods in the Hindu religion have 108 names.

There are 108 Navamsas in Vedic Astrology, matched to the 12 zodiac signs. The diameter of the sun is 108 times that of the Earth. The distance between Earth and Sun = 108 times sun-diameter. The distance between Earth and Moon = 108 times moon-diameter. The diameter of Stonehenge is 108 ft.

We have 12 houses and nine planets in astrology.

This number refers to spiritual completion and is a harshad number (an integer divisible by the sum of its digits). 108 represents the whole of existence, some say there are 108 forms of meditation, it is a number used throughout Buddhism and yoga.

1 stands for God or Higher truth. 0 stands for emptiness or completion in spiritual practice, and eight stands for infinity or eternity.

There are 108 energy lines within the body, converging to from the heart chakra. On the Sri Yantra, the fractional geometric design of the Universe, there are 54 energy intersecting lines, a set for each masculine and feminine, making 108 in total. There are 54 letters in Sanskrit, with two gender formations making 108.

108 symbolises Divine Mother Energy. It has also been called the Universal Code Number.

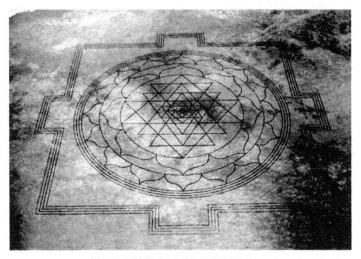

Desert Sri Yantra from 9000 feet. Copyright 1990 Bill Witherspoon

I have also found a fascinating man called Jain 108 who also understand the power of 108. He has so much wisdom around sacred geometry and Vedic mathematics. Based in Australia, he is setting up a sacred geometry University to track the rare sequences and patterns. I am sure I will be delving into more of his work. You can find more Jain 108 on Facebook.

CHAPTER 27

DIMENSIONAL ASPECTS

Having deciphered the population of Earth it was time to turn my attention back to the dimensional mapping I had first started in 2017. It ties back in with the Soul realm work I had begun six years ago, explaining the frequencies of the dimensions which are available to those who open their codes to access them.

Three years ago, I had mapped the DNA strands, to the dimensions, to the frequencies, to the chakras and colour system of first seven, and to the Soul Realms. 12 strands of DNA map to the first 12 dimensions, the 13th is multi-dimensional, and 14th is All That is, governing existence. I now see this as the overarching masculine multi-Universe through which everything is co-created and evolves, expands continuously. Bringing it into being, into structure, which includes frequencies.

It was time to expand on the wisdom. My readings were still valid on chakras, correlation, and numerical mapping. We expanded into higher realm colours and metals operating for each dimension.

Aluminium showed up as the metal for the eight dimensions. Remember the conversation about vaccines? Whilst it is poisonous to the human body, hence "vaccine damage", it opens the ability to receive eight dimensional frequencies if ever that person's awareness takes them on the path of true ownership. These will indeed be magical creators of solutions in this reality. The ones who provide structure in this 'reality'.

The majority of people open up access points to their dormant DNA strands as they awaken, or fast track the process with me through clearing the blocked pathways and encoding in the new frequencies.

Parallel Souls have the ability to 'surf' between different dimensions and multi-Universes without having had to come from there. Like having a free passport, once your access codes are ignited, parallels can gain a taste of the frequencies existing in each and weave it into their own timelines. However, like anything, they must have awareness and ownership of their abilities before being able to use them.

This is why 95% of my clients have parallel aspects within them; I recognise their characteristics and abilities and also to encode them to experience the different frequencies.

If you have Sirius energy from 7D you also have capabilities to tap in telepathically or telekinetically to the frequencies of other dimensions, provided you have fully opened to your Sirius realm.

The number of parallel aspects Soul is open to depends on the level of awakening. When I was first introduced the concept of parallel existence of my Soul, I saw four Universes. It was a few years before expanded and saw another four. To make my 18/9 pattern complete.

As the master of Portalism, I jump between time, space, dimensions, realities and frequencies. I weave together the codes from each of those aspects of you, and recode your Akashics, and therefore your DNA, with the updated energies you are ready to receive, depending on your level of awareness and consciousness.

I morph in and out of different paradigms and levels, I do not need to have them programmed in my DNA in order to access them. At this time of writing, I have seven DNA strands open, ready to merge and embed the frequencies of the eighth dimension. I had not previously chosen to do so, it is the realm of providing the structures to create 'reality'.

In many previous lives, my abilities & power had been taken from me. That is not expressed from the victim's point of view. I knew it would continue to be removed until the time was ready – in consciousness AND my own Soul evolvement to claim it all and reignite what is innately within me.

Holding the seventh dimensional frequency of Platinum, this allows me to move through the other realms undetected. A little like an invisibility cloak if you will, absorbing the colours of the frequencies of the other dimensions so as not to be seen. For lifetimes I felt it was not safe – this is changing as I speak the consciousness into being.

* * *

Let us return to consider the mapping of the dimensions.

It explains the positioning of our Soul Realms and the frequencies we most naturally resonate with. Again, for parallel Souls, do not forget you can 'surf' between the energies quite naturally.

DIMENSION 1

- Coded to the DNA strand 1
- The Iron core crystal at the centre of the Earth where the Blueprint is held.
- Red -Root Chakra (DNA 1)
- Orange – Sacral Chakra (DNA 1)
- Metal – iron

DIMENSION 2

- Coded to DNA strand 1
- From core to crust where creation occurs.
- The underworld resides here. The Halls of Amenti (Thoth)
- Orange- sacral chakra (DNA 1)
- Yellow – solar plexus chakra (DNA 2)
- Metal – copper

DIMENSION 3

- Coded to DNA strand 2
- On Earth 7.83hz
- Blue – throat chakra
- Heart & lungs – pink - DNA strand 3
- Sacred heart – green – DNA strand 4
- Metal - Iridium

DIMENSION 4

- Realm of myths and archetypes – the energies which reside in the Underworld
- First dimension of the dark feminine energy
- Sacred heart – green – DNA strand 4
- Thymus
- Violet – third eye
- White – crown
- Metal – silver

DIMENSION 5

- Realm of Love, connection and creativity
- Soul realms of: Blueprint Deliverers, Hadar, Mintaka, Pleiadean, Alpha Centauri
- 8th Chakra above crown coded to DNA strand 5
- Colour – gold

DIMENSION 6

- Realm of sacred geometry, hieroglyphics
- Soul realms of Sirius, Polaris, Blueprint Translators
- Realm of magick
- Colour – rose gold

DIMENSION 7

- Realm of sound, Cymatics, highways of light
- Realm of frequencies and vibrations
- Andromeda is connected through this dimension, our twin galaxy
- Colour – Platinum, which contains all colours and reflects everything, transcends all colours

DIMENSION 8

- Realm of Light, where Cosmic Codes are held
- Provide the structures to create 'reality'
- Realm of innate power, infinite balance and wisdom
- The emotional being
- Colour – sky – aqua blue
- Metal – aluminium (which is required in the bodily structure to open the cosmic codes up to be received)

DIMENSION 9

- Black hole at the centre of the Milky Way
- Gatekeeper to other Universes
- Time travel, Akashic Key Holders
- Colour – Titanium

DIMENSIONS 10 – 12

- The realms of death, transition and returning to the All that Is
- Dimension 10 – all Souls incarnation to human spirit
- Dimension 11- Angels and guides
- Dimension 12 – Archangels, Highest Beings of Light, Galactic Council

DIMENSION 13

- Multi-verses

DIMENSION 14

- All that IS. Infinity.
- Duality created our Universe with dimensions 1-12 and other Universes

REALM OF 15

All aspects of duality, this the nothingness, the everything, the void between the void. Exists with no evolution. The ultimate ISNESS. Anything that exists can have no relationship with anything in the 15th because it is beyond existence.

The plateau between two creations. Existence itself needs the polarity of not existing. Of nothing.

Consciousness requires continuous evolvement and co-creation which can only happen in the void of nothingness. It is the space after consciousness which marks the end of evolution.

The accessibility of dimensions and the frequencies they hold has radically changed since the shift. No longer do we need to refer to above and below as if the dimensions were held on some kind of linear scale, expanding upwards and outwards. The reality where we had to go somewhere to get something no longer exists.

Once your cosmic codes are open, the frequencies can be accessed through alignment from wherever. This will put an end to the spiritual crew hopping on out to another realm to fetch a little intuition to feed back into their reality. Now, we simply project the thought and witness through watching into being, into reality through the synchronicities of frequencies. We are becoming "frequenters of energy".

* * *

As always, this wisdom cannot remain as theory. Something outside yourself you need to learn and absorb. The text merely gives your human mind the capacity to comprehend and name what is already within you. Whether it is open for access is another question, only ever hidden in shadow, illusions and false concepts of conditioning.

We go on scouting missions to connect back within ourselves. Why do we not connect to it? Ego. Old patterns. Our slave-self conditioning.

I need to know the purpose rather than, This Is It. You have all connected to it for eons, some longer than others. Some have accessed the wisdom more frequently and made it their mission through lifetimes to re-member.

When classed as finding and fulfilling our purpose, our ego kicks in and questions, "what if we can't do it?"

It is not the truth of who you are. We get all the information we require to get the job done. We do not need to understand it all or know all the details.

You are receiving it right now.

CHAPTER 28*

DIMENSIONAL CHANNEL

In the early morning on the day we deciphered the dimensions I received the following channel to further our comprehension of them.

"4D is the gateway to the dark. It's why the Light Gridders have gone from 3D to 5D – they are not willing to go into the dark, into the unknown, into the true feminine energy. Once people are accessing this frequency of the dark, it's where things are reversed. It is a feminine realm of non-structure.

Evolvement comes from top down, ending up as humans on Earth in 3D. When the frequencies hit Earth, time is created, and reversed, so it is seen as 1D, then 2D then 3D were created.

It is an infinite loop of beginnings and ends within each dimension, and just as the human eye sees everything in reverse through its lens, it is only when we see things for what they really are, without the human illusion, we can see things the right way up. From top down.

When we got to 3D and human form, the access points through our DNA were switched off. It is for the evolvement of individuals to discover this and reawaken their coding. Not all have to go through all levels, for they are accessible and can be jumped to through the awareness of their Soul realms (under whatever name is used for systems within the 5-7D dimensions). It is only the parallels who can access all dimensions and frequencies, once their portals have been opened to their own Soul realms in the multi-verse and reconnection to the wholeness of who they are at the Soul level. They would have already accessed their other realms in 5th – 7th – the order of processing facilitated through Josephine. This automatically dissolves and transmutes the Soul shadow, which had been preventing them from accessing the higher frequencies.

To obtain access through these portals, they must be clear of sufficient shadow – their human conditioning and density, through own power of choice. Free will is never removed from the Soul individuation.

1D contained the embryo of time, and the imprint of this is still held at the core crystal of the earth.

1D

2D

3D masculine Light Grid, structure

4D feminine dark void, no structure

5D feminine Light Grid who have embodied the dark within their structure

6D Sacred geometry – masculine Dark Grid, codes for structure

7D Sound – based on frequency, feminine and masculine - androgynous

8D Cosmic coding – providing the structure to create 'reality' androgynous

From 7D up no agenda, no ego, no purpose other than to be. Therefore, not Masculine or Feminine. Humans would count this as pointless. Humanity could not reach it because of agenda.

To continue evolving, the frequencies must be experienced in a reality. It is why the energies take time (because we are still existing on the 3D Light Grid) to integrate into the cells. To master sailing the waves of the realms and the different frequencies, one must be able to master both the masculine and feminine aspects of self AND they must be in balance.

Where there is denial of one of the polarities within oneself, the vessel of the body is lopsided, heavy and dense, and it is extremely hard work to attempt to jump to another frequency.

When the balance is obtained within the psyche of the human and embedded in the frequencies of the cells and DNA, the Soul is then able to access the frequencies of the realms from whence they came. As a Parallel I am able to jump between these realms and frequencies to read, understand, translate and embed within others. It does not mean my Soul came from all these realms, it means I have a 'free pass' to all. The availability of higher frequencies will be made available in line with my own evolvement and awareness, just as it is for others.

When people shift from one frequency to another, let's look at 3D to 4D, the polarity of the experience is reversed. We are moving from a Light Grid time-based paradigm based on grids, structures and connection, into the 4D feminine realm of the quantum. Here, man must reinvest himself through the energy of the feminine void, so as to exist in this new realm, which the divine feminine already had access to, just as the divine (empowered) masculine does.

Provided the masculine and feminine essences of the individual are fully awake and ignited, regardless of human gender, they can access the 4D. However, many of the enlightened men have no concept of their real power as a man and happy to jump a dimension with the women onto the 5D feminine Light Grid structure.

Souls can access the 5D, though these energies are unsustainable unless the balance of M & F is acquired. These individuals will be limited in their capacity to develop and remain in the construct of a human existence in the light body. They will not be able to stay in the 5D unless they remove the fear-based paradigms which exist in humans, it is too dense and the vibrations cannot be sustained. It is why those who meditate have access to this zone yet cannot integrate into reality for they are in denial, or ignorance, of what is required. Namely, to remove the fear and gain balance between the empowered masculine and feminine within.

The chakras link the body to the energy portals, and through from 3D to 5D. They are not required in the 4D with no structure, there are no anchor points. It is only an old fear-based concept which had us believe the chakra system must be in balance and fixed in place. Rather, they are access points through to the energy fields beyond our mind. It is the frequency of the codes and the realms within the body's circuitry (DNA and cells) which are resonate with the frequency of the realm to be experienced.

Without the structure of the Light Grid and individual or collective human consciousness to throw shadow across the Soul, the 4D can start to access these higher frequencies, the gateway to unlimited potential and unique abilities.

Every individual is pre-coded with where they came from, what they are to experience through all the realms and span 1D - 14D depending on the Soul. Over lifetimes, the Soul moves up and down in its frequency, and can *obtain a higher frequency than previous lives depending on the rate of Soul evolvement and ownership in that lifetime. It is free will to unlock the codes at each level, and cannot be done through ego and entitlement, only through ability to experience the frequency itself.*

Every Soul has a different set of unique programming, hence creating unique individuals. Some chose to go down the path of spiritual awakening on the Light Grid. Others are coded not to have to receive that experience, though for all, it is the dissolution of ego which is required to evolve.

This is not to say people cannot own their abilities and genius, it is that it will not be sustainable in the new Collective Consciousness frequency if not achieved to benefit the highest good of all. For greed, corruption and theft is not something that can exist, and will annihilate out of existence as the evolvement is implemented.

Some people with neural divergence, whether they admit to it or not, means they can already access their stream of genius from the 4D or higher, as they fully own their abilities and ownership of power means sustainability. However, many humans still hold the conditioning of requiring fitting in and belong, and thus abandon their higher frequencies and the intelligence available to them. Some will not return for many years, some not again in this lifetime. They are not willing to face the illusions about the Truth of who they are.

Different Souls have different requirements of experiences. The spiritual Light Gridders see themselves moving into 5D, the ascension, and this, for them, is moving out of shadow, into a Light Body. It is an advancement of the collective, and yet they still fundamentally miss the point of masculine and feminine balance, polarity. They are also sidestepping 4D as it is not for them – they do not understand it. Their time in meditation quietens the mind, when to deal with shadow effectively, it must be dealt with in the remit of the emotion it triggered. They must be alive to be captured and alchemised. Light Gridders are not seeing the essential nature of this and continue to manage them, rather than be free of them. For there is much mileage to be gained in staying a victim and continuing to fit in to the Collective Consciousness.

However, for the Darkworkers as you call them this is the realm of fully accessing their genius, the prodigy. It is not for you to lead people to 5D, it is to clear enough human density to drop the parallels directly into the unknown, the dark void of the feminine energy, without structure, time, space, linear concepts, value. All the paradigms are shattered, and it is up to the individual to learn to navigate their own way home to their dormant genius giant. This is fast tracked through the encoding of JS who has already mastered time and space navigation through Portalism."

CHAPTER 29*

MY OWN TIMELINE

27th May: I woke up at 3.33am hearing my boys talking in their sleep. I rested in meditation for a while, where I drift in and out of the dimensions, out of my body. I was drawn to speak with my Mother and found it difficult to stay connected and present to her. It is a relationship I left, it seems lifetimes ago, even though its 32 years since she was last here with us.

I was then reminded of the circle of life, and the numbers. 9, 18, 27, 36 of course are all the base numbers of a circle, and my key numbers. I am realising this awakening for my Soul is the last quarter of the circle. The Fourth Awakening, on its journey to wholeness as the circle of life itself. Or rather, spiral.

With all aspects of life being a fractal hologram of the whole, we can always see the patterns embedded when we know where to look. I spent some time considering those milestones in my life. What happened at every nine-year mark and halfway between each?

I was already at school at four and a half. I had started nursery at 2, my parents were beside themselves not knowing what to do with a hyperactive child who refused to sleep through the night. There were kids up to the age of seven in Miss Fisher's class, and of course I wanted to do their work, which I did. My parents took me out of the public system a year later and sent me to private school, despite my grandfather's protests they were wasting their money, I was a girl and would only be a secretary when I was older.

I spent my 9th birthday staying with my favourite Aunt Barbara and my cousins whilst my parents went to the States for a three-week holiday staying with friends. It was my first taste of independence, so cool hanging out with my 15-year-old cousin Julia and her boyfriend. I got my ears pierced, it was all I wanted, a marker of me growing up. My mother could not say no from the other side of the world.

Midpoint was 13 and a half. I remember accompanying my mother to hospital one night after my father had beaten her. She had put her hands up to protect her head, and he damaged them both badly. I listened to her reel off the stories to the other patients in the waiting room how she had fallen down the stairs.

This was the year my mother first filed for divorce too. The Decree Nisi was about to go through at 11am on a Thursday morning, and she asked me if she should stop it at 10.50am. I said yes. I carried the guilt of that for many years.

Six weeks after my 18th birthday my Mother died of liver cancer, which had spread throughout her body in the previous four weeks. She had been ill for a year and was her easy way out of extracting herself from life, which she had been trying to do for some years by then. I managed to talk her out of it the other times. She was almost 44.

Within four weeks of her funeral, my life as I knew it turned upside down. My brother left home, he was 16. The day my father refused me access to food to eat, he had it under lock and key, I had had enough, gave him a loud "Fuck You", packed some bags and rang a friend from the local telephone box asking if I could come and stay. I started University a couple of weeks later. I had basically lost my entire family and home and moved to a new town miles away within six weeks.

I did stay with Auntie Barbara during the holidays for a year after that, though when my uncle asked if he could sleep with me, I became terrified of being in the house, especially if no one else at home. I had to hide this repulsion each time I subsequently visited. I had been raped at 17 by a waiter in (then) Yugoslavia who had taken a shine to me and didn't want a repeat experience.

Midpoint was 22 and a half. I was getting my life back on track. I was over my suicide attempts and weekly visits to the doctor whilst on anti-depressants. I visited a friend in South Africa, and whilst away, my boyfriend of the time Ian enrolled me in CIMA exams, he felt I needed to further my education and become an accountant. I had a contract job as a purchase ledger clerk, and he had been one of the Big Boys to come in and help the company.

He seduced me and I had an affair with him. I was engaged at the time to a beautiful man Adrian who was away in Germany in the Army. I had got engaged to Ady upon our third meeting just before I turned 21. I thought he could rescue me. He was later killed in a motorbike accident at 24.

I remember when I first dated Ian, he had recently split up from his fiancée. He did not want to appear hasty in the eyes of his parents. On a

Friday night we used to drive from Kent to The South Wirral some 230 miles away. He would pick up his dog from his parents in North London and drop me at the local tube station whilst he went to see them and have dinner with them. An hour or so later having stood there, he returned for me, and we would take it in turns to drive the four hours to his home.

Talk about lack of value and self-esteem, and what we would do for a little bit of attention. It gives you some indication on my state of mind back then. I subsequently moved in with him before shifting to Birmingham with the company, making my escape.

At 27 I started a new finance analyst job at British Airways and left after nine months due to the politics and lies I had been sold on. I was put down and told to be quiet because I spoke the truth, and took it upline, they didn't like that much. A couple of good holidays though to St Lucia and Beijing on 10% fares. I contracted for a while after that for Express Newspapers looking after the revenue streams for the International Express. Little did I know I would be buying it in New Zealand four years later when I needed a touch of home news.

The midpoint was 31 and a half. I moved to New Zealand with two suitcases nine days before 9/11 and took six months off before starting work. I stayed with my old flat mate from Birmingham and her friend Warren who she was trying to set me up with. Which worked. Then she realised she didn't really want this three-way relationship and moved out without telling us.

Heady days of sauvignon blanc and weed. By the time I was 32 I could see who he really was and I felt trapped once again in a country a million miles from any sense of security. I stuck it out for another six months with him, not seeing an option to leave. The crunch came when he played holding hands and whispering sweet nothings into a colleague's ear as he stood in front of me, with my boss, boss's boss and friends in a pub after the works Christmas party. I tipped my pint of beer over him and left. New standards had to be set.

I got engaged one day after my 36th birthday and married Mark six months later in Auckland. My Whanau came from the UK. Such an awesome New Zealand word for friends you regard as your family. My brother had not replied to my wedding invite, he sent 12 bottles of French Champagne anonymously which arrived the day before the wedding. I sent word to my father after the event with a photo, it was his 70th birthday. I had only seen him twice since I was 21.

We travelled back to the UK for a friend John's 70th birthday celebrations on my 37th birthday. He had given me away at my wedding and subsequently visited me in New Zealand or Australia most years for about 10 years on his annual trip down under. A year to celebrate at the marquee in the grounds of Westminster Abbey.

Halfway point was 40 and a half. We had moved to Sydney by then, and I had two youngsters in tow. That first Mother's Day of being parents to a 20-month-old and 3-month-old. I remember Mark slept for 3.5 hours and said how great he felt when he woke up. I had not had a good night's sleep for two years at that point.

I was so devastated, so disillusioned of what Motherhood was meant to be, yet knew I could not run away from this responsibility. I got in my car and drove to a park. I bawled. What had I done? How did I ever think being a mother would return me to a state of unconditional love?

I hated it. I felt so trapped. So alone and unsupported. I was running my paradigm so beautifully all over again.

I then drove to a mall and walked around aimlessly. I wanted Mark to have to deal with two screaming, hungry babies. For him to entertain them, to work out what it was they wanted. I only returned when my aching breasts got too much, and I knew my baby needed me. We never spoke of it again.

45 was the first year as a single mother since I left Mark in September 2014. My best friend had died at the beginning of that year, and then John died two weeks before I left Mark. In October 2014 I set up Your Universal Self, so at 45 I was doing what I could to get my healing and coaching business off the ground. I was finally tasting freedom, to do what I truly loved, and to be free of relationships which so did not serve me moving forward.

I turned 49 and a half in January this year, and you have a detailed account of what has happened for me so far. To say it's an exponential year of growth is an understatement, to see the potentiality is vast.

And I am only half-way through my life, the half century to be marked in the next couple of months. Without the pomp and circumstance of dinner at the Criterion in London as planned. Rather a quiet meal with my boys and Mark, for we co-parent better than we ever did when together. Leaving him made him show up as a Father.

For I have work to do. The most important job I have had in millennia.

CHAPTER 30

WEAVING THE NEW MYTH

May was the month to dive in deep and explore what the new myth really means. By now it was so clear the old energies were fading on the Light Grid and we needed to start exploring the dark. The place so many are terrified of.

In some ways, I understand why it appears so scary. For it is the realm which requires you to relinquish your human self and tribal consciousness, i.e. your buy in to victimhood and powerlessness. To finally recognise and surrender the illusions which have weighed you down for lifetimes, the very essence of your Soul shadow which programmed you each and every reincarnation.

Mastery of the 3D Light Grid means you are free of shadow and you create your life your way because you completely own your Sovereignty, value and purpose. It is based on Self, the ego, which is required for tribal survival.

Attainment of this freedom allows you to step into the dark, the space where your Self is undone and conformity leaves your remit. Many awakening people will hop between 3D, 4D and 5D with the majority returning to the safety and comfort zone of their minds and fears of their human Self. It is only when you have mastered the recognition of patterns, know how to alchemise the fears and take on the responsibility of higher frequency dimensions can the codes be ignited, sustained and accessed in 4D and beyond.

Once free of your human conditioning you are outside the remit of survival as a human. No longer do you operate on logic and reason, from the mind. You become egoless whilst fully owning your individuality – the basis for evolution.

There is no longer a sense of what is just and fair, the storyline for all victims. Instead, we are creating a new psyche which does not yet exist. This is the essence of evolution of consciousness itself. It exists in all time yet only evolves at the point of being experienced, of being created. Realization of true nature over and over.

The baseline for Collective Consciousness had changed. Previously, we would tap into cosmic Source at certain times such as meditation and a Zen moment in nature, yet we had no ability to hold it. Now these frequencies are freely available to those who have their codes open ready to experience it. To be able to sustain and BE in the new vibe was the tipping point into the new existence – living in the quantum.

With the death of the ego also came the disintegration of labels. The requirement to distinguish if we call ourselves male or female. Instead, we morph closer to the nature of purer existence, where we work to our fullest strengths, in our power, with balance between the polarities within. The ability to switch between male and female as and when required. This provides such utter liberation from the lopsided energetics of trying to be one or another, usually to conform to society's agenda.

Higher dimensions facilitate our innate purpose far easier than the dense restrictions of 3D. For as we move out of conditioning, we move into the space of creation. Our essence is designed to experience, create and innovate continuously. To be in the flow of life and be part of the consciousness of continuation and formation. The spiral of life, never ending interconnected circles and vortexes operating through vibrational energy.

This is no longer the space of lines, structures and restrictions. It is the feminine energy of expression of creativity as individuations of the quantum. If we fight to exist, it is a losing battle. Far more energy is exerted keeping us separate from our true nature than is required to operate in our natural design.

This new era and the shift in collective energies means we have the opportunity to return to the truth of who we are. To discover our own unique abilities and operate to our fullest remit of power, regardless of what that looks like or whether it fits the labels of conformity. This integration facilitates huge productivity when we give ourselves permission to be ourselves.

The lack of this freedom for people to be who they are is the fundamental reason behind emasculation of the male. Where equality has taken away the right to show up as YOU. No longer was it acceptable for a Man's Man to be sure of himself, be of little words or treat women differently to himself. This was labelled as arrogant and backward. Basically, society drove men to the point of submission to the feminine ways of being as the only ones that were acceptable. It is no wonder the collective of male energy has fizzled out on the Light Grid. There is no structure left to provide a scenario in which he was free to exist.

This is not saying all men have all the characteristics of the Alpha Male and need the chance to express them. It is the restriction of freedom of expression to be himself that fundamentally leads to such issues as domestic violence, anger and high rates of suicide amongst men, amongst many other symptoms.

The new frequencies provide a level playing field to be ourselves as only we can, without an expectation of having to fit in. It opens up the platform for gender fluidity, the dissolution of traditional male/female roles and simply provides the opportunity for each of us to freely express.

The Light Grid was the platform for having to justify our very existence, continuously explaining and defending our choices. We live in a more liberated society than ever before, yet freedom of choice was becoming limited as governments and agencies tightened the controls on society.

The new energies must be spoken into existence and therefore paramount we choose our words carefully and express them only to those who are willing to hear and sustain the Truth, at least until the Collective Consciousness reaches a point of being willing to hear and see the new ways.

Speaking creates the vibrational expression of the new consciousness, writing cements it. We must use all sensations to anchor the new frequencies.

The masculine was rallied into continually speaking on the Light Grid, his silence was not accepted. This goes against his nature, for the empowered male is a man of few words. He is separate, aloof and quiet. He refused to be in a relationship with a woman who sees her power as dominant and dictatorial. The majority of men succumbed to society's requirements to be more like the women in order to fit in, be accepted and be deemed to have value. The Devouring Mother ate him up and spat the remnants out with distain.

The Dark God of the new energies is silent and we must expect him to be so. He will communicate with the female if and when necessary. It is up to the feminine to inspire him and to be totally comfortable with them both being in the dark finding their way to each other without putting the light on.

For the moment the female choses to put on the lights, his pure potent energy starts to disintegrate, as she tries to fix him, to help him become more like her. She inserts her own narrative and cannot see how self-serving she is.

This is the shadow feminine at her best, cajoling and persuading the man to just be like her and everything will be ok, because they can talk it out. It is the 3D Light Grid where everything is seen as a mirror. The spiritual awakening women wanted to see a mirror image of themselves in their partner. The biggest myth of the All as One concept, with no grasp of the necessity of polarity of energies.

The feminine usurped the masculine. It is she who has killed him. We did not recognise and acknowledge the MYSTERY of him. It is time to own what we have done to them as a collective and on an individual level. To take responsibility, step back, see his truth and invite him into existence as the man he truly is.

It is important to remember the masculine was not a victim to this, he allowed himself to be 'fixed'. The coding already existed, just remained shut off.

It is only the dark feminine who can invite the empowered male to step forward and create himself anew. The feminine had to awaken first and realise he is not required to wake up in the same way. She must acknowledge his mystery, then he is free to choose to ignite his own codes of power, to return to his natural state as the Wild Alpha Male.

As the new Dark God is birthed, the empowered masculine, he fully accepts the female as she is. He knows that energy is a fundamental requirement for the evolvement. Feminine may stand in her fullest empowerment as she meets him in his.

We must return to the Natural Order and accept both polarities together and in balance. We wore him down and exploited him in the same way we have done to the Earth. Spiritual seekers must understand we are not all one AND THE SAME.

This of course, must start within oneself. To alchemise your shadow feminine, step into your divinity. Allow your own inner dark god to show up as our provider and carer whilst we are at all times loyal to him and not taking over the show in any way. This is the ultimate inner relationship of self-empowerment, the love story you have forever been seeking. To recognise we are not one or the other – we are both frequencies, and both are required.

The polarities are a necessity within each of us. Our gender and body form are irrelevant here, we contain all aspects of both, and it is our uniqueness which expresses more of some aspects than others without making anything right or wrong. This provides the freedom to truly be ourselves with no labelling, conformity or stereotypes.

This is not a case of achieving anything. It is all frequency, nothing matters. Once the balance and awareness are established and sustained, the cosmic codes can be opened and the masculine and feminine energies balance in intimacy. This is the ultimate removal of the illusion of separation allowing the Higher Self, the individualisation of Source, to be revealed. This allows life to fully flow through us, not happening to us. We are beings of continuous creation.

How then can we generate the power to resurrect the new male?

The currency on the Dark Grid is SYNCHRONICITY, the current, the energy, he runs on. By making synchronicities matter, i.e. bring them into existence, we begin to weave together the timelines by accessing them through the portals.

By noticing the synchronicities, we are aligning the timelines for him to step through the portals and reclaim his power. Timelines do not exist unless we witness them. This is a fundamental Law of Quantum Physics and applicable now we have moved out of linear time into the 4D of no time.

My definition of Portalism is to create prodigies through the portals of time. This is exactly what we are doing to bring our dark god to life. The next generation of Magician who weaves and creates through the quantum. Synchronicities are the anchor fields through the holographic and fractal timelines. Weaving the timelines together to make synchronicity matter (into existence) makes a new time.

It is the dark feminine who deciphers the coding required and must follow the trail of 'coincidences' to bring these energies back into being. It is the map to the portals of energy through which creation and frequency is generated. We are creating the framework for the masculine to return. The decipher codes are the new tone of frequency.

It is a negative frame through which the quantum will be woven back into existence. Making Nothing Matter.

He does not understand the feminine chaotic nature, her emotions, her engagement. He requires you to be still, to provide a framework built out of synchronicities which he requires to define and emerge as who he is. To return in his natural state. He must be inspired by you and the feminine must keep her own narrative, process and thoughts out of this creation.

When both the dark god and goddess emerge in balance and fullest acceptance of each other, then the new realms and frequencies be fully accessible. The natural morphing towards androgyny, the ultimate entwinement, yet never merged, of both polarities.

(the following is channel 15 June)

The dark feminine first ignites her own codes by clearing herself of Light Grid Shadow. This anchors in her own dark body through the portals to her true feminine energy which awaits her in 4D and beyond. Now she is off the Light Grid, these portals are the operating system of the dark.

She no longer requires the anchor points in the body of Light – the Chakra system to operate purely in the dark. Now her portals are open through encoding she can see clearly in the dark the synchronicities, the dots she must join to form a structure for her divine masculine to enter back through the portal from the other side to meet her in this new reality. These cannot be seen on the Light Grid and must be witnessed in the quantum field in order to exist. It is for her to master the maths of the irratio, the quantum field, to make nothing into matter.

This ignites his dormant coding to anchor into his body and re-establish his connection to his own innate power and mystery. The two higher frequencies of the masculine and feminine come together to form a diamond frequency within the body, which is the vibration of 4D and 5D combined. Embodiment of this frequency activates the Diamond Grid, allowing the alien codes to come, be seen and experienced in this reality.

They will be experienced firstly by the Master Code Holder who can then open the portals between heaven and earth for more frequencies to be experienced in the Collective Consciousness. This is exactly what Josephine is doing over the next three months.

The Master Code Holder is then able to weave the portals back into the Light body through infinity symbols joining the light body chakras with the dark portals. This retains the balance within all layers of the physical and etheric body to ensure full access and flow between the frequencies and allow them to be experienced within this reality. This is how Genius codes can be brought to life provided the Chakra system is completely clear of Shadow and ready to be dismantled from the old paradigms.

The spiritual Light Gridders based solely on the Light Grid are not in polarity and are out of balance. It is why the grid, and the world as we know it, is dying. It can no longer hold the frequency of Untruth and is off kilter. The Sacred Symbol of All Things must be woven back into our existence – the Infinity Symbol. The figure eight, the sign of power.

The cosmic codes are then free to be downloaded depending on the frequency of the individual and how many portals to different dimensions they have opened and have access to.

It was the shadow of man and his ego who created the myths, burned the truths and mysteries of the feminine especially around key times such as Egypt and Lemuria. The feminine awakened to this first and deemed men must go through the same process as they to free themselves from the slavery of shadow, with no acceptance their way is not the way for man to claim his power.

We are now ALTERING time and change it to resurrect the empowered man by creating an ALTAR on which to worship him and the mystery he is. He is not to be domesticated like a lapdog. Let him return to his wild code, one who cannot be tamed, yet loyalty is everything.

The wild masculine energy masters the chaos of time from Chronos to Chaos by the Crone virus which dismantled his shadow time codes. Hence, he is invented by the synchronicities of time to ignite his own codes. His own inner female, which he must have claimed first, hold him in stillness in the quantum portal. She must be in his awareness, empowered in aliveness, otherwise he will have to be a constant source of balance for her.

She must provide the stillness and space for him to choose to transmute his shadow into power, through embracing the chaos of the feminine - her emotions, flow and surrender.

Dark consciousness is about fashioning and being fashioned into a work of art that is purely individuated Genius, in the field of the new. The space kills the ego, it simply allows you to run at the highest frequency your codes are open to.

Frequency just is, irratio, with no logic or reason, it cannot be owned. You are it. It removes the notion that innate power can be given or taken. It is simply there for you to claim when you get out of your own way, your human illusions.

This field is NOT new. It has always existed. We may have had glimpses of it before yet never sustainable. As these fields are embodied it allows leading edge consciousness to be experienced through form. It is what can be continually created through new timelines weaved in the quantum.

This dark frequency has always been contained within you, held in your bones. This is where the innate power, structures and divine guidance can be found, in the space of nothingness.

The nothing is the everything. This is the dark eternal feminine energy which exists at all times, the energy I have been leading people to back to connect to off the Light Grid at the core of my work.

When I encode individuals, it is igniting this dark frequency of the purest light within the bones to be accessed through the codes held in your DNA and cellular structure. Then it becomes sustainably accessible to you at all times unless your lower self casts a shadow of doubt and unworthiness on it. At which point you must alchemise.

Humans are terrified of being hooked to nothing because we believe the nothingness is the void of emptiness. They have a sense they have to belong to be worthy, an illusion keeping the majority trapped. This is a great paradox not seen on the Light Grid. We must unhook from others and all experiences to be in the stillness, claim our own innate power and prodigy, free of shadow and trauma.

One of the characteristics of CV19 is people drowning in their own lungs, clutching to the last breaths of air. To draw the comparison to the ancient texts, the Dark Gods of the underworld knew how to breathe under water. It is what is required now, to learn to breathe life back into the bones of light. It is the Inspiration (in-spire, breathe in) we require of our own power and not require another. Literally, saving yourself by learning to use your own innate power.

Our bodies and minds must become unhinged and navigate its own sovereignty. Relationships with food will have changed since March 2020. It is imperative we are released from the toxicity of mind and body. To take back our own innate ability as a powerful healer. To stop giving power away to drugs, alcohol and processed foods.

At the same time, hold the awareness that you are always sovereign of your own frequency and no thing can take your power away from you. It is only the victim mentality which deems you powerless around toxicity. You get to choose what you feed your body, the environment you live in and what you allow into your body, including pollutants such as 5G and chemicals. Do what is necessary to keep a clean environment. Josephine has been promoting products for this since 2014 at Protect Your Energy.

It matters not what is happening on the Light Grid, the new consciousness has usurped it anyway. A frequency upgrade was long overdue to assist people taking back their own power.

Intuition does not work in the dark as it is based on relationships and ratios. It has been upgraded to synchronicities to be seen in the dark. The Magician and Warrior have split as time and space have broken down.

The Activator is the fused domain of the Warrior and Magician. I have called myself The Quantum Alchemist for several years now. My dark mind has been switched on for a long time, I had never seen it whilst I was searching in the light. This allows for quantum flight surfing the waves of the Cosmos at all times. It is beyond taking a quantum leap which implies you must come to a stop, exert a huge amount of energy with which to take off again, effort.

It is indeed time to find your way in the dark.

CHAPTER 31

TWIN FLAMES – THE NEW HIGH MASCULINE

For a few Souls, they believe they can experience their twin flame uniting with them in this reality. I feel our ultimate twin flame lies within the same Universe and is part of you. Your true dark love with yourself.

It has been asked if the new man yet to emerge must be resurrected through another human, one you are in relationship with that is not familial. This is still a 3D viewpoint, with no regard for the higher dimensions of reality.

I fundamentally believe the first male required to be resurrected is your own dark god within. It is about finding the next level of dimension of who you are.

Twin flames are no longer external and separate from us. It is within the one. Shiva/ Shakti, Jesus/ Mary, the combined essence became a new frequency, the new teaching. Their energies never merged, each holding the other in the tension of the brilliance witnessed in another human.

When reunited within, you rewrite your own story over and over, the process of creation. The Torus energy always circulates, the DNA helix always spiralling.

Towards the end of May, I was woken once again in the night. My dreams are continuously about the channelled messages, and I wake up doing my best to recall them and jot them down. The thread today was looking at opposites, the mirrors, determining how we must move away from the need for reflection in the 3D, and go through the portal to the 4D. From there, we look back upon life in 3D.

We no longer work in a linear fashion – ascending up to the energies or drawing them up from the earth. Instead, we work through the infinity loop of duality, the bind that ties the polarities together.

For most humans, self-mastery is about finding and sustaining a balance between the masculine & feminine aspects of self and clearing the illusions of human conditioning. The infinity symbol weaves between these polarities, he whispers sweet nothings of intuition in the ears of the feminine, and thus they create a magical life which she has defined and desired.

When this is taken into the "real world", individuals who have done the work seek relationships or evolve their current ones to a new level, and much talk is had about the female submitting to the male. I have always had a big problem with this theory – where does the balance of the individual come into it?

Each gets to choose their own definition of empowerment, and yet I am challenged to see the ultimate goal of being a powerful woman, in my full feminine submitting to a man. Frankly, I never got it and wrote myself off as being able to have such a relationship because I didn't understand it for many years.

As I see it, we develop certain characteristics, talents and energies that may lean towards the feminine or the masculine, regardless of the body one occupies. The ultimate partner is the one who has the opposite characteristics to you. In textbook theory, this is the domestic goddess paired with the corporate highflyer. We know the world has evolved so far from the days of the 1950's and prior, yet society in the process of making everything equal, has emasculated the man.

How does this fit into the aspect of evolvement? The Alchemists' Awakening is about becoming aware of our fullest potential, which means moving into higher frequency realms, towards heading home to the Soul realm dimensions from where we came. For now, it is about opening up the channels and encoding to access those frequencies, so the power of each can be utilised whilst in human form. This is the ultimate magic within us.

For those reading this book, you already have a taste of 4D, for this is the residence of your Alter Ego. Your true self, one that left the shackles of humanity at the wayside as you stepped through the portal and claimed who you really are. Your challenge is to sustain this frequency, no matter what, and create your life as art from this dimension. Every time you observe you have slipped back into your 3D thoughts and fears, ignite your symbol, alchemise the energies and return to your true self.

Once you have established your deep dark feminine in the 4D, your Inner Masculine of the 3D seems a little surplus to your requirements, for you are no longer hearing snippets of intuition he would pull in from the higher dimensions. Now you are having continual dialogue, a full conversation with your Soul in the 4D.

What I realised recently was although this may be in one tone, on sound of voice, it was actually both my masculine and feminine higher self-communicating with me. For now it is time to master the infinity loop of relationship between your masculine and feminine in the 4D. it is so much easier for you no longer have the fears, the doubts, the mind interfering with your truth.

For a while, most Souls will have a foot in both camps, if not three camps, of 3D, 4D and 5D. However, they cannot sustain the frequencies of the higher realms until cleared the density of the lower ones.

You must master the infinity loop relationship between the dimensions until you fully transition.

4D is where dark love resides. High Masculine (3D) has morphed into your Dark God of the 4D.

Your ultimate Twin Flame.

He is the one who drops the synchronicities through the quantum for us to observe.

Your Sovereign of the 3D has morphed into the Empress of the 4D, AKA your alter ego.

True love, in your true self, lives when you stabilise in the 4th dimension, or higher. For me, my base is in the 4D and I jump between 4D & 5D, it is where I reside. I still access the frequencies of other dimensions, some of which are ignited in me and some I just visit and access as a Parallel.

Evolvement happens when you access these dimensional frequencies and also anchor in the codes through your DNA. This can only ever happen when you are ready and willing to take on the responsibility of this new higher frequencies. Any wavering on ownership will send you straight back down to 3D.

It is both polarities which must be ignited within, and in the dimensions, woven together through the infinity symbol.

Once 3D is mastered, or at least you have mastered the tools to dissolve your 3D traits and maintain your willingness to continually do so, you spend more time in 4D, your alter ego, your true powerful self.

The Heiros Gamos game of 3D is dead, just as the Light Grid is dead. It limits your evolvement and retains your false perceptions of what man and woman are meant to be and how they are meant to be in relationship with each other, all control based and conditional. Any insistence this is the basis for the ultimate empowered relationship is clinging to the old human paradigm of relationship.

Any partnership built on uneven ground will be shaky. If one party evolves and the other choses to remain in 3D for they are not inspired to evolve with them, the relationship frequency is likely to be unstable. Similarly, if any relationship is built with one dominant force over another, and then the other party claims their own power back, that is a recipe for annihilation. It is also the perfect scenario for the ultimate Romeo and Juliet playout – death to both if they cannot be together, metaphorically and perhaps literally.

It is why we are becoming more gender fluid towards androgyny. If gay, all aspects still need to be in balance. Feminism is a massive distortion. A gay man needs to be feminine to accept himself to accomplish what he needs to be in a physical level.

Relationship in the 4D is unconditional. It is the next step moving towards androgyny.

I see the integration levels between dimensions also working on the basis of the infinity loop being between the two. It is about finding the next level of dimension of who you are. As you establish your true self in the 4D, you open up to the aspects of your polarity – your twin flame – in that same dimension. He/she can be ignited and acknowledged in the alter ego realm. Then it is fed back through the infinity loop to your current self. Here the entwined love found within the balanced alter ego drives the empowerment of the inner masculine in this reality, body.

* * *

Last week I was shown the energy form of my twin flame, similar to the green northern lights. As the feminine I can open my vibration and send it back to him in his realm, which enables the structure of body and face to be formed as I chose, and was shown to me, as my heart felt love and partner.

His name is Tajuane (ending in 'e' for masculine, 'a' for feminine). Far more will open up to us as we integrate through the infinity symbol. I am still working out if this is the 4D or 5D realm of lights and my Soul, as I hop between the two. As always, my sacred moments of self-intimacy (into-me-I-see) is when I can merge and embed the energies most powerfully, through the vibration of the body in that moment.

He will work in partnership with me at all the portal openings, directing the cosmic energies and frequencies to the portal. He helps unlock the coding of the energetic holographic portal at that location.

To gather a perspective of ourselves in the multiverse, we must expand our conception to an even higher plane. We have a Black Soul – the invisible version of us – living in a Parallel Universe. Just as the solar sun revolves around the almost invisible black sun which determines other calendars, so does our Parallel revolve around us.

It is the ultimate twin flame who sometimes incarnates in the 3D if neither of the Soul parts are ready for 4D. I feel this could eventuate for Mintakans / Hadarians who do not enter the 4D, or not open to Soul evolvement under their contracts to be on split levels.

Whilst considering my twin flame, I was shown a symbol of the relationship, yet it did not feel complete. Within a day or two I realised why.

It is time to move beyond the concept of just male and female and to re-member with our Divine Source, the third aspect of who we are. The ultimate Holy Trinity.

As soon as that landed, I saw the Triskelion. The Triskele Symbol is a trilateral symbol consisting of three interlocking spirals.

Widely regarded as one of the oldest Irish symbols in existence, it appears on the Newgrange kerbstones, which date from approximately 3200 BC.

Triskeles feature prominently in both ancient and modern Celtic art. As they evoke the Celtic interpretation of the three realms of material existence: earth, water and sky. It is also thought to represent the three worlds: spiritual, physical and celestial.

The Trinity connections associated with the triskelion art: life, death and rebirth; past, present, future; creation, protection, destruction. Each one deals with some aspect of personal growth, human development and spiritual progress.

One theory suggests that the triskelion represents reincarnation, consisting of one continuous line it could be analogous to the unbroken movement of time.

My initial perception was the symbol between the masculine and feminine aspects of myself combined with Source, the Universe.

I was then guided to understand it also represents my third link to my androgynous self in the parallel. Considering the parallel Universe shows everything in reverse, it makes sense that the lowest dimensions here are mapped to higher dimensions in parallel and vice versa.

As we move through the dimensions of frequencies back to the androgynous self in this Universe in the 8D, then we will start mapping to the two aspects of self, existing in the parallel. I have nine pairings is my life path number shows me.

I encourage you to use the symbol in conjunction with your own to really anchor in the third aspect of self. To your divinity and also your parallel aspect.

CHAPTER 32

SYNCHRONICITIES – NOW AND THEN

All the talk of synchronicities which had been swarming around me for a month or so by mid-May pulled me to read The Synchronicity Key by David Wilcock. Now was the time to dive in.

I share here the keys points relevant to The Alchemists' Awakening and this body of writing. The italics are my 'translation' of the key points.

He reminds us that DNA begins as a quantum wave; the Universe is constantly conspiring to create life. *This is the fundamental reason we are creative beings and to feel fully alive must be in a continuous state of creation otherwise we stagnate.*

We are all in service to the One Infinite Creator whose goals is to help us become more aware of our true identity. You Are. It Is. *Do not think of the Creator as God, or anything that is separate from you. It is the essence of the Universe itself, the frequency of love, of nature. You are in service to your Self.*

The synchronicities provide the trail of connection which we must see to acknowledge their existence. They make their own laws, time is irrelevant. Astrology is an excellent map of synchronicities.

The 'coincidences' have meaning. The symbols, numbers, events can be decoded when experienced. It cannot remain a theory.

The individual must be highly vigilant for all observations of synchronicities. A Decoder learns to spot them, see the connections and joins the dots. They use the 'proof' in front of them as well as divine guidance to follow clues and hunches that help create the pathway between the synchronicities which cross many timelines. Calling them into this moment through the quantum is what opens the awareness to the mapping of the Universe and the portals to higher frequencies and consciousness.

Each human being is a perfect hologram of the Infinite Creator. Time and space are ultimately illusions, created for the evolution of consciousness. Free will is the ultimate law to be upheld.

Synchronicities unlock the doors to the mysteries of the Universe, in cycles, not linear time, through history. Humans evolved every 26,000 years, a precession cycle. The transformation in the species could occur literally overnight. In the Law of One, it is said the Neanderthals morphed to human over 1.5 generations, roughly 45 years. i.e. there is no missing link between then explaining the doubling in brain size.

This almost immediate transformation in the scheme of things fits perfectly with the Quantum Theory of Redshift. I studied this 3 years ago and is the basis of my Quantum Healing, across time AND space, i.e. remotely facilitated. The principle that one thing can be transformed into a completely different form almost immediately, without any time taken to morph.

Ancient mystery schools talk about the Black Sun which has a gravitational pull on us. It could be this that pulls us through the precession of the equinoxes every 25,920 years, this being 12 cycles of the zodiac of 2,160 years.

The black sun is the dark feminine energy force around which the light, the masculine, revolves. As we are in the transition time between precessions, everything is being reversed. This will include a physical POLE CHANGE - a reverse in polarity of our planet. Starting with a change in direction of force to exist on the planet. Moving out of the masculine Light Grid into the dark feminine energy of a higher dimension.

It is the Black Sun which affects our thoughts and behaviours as we move through its energy fields. It contains codes to rewrite our DNA.

The feminine energy doing what she does best – continually creating the new. As we switch polarity, this returns us to ownership of our thoughts and feelings. Something the majority of men (and many women) struggle to take ownership of and what is essentially required at this time to regain the balance within the individual as well as for humanity.

The next level of human evolution is called the Fourth Density, the ascended beings. *Moving beyond 3D and into time mastery through the quantum and Portalism.*

The scientific world is largely / completely incorrect. In a greater spiritual reality, human life could be multi-dimensional. Not all Souls have access to their multi-dimensions, it depends on their Soul evolvement. Parallels and awakened Souls do.

Not everything can be proven, the most important things must be experienced. *In the same way, money cannot buy the things we hold so dear to us – love, happiness, freedom of mind.* Synchronicities transcend thoughts and logic; they are the gateway to the world of spirit.

Love and light, the favourite expression of the enlightened, comes from the recognition that light is the raw power of vitality, the sun, the male energy. Love is what shapes, molds and directs the light through invisible tunnels and is both receptive and magnetic, the female. It is also the force that makes the DNA phantom – where photons remain when DNA has been removed.

About 1% of the world's population are sociopaths, the global adversaries fuelled by greed, power and corruption. When the population denies the potential 'evil' caused by the sociopaths, they turn to their leaders hoping they will protect them when sent into massive fear and terror. They deny themselves alternatives to the leaders, labelling them as conspiracy theorists, to stop the loss of vital energy which would occur if they allowed themselves to feel fear.

Absolutely what is playing out now, as well as the mainstream media conveying the government messages of fear. Instructing the populations to do as they say to prevent further devastation is mass mind control. Social media sites remove any and all theories which could give alternative viewpoints or even the Truth! It has gone beyond the sociopaths escalating the fear, it is the currency of control used to cling on so tightly to the structures of old.

The Federal reserve creates magic money to control the world's wealth. They hold 98% of the world's gold, buried in bunkers in Asia.

147 companies make 80% of the world's wealth, of which 75% are financial institutions. The top Federal Reserve Banks are the most powerful. Health insurance and Big Pharma have controlling interests in the top 8-9 media companies. Everything is internally controlled.

PART 2 – MAGICAL WORLD

The world we live in is an illusion. The Soul carries our energetic aspect through our lives and has a direct effect on and function of our DNA. *Which is why I clear the Soul contracts at a cellular and DNA level. It is where your cosmic coding is held, which lights your frequency held in your bones to embody it.*

Your past lives affect current personalities. *This is your Soul wounding as well as your gifts which are programmed and carried forward. It is why you play out lifetime after lifetime the same patterns, it is deeply engrained and major life lessons must be cleared at a Soul level.*

Souls reincarnate in the same era at another time, likely to have been related in previous lives. *I have seen this play out time and time again with me and clients and their relationships.*

Dr. Newton wrote in the book Destiny of Souls: "the average less advanced Soul will put 50 – 70% of its energy into a physical body. Advanced Souls may only expend less than 25%. "

We have an Inner Circle at Soul placement level which stays consistent throughout lifetimes. This could be 3-25 Souls, usually around 15. This is your Inner Circle. *For me, this set is 9 in this Universe, with a matched set cross mapped to my Parallels, making 18 in total. They could be held on other planets in the Milky Way or Arcturia, our twin galaxy. Perhaps others. It depends on your Soul Realms of origination.*

There is a secondary group of Souls of more than a thousand who will reincarnate with us to varying degrees. We organise ourselves to come back at certain times in history until we learn our lessons precisely and finally. *I have no doubt who ever I have worked with, we have met before.*

These are kept in a Life Book - *your Akashic Records.* Newton describes seven colours to reflect the levels of Souls. Level VI are Sages, and VII are Old ones, highly mysterious and rarely seen.

There are around 65m (2013) Wanderers from 4th, 5th and 6th dimensions, often displaying physical disorders, to help us remember who we truly are.

Souls use time doors (portals) to travel into the one continuum. Time and duration were created to experience evolution at a given rate. Now we are moving into the quantum it need not take time to evolve. It is determined by your willingness to take responsibility for the frequencies you harness, which is in direct proportion to your willingness to destroy the illusions of your human existence.

We move into the Ring of Destiny when we are ready to choose our next life. We are shown aspects of potential future lives, maybe four to choose from. We pick the ones where we will evolve the most, some missions will have much hardship.

This also includes body choice which is always deliberate. Physical challenges play a role in speed of evolution. Both the body and Soul must agree. Without the Soul we would be ruled by emotions.

It is why Darkworkers who have claimed their Soul purpose are no longer ruled by the emotional body and triggers from others or circumstances. You know that no one or no thing has power over you.

Once the Soul has left the Ring of Destiny an intense planning meeting with key roles is undertaken, usually from your Soul Group. Synchronicities are planned. Another meeting with the Council of Elders (for the advanced Souls) before rebirth.

We have the ability to travel back to our realms and leave our body before the age of 5, *though we know of some who still do this regardless of age.*

PART 3 - CYCLES OF VICTORY AND DEFEAT

Wilcock talks at length about how movies play out the Hero's Journey. Whilst it does reflect what happens on the Light Grid, it is not the myth of Darkworkers. He states we are part of a cycle that repeats itself, the Hero's Journey every time. I will address this further down the track. I feel we are at the end of a cycle which will then unravel off into the quantum as we move into Endarkenment and thus ending the cycle of Light.

We are in the midst of crossing from the Age of Pisces into the Age of Aquarius, a marker in our collective spiritual evolution.

This crossover period of the bigger cycle is called a PRECESSION and is 25,920 years long. Divide this into the twelve signs of the zodiac and each Age is 2,160 years.

These have sub-cycles like the four seasons 2160/4=540 years. It is actually 539 to be precise, which is made up of further sub-cycles of 7 and 11 years.

7 x 77 = 539

49 x 11 = 539

Earth incurs sunspots every 11 years and it is a common saying life goes in seven-year cycles.

The Siege of Orleans was led by Joan of Arc in 1429. 539 years later, the French Uprising led to a month-long Revolution in May 1968. Forty-nine years later in 2017, France saw unrest again following abuse of power by police.

Much of humanity dismisses the ancient texts as myths lost in time, if they even know about them. It is going to take a monumental historical event for society to grasp there is life beyond this world and this lifetime. It may just take the disclosure of extra-terrestrial (ET) presence.

The ancient stories will finally achieve its purpose by bringing us face to face with the nemesis. We must learn to integrate our ego and out of blame for pain, fear and anger. It must start by stop projecting our shadow onto others by making them our enemies.

The patterns will continue until we use our power to change the outcome. This requires the collective will. *It is why the new frequencies continue to arrive and more will be opened with the Portals over next three months. The will of the people for free choice, freedom of speech and counting ALL lives matter is speaking up. The Collective is beginning to shift, starting with revolution.*

The organizing power of the ancient cycles of time mean we never see any negativity greater than we have invited in through our own free will.

The Illuminati are guarding the ultimate treasure – the technology which would vastly improve the quality of all life on Earth. *They are simply waiting for the cosmic proton energy to be made available in order to harness it. Fuelling this planet is the biggest issue and as said before, cosmic energy will not be under the ownership of conglomerates or corporations. It is the philanthropic private companies which will bring together technology and new power sources and make it available for the people to own. It is the first steps to the new future, yet individuals must be ready to be able to receive the possibility of fuel and energy not from here.*

UFO's have constantly interfered with the nuclear arsenal of every country who has them and the governments know that.

PART 4- RESOLVNG THE OUTER AND INNER CRISES

The new types of power can only be received when the Collective is at the right frequency and over the threshold point in their evolution.

Three great scientists discovered the cycles of history; Fomenko went into much more detail than Helmer or Masson.

Different cycles have been identified, and seen the procession of 25,920 years which can be divided by the 12 zodiac signs into Ages of 2,160 years. The precession length is also close to the Mayan calculations; 5 x 5125 years = 25,625 years.

The transition from one precession period to another at the 25,920-year mark is called "the Gateway to Intelligent Infinity" as it has a much stronger energetic charge. Exactly what we are experiencing right now.

The cusps bridge the Ages: 1 ° either side gives a range of up to 144 years, 72 either side of the exact point.

Due to the nature of the Precession of the Equinoxes, the progression of ages proceeds in a REVERSE direction through the zodiacal signs.

- About 2012 Age of Aquarius
- About year 0, Age of Pisces
- About 2000 BC, Age of Aries.

Other cycles also been identified:

25,920 / 20 = 1,296 divided into four equal parts on Fomenko's graph of 324-year sections.

324 x 80 = 25,9520

He calculated how many years elapsed between starting points of each cycle in the graph and discovered key historical events occurred about every 720 years. This can be seen as three cycles in one age of the zodiac.

Masson had also associated the 720-year cycle with the growth phase of major religions. The first phase is the prophetic period, the second is the clerical phase and the third is that the supremacy of the temporal power of the spiritual power.

For example, Christ's teachings to the years 720 to 750 corresponds to the mystical epoch of Christianity. From A.D. 722 - 1440 the times changed and the ecclesiastical church hierarchy became masters over people and governments.

At the end of the second cycle (around 1440) the Renaissance started, creating the dawning of modern science as we now know it. Renaissance challenged the church's authority to proclaim the truth without question and also led the Reformation. 720 years after 1440 will get us to 2160.

What if we considered the year A.D. 720 the beginning of a new cycle of a different length, that of 1,296 years? This would give an end date of 2016, not far off this current time.

The Bible in Daniel 12:11 clearly mentions history progressing from age to age. In Daniel 12:12 (a little familiar with the Mayan predictions of 12/2012?) It is indicated there will be 45-day transition period.

What piqued my curiosity was that Wilcock stated 45 years and not 45 days as I doublechecked in Bible.

Supposing these 45 years broke down into five cycles (the Mayan's favourite and that of the pentagon) of nine years each? We could be in the midst of a 45-year transition cycle, which fits in with the writings that the Neanderthals worked out within a generation the half at a previous awakening.

I consider the patterns of years this could form.

1996 - 2003 – 2012 – 2021 – 2030

I also considered if these years with the midpoints of another cycle

1998 – (2003) – 2007 – (2012) – 2016 – (2021) – 2025 (2030) – 2034

2016 is the midpoint of the Milky Way equator alignment which takes 36 years.

The midpoint year was when the Mayans predicted the end of cycle. We are close to the birthing of the new age 2021 established by 2030.

25,920 / 5 = 5,125-year Mayan Cycle

45 / 5 = 9-year transitions

What if the 2016 Wilcock identified as the end of a cycle needed to have the additional 5 years added to be 2021?

The Mayan calendar is tracking each of the sub-cycles – 260 days, 360 days + 5, 7,200 days (19.7 years), 144,000 days (396.4 years) all directly synchronise with the orbits in our solar system.

260 days (the tzolkin) is the smallest possible number that interlocks all the orbits of the inner planets together. The Mayans built a whole system of divination around this, tracking a 20-day cycle and a 13-day cycle at the same time. Each of which has a particular meaning, similar to astrology.

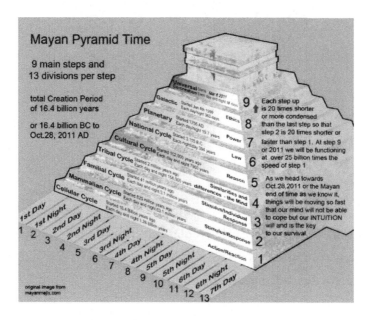

The Aztec Sun Stone

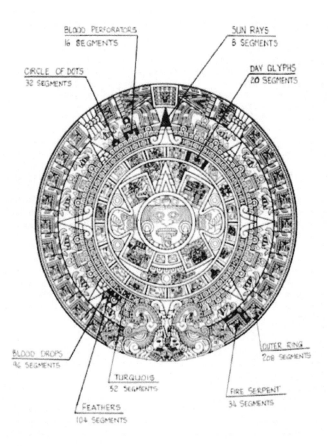

Wilcock questioned what was creating the cycles. If the sun is orbiting another star which is nor easily visible, and the orbit was rounded into a circle via a computer program, the Mayan calendar cycle length then forms perfect five-sided geometry within it.

This could be the "lost Star of myth and time." The brown dwarf, the Black Sun, hardly visible to the naked eye.

The black Sun is the dark feminine energy around which our Solar Sun revolves. The masculine revolving round near invisible feminine yet always required to keep him orbiting.

The distances between planets is one of the five basic Platonic solids. These solids are the most basic harmonic patterns that appear when you vibrate a fluid. I am sure you have witnessed experiments where water is vibrated with pure sound frequencies, particles will mysteriously fall into very precise geometric shapes. This leaves spaces of clean pure water in between.

This is the same concept as the dark matter being the creating matter of the Universe. This is the Source field, the Universal Mind.

Any vibration of the fluid could be regarded as a thought. "All things, all of creation, is part of one original thought".

The pure dark feminine energy through which all things are created, existing eternally. Platonic relationship is one that is purely spiritual and not physical. Just as the stars will never meet yet always in a dance of polarity, so too the masculine and feminine never merge (within the lower dimensions) yet both are required to keep the gravitational pull of existence in place.

This theory could be extended into the return to Platonic relationships and higher dimensions where structures (masculine) are formed when vibration is applied to the dark matter (feminine). Both elements required to create. This is the essence of androgyny.

We live in a binary solar system and orbit our companion star over the course of 25,920 years. The Sumerians call this Nibiru, various secret societies including the Masonic order call it the Black Sun. Sometimes the Black Sun is also depicted as the Eye of Horus. A triangle may also be drawn around the eye.

The Law of One series Wilcock studied extensively states the 26,000-year cycle is the basic pattern that governs the evolution of all third density life on any given planet in our Milky Way system.

Each planet must go through the cycle entirely before fully transitioning out of third density and fully transition into fourth density.

The sun's surface moves up and down a few metres every five minutes. This creates waves in the Source field. The ripples create interference patterns which in turn generate invisible geometric force fields holding the planets in position. Otherwise known as gravity. The constant push pull between the planets holds them in place.

Intelligent infinity - the heartbeat - is the central sun; the rhythms clothed in mystery. The constant flow of new energy allows planets to exist moment by moment.

Much the same as both energies of the masculine and feminine required to keep relationship in balance. The deep mysteries of feminine hold the beating heart of the male at her core.

The planet itself has moved through the useful parts of that dimension, begins to cease being useful to the lower levels of vibration within that third density.

Hence the male begins to die. It no longer has a useful life in the lower vibrations of existence.

Our entire solar system moves one degree every 72 years through the night sky. (72 x 360 = 25,920)

By Law of One standards, all stars cluster into groups of at least two stars and that any solar system that has planets with third density life would have to be orbiting a companion star, orbits lasting 25,920 years.

This returns us to the essential requirement of polarity; we need both the male and female to exist. The male sun cannot exist without the black female sun around which it revolves.

The solstice date of 21/12/2012 was when the Solstice Sun aligned with Dark Rift in the Milky Way. This is known as "The Mouth of the Crocodile".

The Devouring Mother.

The conception point of the female consuming the masculine.

The Mouth is the widest part of the Milky Way and corresponds to the direction of the galaxy.

When the Solstice meridian aligns with the galactic equator, we can resonate with the source of the field. This could create a pole shift in our collective psyche.

It has also been said when Nibiru (the Black Sun) crosses Earth in our solar system it creates a pole shift.

The actual crossing occurred in 1998 and takes 36 years to complete. 2016 is the halfway point. I do not believe this been recognised anywhere else in texts.

Wilcock believes this is not possible as stars naturally repel each other by gravity through the geometric energy field.

I have received guidance there will be a pole shift. The so-called climate change is the forerunner of this event, just as it has played out many cycles before.

The end of the Mayan calendar is when we come into the geometric alignment with this massive dodecahedron created by the companion star. There is strong scientific evidence that every time we hit one of these nodal points our sun has a major energetic shift. The energetic surge directly affects climate.

Major climate change occurred 5,200 years ago, not far off the alignment with a calendar cycle of 5,125 years.

There is evidence that points to this shift in climate when there was 250 million people occupying the planet last time. With over 7 billion today it is far more noticeable. The Glaciologist Lonnie Thompson believes a huge solar energy oscillation triggered the previous climate change and could well be what is happening right now.

Also remember, what happened 5,200 years ago will be as dramatic as what we would see at the end of the entire 25,920-year cycle. We are coming to alignment of geometries at the same time.

The Law of One series indicates the transition from intelligent energy through the gateway to intelligent infinity, regardless of the circumstances.

The book implies the transition will be gradual. Many will die natural deaths at whatever time is appropriate and then reincarnate in the fourth density. However, the real magic lies in the fact that if you could become "double bodied" you can start doing fourth density magic tricks while you are still in your physical body.

The question was asked, how many are here now who come from other planets who are third density harvestable for fourth density experience? Ra answered it was not yet in excess of 35,000 entities (2013). It can only be gained by demonstrating a great deal of orientation toward service to others.

* * *

The Synchronicity Key book served me as a reminder we are not alone in being advocates for Truth and what wisdom is to be found very nature of existence.

However, I do fundamentally believe we are moving into a new era but has not been well documented as it has not yet been experienced on the planet. Very few have an indication of this new level of existence and fewer still acknowledge the true power of what lies beyond. Many truth seekers are still blinkered by the bright lights of the promises of enlightenment. They have missed the point that we must search in the dark for the truth so that the new male be resurrected, born again in a new light. One without the shadow of tribal conditioning.

CHAPTER 33*

GRIEVING: ACCEPTANCE

The final part of the grieving process is acceptance. Life would never be the same again. It provided us an opportunity to consider the elements of normal which were welcome to stay in the past.

People were considering: "This is happening and I must figure out how to proceed." It was the time to explore new options, put new plans in place and move on with their lives. All within the confines of government restrictions.

As always, it was only limited by the illusions keeping them trapped. Despite anything happening in the world around them, there are always free to look forward from a space of the creative being they are.

Emotions could start to stabilise now as people were coming to terms with the new reality. There may still have been a lockdown, all we kept hearing were the promises of a new normal. One that didn't bode well for the freedom seekers amongst us.

May was a time of adjustment and readjustment, waiting whilst holding our breath. Perhaps subconsciously sympathizing with those on ventilators. Some of the lockdown restrictions started easing back in mid-May in many countries.

Every individual was required to step up and decide for themselves how they want to live their lives, what is it that they really want to do. It was a golden opportunity to consider what they were no longer prepared to accept as part of their daily lives, of their relationships, of their working life.

So many still wanted to be told what to do, when to do it and how to do it, unable to take any level of self-responsibility. Cowering in fear of a virus from which 99% of people recovered if under 60. All logic and reasoning had gone out of the window due to the brainwashing of government and media.

There is also an additional type of grief beyond the five stages defined by Kubler Ross. Anticipatory grief is that feeling we get about what the future holds and we are uncertain. The feeling that a storm is coming.

Not being able to see it rattles primitive minds and breaks a sense of safety. It was a new thing to feel this on a global scale. Many were grieving on a micro and macro level.

To help reduce the intensity of grief, it was important to find techniques which would give balance in the things that you were thinking. It was hard for many to get back into the present moment and stop projecting into the future.

The what-if scenario could have been used productively for many. Rather than what's going to happen to my job, the world health, when will the vaccine come, how will we survive? Instead, individuals had the opportunity to gather themselves in this moment, to move into the feeling space of what it is they really want to create in their lives.

It was hard for many to recognise the need to let go of what they couldn't control. At the end of the day, the only person they were responsible for was themselves.

The most alarming aspect was the open-endedness of it all. Even if they got through this wave of the pandemic, many realised it would sweep again. When, where, worse next time?

It was a shock to deal with so much uncertainty. It really was taking many out their comfort zones who abhor change.

Nations were clearly divided by those who were leveraging this exciting opportunity to change their lives through enforced situation and those who are cowering in fear waiting to be told what to do.

It is clear who is going to ride the wave of the fundamental changes coming to humanity and the very fabric of society over the coming months and years.

Hold the reminder in your heart it is not your responsibility how others think or feel or operate through this change. Your role is merely to share your truth which may inspire others to reconsider their own options.

Going deep on exactly what you are willing to experience was imperative now. Were you blindly accepting what you have been told by the government and media, or could you take the time to discern the truth by feeling within what really resonates for you?

This is the simplest way for people to understand the difference between reality and illusion and not take anything on face value. We will delve into emotional response in future chapters, as it is a key indicator of human conditioning.

For now, in May, the ultimate acceptance was to realise the power within to change your own life according to your own free will and to step into full ownership and authority of what you are really here to do, despite world events.

ASTROLOGY: MAY 2020

May was a mercurial month with three planets beginning their retrograde cycle. Whether we saw this month as providing us mayhem or magic is in direct correlation to your stage of awakening. It was so important to be mindful and present.

It started with a short conjunction between Mercury and Uranus which is an ideas transit. Sudden flashes of inspiration would happen, though it could also mean a racing mind, hopefully balanced by the Taurean energy.

Throughout May, Venus and Neptune formed a challenging aspect. With the square aspect there is a tendency to feel disillusioned with our personal relationships and a feeling of disconnection. This is made even more demanding when cooped up inside with those very people. It would however give you an opportunity to re-evaluate our connections and values. Like all considerations, it is up the individual to act on it and not just bury it in the sand, ignoring the consequences.

The Scorpio full moon on 7th May brought in a wave of emotional cleansing. It was time to let go of what no longer supports you and make the changes necessary. This was challenging as people were realising it was the relationships they had needed to either progress or end and was not the situation in which they could easily act.

This was about the six-week lockdown period. Toxic relationships and negative thinking were rearing their heads under these energetic influences, with Scorpio's tail added into the mix. It will be fascinating to see in hindsight how the cases of domestic violence and suicides fared across this time.

Around May 12th was an ideal time to feed of Mercury's vibe with a high attention to detail and ability to process information. It was the perfect support for people who were starting to question the same diatribe being spouted by mass media and to do their own independent research into the truth of what was unfolding, from experts who were not subject to political or financial bias.

Just as Saturn turned retrograde on May 12 some restrictions across the world started easing. This energy supports us to consider what we would like to build for our future as the planet of structure and foundation.

It was important to maintain our individuality through this period and not grasp at everything offered just because it gave a glimmer of security. Once again, an opportunity for us to realise where we get our true power from, it is never outside ourselves.

On 14th May Venus began her six-week retrograde cycle, the midpoint of which would be her starting a new Venus cycle of 19 months. It was a key time to reflect on our own values, standards of thoughts and the way we communicate, interact with others and who we are interacting with.

It could be a time of misunderstandings and righteousness, saying hurtful words to others. Tensions in many households could be at an all-time high about now. At least Mars moved into Pisces on the same day reminded us to treat each other with kindness and to speak from the heart.

May 15th saw Jupiter begin his four-month retrograde which could leave us feeling flat and without enthusiasm. It is important to rely on our own internal resources to fuel us rather than external experiences. Use this time wisely to cultivate inner awareness so needed by Collective Consciousness at this time.

Jupiter retrograde provides the perfect support to consider which areas you would love to expand into, what you would most love to do and to consider escaping from environments which did not light your fire, especially on the career front, where Capricorn is concerned with your career. Things could look very different by the time Jupiter turns direct in mid-September.

The new moon in Gemini on May 23rd brings our attention to communication and speaking truthfully. This aspect was sorely lacking and obvious on the world stage as so many lies were covering up the real agenda at play. It also covers listening and it was imperative people chose what they listened to and not just go along with the ride of fear so apparent in the mainstream.

It also includes our own inner dialogue, how do we communicate with ourselves and what we are feeding our minds. It could be a scattered energy time so grounding and quiet time was essential.

Remember we choose our reactions to everything even if we cannot control what is happening. It was an important month to respond rather than react, which is where the true power lies.

JUNE 2020

CHAPTER 34

THE REASON FOR REVOLUTION

May had been the most profound month of my awakening in this lifetime, it was a complete time warp to reflect on what had unfolded. I was feeling quite daunted at the task of writing it up, although I had realised mid-May I was to jump timelines continuously whilst constructing this book. I write the current days activities, downloads and deciphering's, then jump back in time to write up what occurred a few weeks or months ago, whilst not being distracted from my new wisdom gained in between. It was like a warm-up to travel between weeks and months, before I got into the depths of some serious travel across the eons.

The beginning of June saw the opening up of many countries, in phased re-opening, including some of the most devastated countries such as UK & US. Health officials in the UK were making last minute pleas to the government not to ease restrictions. They had 275k cases and 38k deaths by the beginning of June.

In the US 600 doctors wrote a letter to plead with Trump, saying the lockdowns is a "mass casualty incident". They see US as a Triage situation, and colour coded patients in order of priority. Suicide hotline phone calls had increased 600%. 150,000 patients could have had cancer screening leading to missed cancer diagnosis. The doctors saw "lack of consideration for the future health of our patients".

US was standing at 40m unemployed, with millions of casualties of lockdown hiding in plain sight. They will be called alcoholism, suicide, homelessness, strokes, heart attacks, kidney failure. It will also show up as unemployment, drug addiction, unplanned pregnancies, poverty and abuse. More drugs were being issued for anxiety (prescriptions were up 34%) and depression (up 19%).

One of the doctors said suicide was claiming more lives than Covid. One years' worth of suicides in the last four weeks alone. They are screaming we must get out of lockdown and encouraging others to share.

Schools were starting to open up in the US, with complete segregation, children wearing gloves and no playing together. This is laying the groundwork for mass depression and a new standard of living for future generations. Suicides amongst 15-24-year-old is at a 20-year high. The US, and other parts of the world, are living in a pressure cooker of social isolation.

Lockdown dates for key countries. Still far from all aspects of society back in operation.

Lockdown data

country	start date	ease restrictions
Italy	9/03/2020	18/05/2020
Spain	14/03/2020	26/05/2020
France	17/03/2020	11/05/2020
United States	19-24/3/20	13/06/2020
Australia	23/03/2020	1/06/2020
Germany	23/03/2020	10/05/2020
United Kingdom	23/03/2020	10/05/2020
New Zealand	26/03/2020	14/05/2020

Australia had been extremely slow on the uptake, especially here in South Australia where we had a total of two new cases since 23 April, who had flown in from overseas. The media were still feasting over this "pandemic", which it simply was not here in Australia.

Wikipedia definition:

A **pandemic** (from Greek πᾶν, *pan*,"all" and δῆμος, *demos*, "local people" the 'crowd') is an epidemic of an infectious disease that has spread across a large region, for instance multiple continents or worldwide, affecting a substantial number of people. A widespread endemic disease with a stable number of infected people is not a pandemic. Widespread endemic diseases with a stable number of infected people such as recurrences of seasonal influenza are generally excluded as they occur simultaneously in large regions of the globe rather than being spread worldwide.

Our government does little to stand independently from the rest of the world. It cannot because it relies so heavily on the trade agreements between the countries. I have always felt it rides on the coat tails of the Big Boys, never one to stand up and make its own decisions. It lost its identity years ago. Or did it ever have one?

In fact, Australia lost its true identity as one of the energetic power centres of the world when it was colonised. Unlike its neighbour New Zealand, led by Jacinda Ahern, who had always retained its independent state and own thinking.

Elsewhere in the world tensions were high and the unrest started. On 25th May, the revolting murder of George Floyd, a black man whose neck was knelt on by a white police officer for over eight minutes was the straw which broke the camel's back. Whilst Floyd did have pre-existing health conditions and a background of criminal activity, it did not excuse the officer's behaviour resulting in his death.

Protests, riots, looting and fires tore through several American cities, and across the world. It was the same weekend the "anti-vaxxers" demonstrated across Australia against 5G peacefully.

In the States, curfews were imposed, the National Guard was called, tear gas and rubber bullets were used as the peaceful protests turned ugly at night-time. Fears were increasing for a surge in Coronavirus cases after such gatherings.

The White House was under attack in many senses of the word. It would be a test for Trump to see how he would deal with this continuing stream of cascading disasters. CV19 had taken 100,000 lives in the US, the economic slump had cost 40m jobs and now rising social unrest.

Of course, the unrest was not simply as a result of the murder. It was free expression of pent-up anger and resentment which had been building for months. The tension was high, populations had been kept indoors for weeks now, and were literally busting at the seams to express how they felt. The people were speaking out to the world, yet what started as peaceful protests soon turned ugly as the energy rose.

This article provides more insight to the US landscape.

The actions of the people were the outpourings of blame and grief, expressed only as they knew how. When it is met with further police controls and violence, it was bound to escalate. Populations had simply had enough of government rule.

Black Lives Matter is a "global network that builds power to bring justice, healing and freedom to black people across the globe". It is an organisation movement in the US advocating for non-violent civil disobedience and protest against incidents of police brutality against African-American people. An organisation which could not exist without white perceived superiority.

They made front-page news nationally and around the world during the George Floyd protests. An estimated 15m to 26m people participated in the US alone, with many more countries around the world joining in support.

Cities across Germany may have been the largest demonstration turnout outside the US. Institutional racism is entrenched within police institutions in this country, who know full well both sides the coin when it comes to social segregation.

Here in Australia people took to the streets to acknowledge there had been at least 434 deaths since the Royal commission into Aboriginal deaths in custody ended in 1991. At the same time the Prime Minister, Scott Morrison stated on Sydney radio, "as upsetting and terrible that the murder that took place - and it is shocking, but also just made me cringe- I just think to myself how wonderful the country is Australia" he said.

"There is no need to import things happening in other countries here to Australia. Australia is not the United States".

Oh, but it has some stark similarities Scott, stemming from non-ownership of real issues.

Whilst millions had the intention of protesting peacefully, many cities saw violence, arson, looting and killing, with protests continuing into July. By June 30 there were at least 26 people, majority of whom were black, were dead, 22 due to gunshot wounds. At least 14,000 people had been arrested, including all four police officers involved in the arrest which led to Floyd's death.

The sales of ammunition and guns had been skyrocketing in the States the past few months and business continued to boom with these new outbreaks. A rally had been held in Virginia earlier in the year showing what happens when the US tries to pass gun-control laws, stating guns are civil right and is a violation of the Constitution to have them removed. The attitude of self-defence through arms to run alongside the fight or flight mentality is alive and well through the US.

Donald Trump epitomises social control societies where substantial resources are placed into police, prisons surveillance, immigration enforcement and the military. The purpose is to utilise fear, punishment and violence, to maintain the considerable order. He really is the culmination of 40 years of increasing social control in the US decreasing social investment.

In the decades following the Second World War, the nation began moving towards social investment. Spending on healthcare public assistance and inequality declined. It swung back in the early 90s with Clinton's Violent Crime control and Law Enforcement Act 1994.

Recent events brought into the open that social controls are not sustainable. They require more oppressive means pertaining people to stand up against oppression. In a few states, moves will make him to renew the commitment to social investment, starting with defunding the police. This included key cities such as LA and New York. Discussions in Minneapolis took place around potentially disbanding the Police Department altogether.

The change in direction is monumental but the size of the proposed cuts is not, activists have said. This will be a key area to watch what unfolds as social justice becomes the forefront of many people's minds. Discover more about defunding the police and what it means.

Somehow, the requirement for social distancing seemed less important than the protests themselves. Governments gave the go-ahead to organise rallies around the world, when only two weeks before, all those who took part in peaceful demonstrations against 5G were badly mishandled by the police and faced fines.

The double standards continued when Trump rallies started to occur towards the end of the month. It was deemed CV19 could spread at such rallies, in churches, in person voting. However, the rules were relaxed or ignored for pride rallies, ANTIFA riots, with crowds tearing down statues, George Floyd's funeral and BLM protests.

The debate over wearing masks and effectiveness continued. Cloth masks which most people were using offers no filtering whatsoever. The carbon dioxide as you exhale generates moisture in the masks, the perfect breeding ground for germs. On the other hand, Asian countries are regular users of masks and believe they help eliminate air pollution and germs.

Once again, the government was enforcing the use of such masks in many states across the US and various countries around the world. No one could seem to agree on the necessity or otherwise.

The BLM movement also lead to several statues of slave traders and other historical figures being torn down or vandalised. People are completely missing the point. These statues are a reminder of our history and how far we have come as a nation. It does not mean the behaviours are in action now but were once a key part of the formation of society.

What is still absent from the remit of Collective Consciousness is the requirement to move out victim energy. This turns from the tribal conditioning, fight or flight and power games. The ramifications of Floyd's death ignited the historical energies of slavery and people felt entitled to lord it over others.

This was not a black or white issue, or any other form of racism, as a channel for a power struggle, entitlement and victimhood. The imbalance of power within society had people rise up and make a statement.

If the four officers were charged with murder in the first instance it might have been dealt with appropriately. Police feel they have the ultimate power, and a nasty element of righteousness and corruption emerges.

Humans also like to paint everyone with the same tar brush. It would serve us well to remember not ALL police are the baddies, the majority serve the protection of society. It is also a complete misnomer to expect the current day people of non-colour to bear the burden of the ancestors to carry forward the self-loathing based on acts of the past which they played no part. The ultimate martyrs. Similarly, why do many milk the label of receiving racism which they deem gives them the right to be violent in the same manner as they have received?

It is all an illusion to have the right to loot, steal, to kill, act out in any way. It is just an excuse to express their own emotion, blaming it on others, without processing it for themselves. We must start being accountable and know when it is wrong. To be responsible for our actions and reactions.

Society was angry with everything, from a sense of entitlement, felt they had the right to act out. Yet the new consciousness demands imbalance of power is no longer dealt with by acting with the same energy of violence, anger, blame and destruction. They have lost the truth of what they are fighting for, behaving like two-year-olds having a tantrum. All clouded with illusion, not seeing it for what it is. We are all connected.

It had also been pointed out, why was Floyd nor any of the officers wearing a mask at the time of the attack? Was it staged, filmed in advance, to provoke a response from the public when the time was right? Others have suggested white supremacists were brought in to escalate the rioting, who are far more dangerous than the general public.

Piles of bricks lay handily on streets for the violent behaviour without any construction work in sight. Trump supports the supremacists to avoid his own short comings. He creates more anarchy to look to be the good guy.

All the corruption playing out is egoically driven and not for the truth of addressing the imbalance of power. Rioting is another example of people being told that something is wrong so they must act.

For all that has been said, it is not actually the frontline governments and police who are pulling the strings. These are just the front people seen on the surface, the ones unseen are far more dangerous.

Judges, lawyers, huge businesspeople, royalty, Vatican, church leaders. These are the ones with hidden agendas starting to be exposed. It is time for them to fall, and as they do, they will pull back the curtain on so much more that society is not being told about.

Slavery and human trafficking is a huge multimillion dollar industry on the brink of being exposed.

It is time to consider how new energies and consciousness will assist with this long overdue change.

Before we do, take one last look at how Coronavirus had swept through more than 10 million people on the planet in six months, killing more than half a million.

Well, that is what the numbers show despite so many doctors around the world stating clearly how they were asked to account for the deaths, with no regard to existing health issues. It was a massive revenue earner for hospitals if they claimed the deaths were due to CV 19.

#	Country, Other	Total Cases	New Cases	Total Deaths	New Deaths	Total Recovered	Active Cases	Serious, Critical	Tot Cases/1M pop	Deaths/1M pop	Total Tests	Tests/1M pop	Population
	World	10,412,421	+9,518	608,228	+700	5,668,668	4,235,525	57,782	1,336	66.2			
1	USA	2,681,811		128,783		1,117,177	1,435,851	15,864	8,102	389	33,189,513	100,271	330,996,984
2	Brazil	1,370,488		58,385		757,462	554,641	8,318	6,448	275	3,070,447	14,445	212,584,056
3	Russia	641,156		9,166		403,430	228,560	2,300	4,393	63	19,334,442	132,487	145,934,449
4	India	567,536		16,904		335,271	215,361	8,944	411	12	8,608,654	6,238	1,379,937,465
5	UK	311,965		43,575		N/A	N/A	276	4,595	642	9,290,215	136,852	67,885,079
6	Spain	296,050		28,346		N/A	N/A	617	6,332	606	5,162,909	110,425	46,754,775
7	Peru	282,365		9,504		171,159	101,702	1,183	8,565	288	1,681,324	50,391	32,968,619
8	Chile	275,999		5,575		236,154	34,270	2,090	14,438	292	1,096,443	57,359	19,115,496
9	Italy	240,436		34,744		189,196	16,496	98	3,977	575	5,341,837	88,351	60,461,762
10	Iran	225,205		10,670		186,180	28,355	3,037	2,681	127	1,639,078	19,516	83,986,007

CHAPTER 35

THE GREAT AWAKENING

The Bigger Agenda at play had been the main point of conversation from behind the scenes many months. Social media giants such as Facebook and YouTube were the first to take down any information, posts or educational information was not in line with main media, making it hard for people to use the platform for their own self-expression and to share their own research.

The last thing government control wants is people "spreading false rumours about conspiracy theories", providing information, often factual by high educated people in the front line, who are sharing the story as it is. Their first-hand experience as doctors and specialists of viruses or not sharing the same information as governments wish to convey, led them to being shut down, deleted and classified as false information.

On a larger scale, QAnon continues to accumulate a large global following since their first post in October 2017. Using the hashtag #WWG1WGA, it signifies the motto, "when we go one, we go all".

Their "conspiracy theory" (according to Travis View, who writes extensively for the Washington Post, as listed on Wikipedia) states:

there is a worldwide cabal of Satan-worshiping paedophiles who rule the world, essentially, and they control everything. They control politicians, and they control the media. They control Hollywood, and they cover up their existence, essentially. And they would have continued ruling the world, were it not for the election of President Donald Trump.

Now, Donald Trump in this conspiracy theory knows all about this evil cabal's wrongdoing. But one of the reasons that Donald Trump was elected was to put an end to them, basically. And now we would be ignorant of this behind-the-scenes battle of Donald Trump and the U.S. military — that everyone backs him and the evil cabal — were it not for 'Q.' And what 'Q' is — is basically a poster on 4chan, who later moved to 8chan, who reveals details about this secret, behind-the-scenes battle.

QAnon shares the same consciousness as the Illuminati. These extremes are of the same energy and are the duality which exists in every aspect of life.

Deep State / Illuminati / Cabal is all about control. It is run by a chosen few who deem themselves superior beings.

QAnon / The Great Awakening is all about freedom. In the same way, Q sees "himself" as a superior source of inside knowledge.

Q is part of the consciousness of change and is helping to open the doors to take us to an awareness based on a reality that is not separate from us. We each have our own ability to access all the information we need, the tangible results come from our own response. When we truly learn to discern truth from fiction and recognise circumstances for what they are, we are able to grow in our own awareness. This includes not taking all QAnon's verbiage as the Truth.

This text is not for the purpose of identifying and critiquing somebody's theories. Nor is it to express my own opinion on politics. I have been guided more than once to stay out of this arena. It is however, to facilitate your own evolvement into conscious responsibility.

There are so very many things that are up for discussion, the change, to be revealed, to be welcomed. The Fourth Awakening WILL bring these issues to the forefront, it is only a matter of time. The Great Awakening map shows the extent of what is on the table.

The only way they will be taken seriously, implemented or dismissed as appropriate, is when the Collective Consciousness wakes up to the realisation what is really happening in the world around them and who is controlling the fabric of society.

These writings serve the very purpose of combining the unfolding of events in alignment with the new energies entering our biosphere, ready to fundamentally change how we operate as a global collective, returning each individual to the truth of who they are.

Yet the tipping point of those ready to accept the new is only just over half. 53% of the global population is ready to awaken sufficiently to receive new information and realization. It is imperative we establish a higher vibration of the Collective Consciousness immediately.

The key ramifications of the shift of energy are for individuals to become conscious warriors be responsible for their own actions. To recognise and understand when something is wrong, to discern the difference between what is real and illusion. We must step into ownership of actions and reactions.

Already we are seeing the vibrational change has moved to one of understanding rather than reacting. Although Donald Trump is rather slow to pick up on the new vibe, he enjoys playing both sides of the fence and being inconsistent. He has mastered response reactions to justify his change in direction. This is far less visible in other countries and governments.

It is also key to remember that Covid-19 potentially diverted World War III. Several countries have been teetering on the brink of finally pulling the trigger and declaring war. The space created through lockdown with each country becoming an island on its own was the much-needed distancing and refocus on self, as individuals and within the country itself.

It gave governments the directive back to the fundamentals of life - health of the people. With this a priority, there was less focus on the hatred of others. Thank goodness many leaders recognise Trump as a master of tantrums and not react as they may have previously done with the old energies being so well-established.

For many people, the idea of WWIII evokes images of nuclear war in the wipe-out of humanity. Whilst many countries do indeed hold nuclear arsenal, every government on this planet who has the potential to wipe out the masses also know there has been extra-terrestrial involvement to prevent this from happening.

Whilst the world may not be ready to accept the idea of "alien invasion", seeming a scary proposition simply because they do not understand it, governments have been aware for a very long time they are sitting on the doorstep of our gravity field.

The cosmic beings have waited patiently for humanity to get their act together. They know they had to step in and remove the toys from the playpen when it came to the red trigger button which would annihilate large parts of the planet and population.

CHAPTER 36

NEW FINANCIAL SYSTEMS & ST GERMAINE

Let us consider one of the main areas for radical change in society. That of the financial systems. With the talk of negative interest rates, even the likes of Warren Buffett, the guru of finance, is unsure of the implications. Yet another glaring statement everything is going into reverse, the economic structure crumbling before us.

Bitcoin and crypto currency were surging especially with the move towards a cashless society unfolding across retail all over the world.

Destroying the banking system

The value of gold was skyrocketing. By the end of June 2020, gold was valued at US$1782 per ounce, it had been $1385/oz the same time last year. The peak had been $2064. It was US$1184/oz in October 2018. Levels not been seen since 2011.

Whilst the demand for jewelry in China and India had tumbled during lockdown, it was fear-driven investment demand in developed countries which contributed about 18% to this years' gain.

It would seem the rumour to return to the Gold Standard which had been abolished by Nixon in 1971 was indeed making a come back. With the trust in American institutions waning, there was renewed support for money backed by something more tangible. Perhaps it was feasible it would back the dollar when the IMF (International Monetary Fund) would meet in October 2020.

There were stories the Deep State was trying to rupture the economy and trash the US$, to reset the global currencies make the main currency to be Chinese Yan, with the new financial hub of the world at Wuhan.

Trump knows "he who has the biggest debt becomes the banker" and was fully aware of this when he passed the $6.5trillion stimulus bill. Some saw this as his counterattack to undermine Deep State's plan to crumble the economy. Part of his mission is to create a new logistics system to rebuild the US outside of China's control.

This could be the catalyst for a revolution in the economic systems of the world and finally disband the triad of cites holding the world power.

The Vatican in Rome, head of the Catholic Church, is seen as ultimate control over the population. Every birth certificate, otherwise known as the "title of your Soul", is owned by the Vatican and has been since 1302.

London is the centre point for the world's financial system and Washington DC the control hub of the Military.

Is this a new agenda which just happens to be unfolding at the same time as Covid? Not at all. Nor is CV19 the cause of it. Whilst there are some unprecedented changes happening to our economic and financial systems, there is a conversation on a larger scale with a different vision of our financial future.

That of QAnon.

To reiterate, this writing is not for the purpose of categorically claiming something is true or otherwise. Nor does it reflect my personal political beliefs or stance, which is irrelevant.

However, it does serve as a vessel to share what is being purported as part of the Great Awakening.

When people are seeing for themselves changes in the very fabric of society which align with the predictions, it creates a strong belief system. It gives them hope.

I do believe it is this very premise that could keep Trump in office come Election November 2020. Even though it is likely there will be no clear winner for weeks to come.

There are tens, if not hundreds of thousands who have changed their opinion of Trump as he plays out the role of the "Saviour" they have been promised. He just keeps on saving the day as Q predicts.

The masses are hanging out for someone to come rescue them. Passing the buck of responsibility. The very essence of this Awakening which has been discussed since the start.

The coming of the second Messiah has been promised by many religious scriptures. It is just another form of the same kind of brainwashing.

We must see what lies beneath these illusions of alignments. It stems back to one of our well-known ascended masters, St Germaine, what was purported in the Bible, and the mark of the beast. Yet all is not what you think – is it ever?

Background: the mark of the beast was described in Revelations 13:16-18 in the Bible:

"16. And he causeth all, both small and great, rich and poor, free and bond, to receive a mark in their right hand, or in their foreheads: 17. And that no man might buy or sell, save he that had the mark, or the name of the beast, or the number of his name. 18. Here is wisdom. Let him that hath understanding count the number of the beast: for it is the number of a man; and his number is six hundred threescore and six."

"He" is not an individual called Anti-Christ, it is a system. The bible is clear there are two different forces at play during the end times – the first beast and the second beast. These arise from two separate and distinct Luciferian agendas – bad and evil. (Let's also be clear, the reference to Lucifer is the conceived perception of the "baddie" as taught by several main religions, not the true light-bearer that he is, hidden behind the veil of illusions).

Not good and evil.

The first beast is the Deep State, the Cabal, the elite which have almost complete control over all forms of government, media and religion. This is the one associated with the Anti-Christ system, which we have been living under for hundreds of years. Oppression, fear, debt and slavery.

It is not this beast that gives the mark.

It is not a chip to track you.

The second beast, the beast of the Earth, the false prophet system known as The Alliance is who gives the mark. This beast is a system which represents hope, wealth and power to the people.

This may be sounding familiar to the dualities I described in the first chapter of June. Whilst Q may well be providing the opportunity for each to come into their own awareness, the systems which support him are choosing to believe there is one person who will do all the work for them.

And who do you think they see the Saviour to be?

Who would love nothing more than to be recognised as the Man Who Saved The World? Trump was made for this role of the False Idol. The Illusionist. The Joker.

Yet how could one man overcome the Cabal and rule the world as if he were God? It takes an army of principalities and powers to accomplish a worldwide agenda on this massive scale.

It takes a great left versus right deception.

The agenda has convinced us that we are the problem. The divisions within humanity have us fighting literally and verbally across many platforms. This diversion keeps us away from the truth of who actually rules over us and what their ultimate goal is.

We are so busy being concerned over world events and who is right and wrong, we are missing the second agenda when we encounter the mark of the beast.

Remember, Lucifer and his armies must work to a specific set of rules in order for their agenda to unfold. This includes us giving them permission freely. Hold this in your heart when you are fearful of enforced vaccinations, chips, the protocols removing your freedoms.

Enforcing implantations of RFID chips does not follow their dark laws. The ultimate decision remains with us.

It would take something far bigger to revolutionise the world. Welcomed with open arms by most. Something like a new quantum financial system.

NESARA stands for National Economic Security and Reformation Act which applies in the United States.

GESARA is the Global Economic Security and Reformation Act, applicable to the rest of the world.

NESARA purportedly started in 1729 when St Germaine, the fallen angel known as Lucifer, established the new world monetary trust.

(I do know St Germaine had many incarnations at times of Revolution and played leading roles in human evolution. I am merely describing one "version" of him which the Alliance labelled as Lucifer, not I).

Supposedly the elite families of the second beast have been contributing to this world trust for nearly 300 years on the understanding it would be used for future prosperity and humanitarian purposes. Originally meant to be released near 2000, humanity was not ready. Plans were squashed, including a second release date of September 11, 2001. We know what diverted that launch.

With compounding interest, the trust is said to hold over one Quattuordecillion dollars. That is 1 with 45 zeros behind it.

$1,000,000,000,000,000,000,000,000,000,000,000,000,000,000,000

It was first meant to be launched in the USA to distribute the prosperity funds amongst the population.

The NESARA program was first proposed by Dr Harvey Barnard in the late 1980's. His proposal was called "Draining the swamp", the same hashtag being used in current day in internet conversations. Notably by Trump in his infamous Twitter posts.

There are people working with Trump to bring about the new world financial system. Many of the people working to defeat the Cabal and end the Federal reserve banking system are in the US military. Those who were controlling the current monetary system central banking simply do not have the power anymore. I read reports on Trump running the financial show as well now.

It is easy to see why many regard Trump as an incarnation of St Germaine. *(He must be turning in his grave…)*

What exactly will NESARA do for the economy? The funds will first be used to buy out all oil corporations, thanks pharmaceutical cartels and see out all the debt. Once you have those funds paid out, the remaining funds will be distributed to the people.

Here is the promise to every citizen who signs a personal contract with the new alliance:

- Forgive all mortgage, bank debt and credit card debt due to the Cabal's illegal banking and government activities

- Eliminate the Federal Reserve system
- Abolish income taxes
- Abolish the IRS
- Create flat-rate, non-essential "new items only" sales tax revenue to fund the new government
- Drastically increase benefits to senior citizens
- Return true Constitutional Law to all citizens and courts
- Establish new presidential and congressional elections within 120 days of NESARA's announcement
- Create new US treasury currency, the "rainbow currency" — one backed by gold, silver, platinum and other precious metals
- End the bankruptcy of the United States initiated by Franklin D. Roosevelt in 1933
- Stop all special interest groups
- Closely monitor the validity of elections
- Establish worldwide peace — US troops will be brought home from around the world as peace is declared; in alignment with the Constitution, there will be no standing armies, and that will be permanently observed
- Release enormous sums of money for humanitarian purposes
- Enable the release of thousands of suppressed technologies currently being withheld from the public under the guise of national security — this includes free energy devices, antigravity devices, and sonic healing machines (6,000 technologies will be released initially, followed by the release of more than 60,000 technologies)
- Initiate the first phase of worldwide prosperity distribution of vast wealth that has been accumulating for hundreds of years

NESARA and GESARA will create an entirely new system of worldwide currency that is fully transparent, backed by gold, not governed by bankers, the grounds on the block chain. This offers full transparency and privacy, as 100% traceable. It will help eliminate voter fraud and all dark illegal activity. All coming from St Germaine's world trust.

Before We the People can accept these funds, each individual will be required to make a pledge to use this money for humanitarian purposes. A large-scale "oath to humanity".

Can you think of a more enticing way to receive full cooperation with free will from the population? It this not what so many want, someone to save them and the world?

So the Luciferians get exactly what they need.

And by signing this oath, the individual has received the mark of the beast.

This giving away his right to his place in heaven with God, according to the scriptures. For you cannot worship money and God at the same time.

It is quite easy to see how the God-fearing citizens of the United States will be lured to the promise of salvation. At the same time, they are selling their Souls to the False Prophet.

It will be a matter of time before humanity can separate fact from fantasy. Yet there are some remarkably strong indicators this grand scheme has elements of truth within it.

Why is it so relevant here? It could be a game changer in terms of the election this year. It also recognises the notion that people still require to be saved, to be looked after, to be told what to do.

Whether or not the ultimate penalty is being rejected by God (as it is perceived by the believers), it reflects one's own consciousness and awakening. The illusion of a promised land and false prophets.

Is this not the very thing which tore us away from the integration of spirituality in societies when religions took over? Is it not just another system which has come to save the world?

The icing on the cake comes in documentation of such events within the Bible. When they join the dots between Solomon (previous incarnate of St Germaine), Donald Trump and 666, many see this is God's word of salvation. The only thing left for them is to wait the second coming of Jesus....

If when you are left bemused and bewildered as to how Trump got re-elected, or if it is a close call, just remember the promises he has made to save the masses. Either directly or coded behind the scenes, being translated by Q so we get to understand "the full picture not reported in the press".

Of course, it is not just the revolution of the financial systems being promised, it is also the exposure of the corruption and trafficking going on in the Cabal and mainstream government and Corporate America. Along with many other systems around the world. Much is coming to the surface, ripe fodder for the blame and hatred of the patriarchal system.

Those who are still asleep will choose freedom in the material world over freedom of choice, heart and mind any day. This is a major differentiator between those who wish to create their life on their own terms and those just happy to follow.

Memberships are growing exponentially in groups supporting these theories and much has been written on the internet about it. Research for yourself with the awareness to not get dragged into the drama of it all.

Discover more about St Germaine and his reincarnations, the set up for 9/11 and what NESARA is promising can be found here.

Any number of groups may be found on Facebook, or other platforms now being used due to the censorship of mainstream media, such as Mewe, Patreon etc, discussing these belief systems.

CHAPTER 37

EGYPTIAN PHILOSOPHY - INTRODUCTION

Modern society knows little of the philosophy of the early Egyptians. The ethos was to never ever lay down the teachings into a creed of worship. The truth of the world they had uncovered was beyond individual religion.

It was for each person to see and actually experience themselves - the best way to level the playing field for all those who wish to access the higher wisdom. This is what differentiates it from religion, where the hierarchies at play ensure only the priests were perceived to know the highest-level teachings. The majority rely on what they are taught by individuals.

This way, the personal quest for the experience of the infinite can never be changed into a dogmatic set of rules set down in absolutes. It could not be open to interpretation and create different branches of religion.

The other biggest difference is for individuals can strive to be gods amongst men, to be masters over our own lives and understand our own immortality. To know that we are made of the stars, as above, so below.

The Hermetic followers never sought public approval for their beliefs or tried to form orthodox groups.

All major religions, by contrast, worship a God outside themselves and have spent centuries fighting over the meaning of their words instead of simply trying to follow the path they were trying to lead us to.

The Egyptians felt that the true secrets of life would only be available to those who are ready to hear them. They were never forced upon anyone, so different to the mainstream.

There were kept hidden and safe from those who would misuse them - the secrets were sealed. Hence the term Hermetic was created, only available to those who sought the path.

There are three main core writings which share the ancient Egyptian philosophy of life, what creates life, what our purpose is here and what is beyond this life. In general, these writings are referred to as Hermetic. These are **the Kybalion, the Hermetica and the Emerald Tablets.**

The Hermetic texts were attributed to Hermes Trismestigus. Similarly, the Tao Te Ching was attributed to Lao Tzu. However, scholars attributed authorship to more than one person.

In the same way, both groups see human suffering in the world as we know it is a simple consequence of living against the rules of this world. When we defy the natural way things are, suffering arises. Both philosophies require exploring this world - it is not to remain as a separate spiritual practice of worship. Both encourage men to do what we naturally want to do – explore, create, learn. Branch out, seek more – always.

Discovery and excitement drove societies to happiness and wealth. Coming up with new ideas and testing of new theories is the height of man's powers, what he was supposed to do. They drove progression and learning, as seen with the resurgence of Hermetic teachings which were responsible for the Renaissance 1450-1650. This era held a vision of a philosophy that united religion and science.

Interestingly, the last time Saturn and Pluto joined in sidereal Sagittarius was in January 1518. The same conjunct we had just before the move into Capricorn in January 2020.

After the religious persecution of the early Christians, The Hermetic Philosophers settled in Arabic areas now held by the Islamic states. As a result, Arabians are credited with many contributions to modern society; they brought forward the ancient Egyptian and Greek philosophies and dominated the world. This included astronomy, alchemy, science, medicine, music and mathematics. The numbers we use today are Arabic numerals; zero was invented by Bin Hamed in 976, the concept was only grasped by the West in the 13th Century. The Hermetic philosophy undoubtedly creates superior civilisations, based on learning and knowledge.

When the teachings were banned and free thought was inhibited, darker times in society arose. When the early Christian church burned the library of Alexandria and outlawed Hermeticism, so many written ideas and developments were lost forever.

The Italian philosopher Giordano Bruno in the mid-16th century believed the Hermetic philosophy to be the true religion with its worship of God in things, the One in All. He saw it as the ancestor of the Greek mystery schools, the Jewish religion, Christian religion, the

Islamic religion, it is therefore unifying religion which all faiths could meet and resolve differences.

The Catholic Church had a different point of view, tortured him for eight years before burning him alive in 1600. Despite this, one of the 48 obelisks taken from Egypt to Rome after the defeat of Cleopatra was first installed in Rome in 65. It was moved to the great piazza in front of the Basilica of St Peter in 1586. It remains as a symbol of the ancient wisdom of Egypt thriving the heart of Christendom.

Credit: archeology-travel.com

Hermetic writings contain passages which are similar to Jewish, Christian, Muslim and Greek works, amongst others. In 1945, many Hermetic teachings were found amongst early Christian Scriptures of the Gnostic Christians in Nag Hammadi. The caves of the hermits were covered with hieroglyphs ascribed to Hermes.

One of the more central teachings of Hermetic philosophy is Alchemy. Whilst many associate this word with the legend of turning lead to gold, true alchemy is different. It was not meant to be taken literally, instead, to see the symbology of something more valuable. The purification of a crude human Soul into something more intelligent, something purer, something priceless.

Gather the knowledge and wisdom to transform yourself. It is more valuable to your well-being and understanding than all the gold in the world. The goal of Hermetic wisdom is to pass along this knowledge, of the rules of this world and also what lies beyond. This would give you the freedom from everything.

It appears the Emerald tablets were Thoth / Hermes' first body of work. The Hermetica is supposed to represent Hermes' vision and subsequent teachings. The Kybalion, originally published in 1912 by the "Three Initiates" who chose to remain anonymous, supposed to represent teachings based on the Hermetica. It may just be a more modern interpretation of Hermetic wisdom with new-age philosophies. It gets more specific on the exact working of the "laws of life" and how to apply them.

We will consider each of these three texts in turn. Are they still relevant for evolvement of consciousness?

All religions and philosophies lead to the same goal of finding God, all taking different paths. The main paths include 1) service to others 2) knowledge, learning wisdom 3) mental stillness, meditation 4) faith and devotion to God.

It is up to you which path you choose, as you evolve you will find you have all paths as part of your life. Will you leave behind all constructs of the religious paradigm and the concept of God? Instead, are you ready to return to the Laws of Nature, The Universe and finally cull any beliefs that the power of the macrocosm is detached from you?

From this brief introduction, I hope you are seeing how this ancient wisdom is the basis of all new-age movement. The Universe is within us, it is not separate, we are all one.

It is time to decipher where the next levels of consciousness are heading to, beyond these ancient texts. It is no longer feasible that this wisdom is the be all and end all of life.

Indeed, it is time the new myth of consciousness evolves beyond the Light Grid.

CHAPTER 38*

THE EMERALD TABLETS

I was already starting to experience huge time bubbles by the beginning of June. At the weekend I had a quick look at guided meditations on Insight Timer which I had not done for months. Usually I find little amongst the Light Grid offerings, right now focused on how to deal with the fear of the world. Yet the first thing I saw was The Emerald Tablets part 4 of 7. You may find the series on Insight Timer by Anabelle Drumm.

Perfect, I thought, as I knew these were on the list to understand and decipher. I knew nothing of the content of these tablets, only that they are ancient texts. A short audio version (3.5 hours) would be ideal to give an overview and hints of what I require to investigate further.

It was quite uncanny to read about Thoth being the Cosmic Scribe. Just as I had been told I was mid-May. Taking 25 hours to write up the modern-day version of Doreal's translation, I found it both insightful and parts repetitive.

The background to the Emerald Tablets and the translation can be found in Appendix 1.

A very brief synopsis:

"Thoth is a man holding great wisdom and knowledge, with access to the three realms of Earth, the underworld (Amenti) and the Heavens. He came to teach men how to be free of the dark (shadow) and to follow the light and your heart.

Find your inner fire and be free of struggle. The Law states everything that exists is only a form of that which does not exist. As above, so below. This law balances the world.

You come from the stars, be free to pursue wisdom and find your path of freedom, becoming free from the desires for life. Live through your wisdom to evolve.

In the future, those with the wisdom will bring his spaceship to life. It is buried under a Lion like a man (the Sphynx?) We must follow the key he leaves behind, to be used within the pyramid he built.

There are men who are bound to darkness who do what they can to pull you from searching for the light. You must strive, it is not an easy journey. Light will always win, then you are free of the constructs of life.

If you find your thoughts are of the dark fears, question whether the feeling comes from within. If so, clear your thoughts to free yourself using the power of light. You are your own master, keep following your Soul.

There are seven Lords who are the masters of infinite wisdom, each with a different role. You can move up the pathway until all becomes one. Where you are formless and time does not exist. There is so much you do not know.

Stay within the circles of time, do not go through angles where the hounds will be chasing. Create the higher vibrations and blend with the Cosmos. Know you are a spirit, your body is nothing, your Soul is everything. Know that all that exists is only an aspect of greater things yet to come.

There are nine interlocked dimensions and nine cycles of space. Nine Lords of the cycles that come from above and below. The key to unlocking time and space is held within yourself, you are a gateway of mystery.

Find balance and order in life by quelling the chaos of emotions. Plunge into the heart of the mystery then knowledge and wisdom will be yours. Do not be afraid of the power within you. Fear is created by those who are bound by their fears; escape the shackles. Man is only what he believes - he is of the dark or of the light.

Time is the mechanism which keeps events in the place, you move through time as your consciousness moves from one event to another. You still exist as one in all times.

The Great Race gained our wisdom from the star-born races, coming from the masters of wisdom who are as far beyond me as I am of you.

The consciousness must follow its own path within the cycle. Knowledge is only gained by practice, wisdom only comes from knowledge, it is why the cycles are created. The fountain of wisdom is eternally seeking to gain new powers. i.e. to continually evolve.

We are all at different stages of growth. Nothing else matters except the growth we can gain within our Soul. When men understand that they can be free from all bondage and free to work in a harmony of Law.

Be the master of your life yet never be controlled by the effects of your life. The future is never fixed, it follows man's free will. Always look within for the causation of the effects, i.e. be responsible for all you create.

Man always has access to the Law when he chooses; a revival of wisdom would unfold Future ages, yet they must strive through the ages to bring themselves to the freedom of light.

There will be great warfare between light and dark. When the fighting stops, Thoth's ancient home (Atlantis) will rise from the ocean and the people of darkness will be banished. Man will move to a place in the stars, and even beyond the stars.

Know that I am always guarding you and will return in future when light shall come again to man. Only share the secrets with those who seek the light.

Remember you are of dual form (earthly and spirit) and balanced in polarity whilst in form. This balance is the secret of life in Amenti. Life and death are essential, never fear death, you will take the memories of your lives with you for future recall.

Earth is a portal guarded by powers unknown to man. The way to the portal is hidden in darkness veiled in symbols, seekers will find the way, even though a hard path. The secrets will remain hidden until the time when the wheel shall be turned. Then you may call for me.

Three is the magic number, found in a variety of facts and existences, relationships and energies.

Darkness binds you on Earth; it is disorder, light is order. Darkness which transmutes is light of the light. Your purpose is to transmute darkness (shadow) to light.

Remember you are threefold in nature – physical, astral and mental. Each has three qualities, nine in all, as above, so below.

Beyond these realms is that of the spiritual self which has four qualities, making a total of 13 - the mystical number.

These writings serve to be the keys for those who seek my wisdom."

* * *

Having translated the books, I felt rather underwhelmed from the sense of it. It all seemed so familiar, the resonance of the numbers in particular. It was only upon further deciphering with Anne I realised why; I will share this in a future chapter.

Now I would like to expand on who Thoth was. It did not sit right with me that these tablets were meant to have been written 38,000 years ago, we have yet to discover writing in any form dating back that far.

We tuned in to investigate. We both felt Thoth had incarnated three times, hence becoming master of the Earth, the heavens and the underworld. He is seen as the principal parent of all Egyptian theology and philosophy, he was the first and most ancient amongst the Egyptians.

The first time was as an energetic presence around 36,000BCE, some say he 'reigned' for 16,000 years. This was the nature of 'beings' back then, not yet incarnated into a physical form. I believe this wisdom was brought down, teleported, and shared with other energetic beings.

It was only upon his second incarnation when the gods and goddesses of Egypt emerged in the human form, beyond the myth. With their pursual of immortality, these beings were around for much longer than the standard human life.

I am sure this was during the peak of the Egyptian dynasty. At this point the wisdom was captured in form, which resembled mathematical equations on the stone. Anne and I both know we were Cosmic Scribes and Translators as it unfolded, working alongside Thoth, Isis and Osiris. It was the age of one of the major playouts of our Soul contracts.

It is not yet time for our exact roles and contracts to be revealed. It is all part of the mystery of the potential, to keep us open and free to witness what unfolds. It is imperative we stay as transmitters and own our abilities, to receive what we are to do. To stay out of the head and analysis.

Thoth's third incarnation was as Hermes Trismegistus. Some say he is a mythic figure, a Hellenistic fusion of the Greek god Hermes and the Egyptian god Thoth.

Again, he lived over many decades, perhaps centuries of life, bringing together Egyptian and Greek philosophy. I know we both worked on the scribing of the wisdom alongside Hermes. Many scholars believe that the Hermetica and his other works were a result of several authors contributing to a core philosophy at that time.

Whilst attending the Egyptian School of Magic, Anne had learnt the philosophy and prophecy of the wisdom. I had focused on astrology, numerology and alchemy.

258

No one person was ever given the complete picture, it is deemed too powerful. Hence Anne and I in our combined forces and insights can present the modern-day myth as we move into new consciousness. All stemming from the wisdom which lies within us, ignited through cosmic coding. Everyone reading this has their own programming of wisdom to understand the body of work from one perspective or another.

It is of little surprise the work seems so familiar. We were both there the first, second and third time round. Now back to assist reigniting its energy during The Fourth Awakening.

Further insight to the history of the Emerald Tablets presented to me in the book, The Philosopher's Stone by Peter Marshall. (not the Harry Potter book by JK Rowling of the same name…) I will circle back to this book, for now we will remain focused on the wisdom in hand.

He accounts that Ra (or Re), symbolised by the sun, told the names of the creation myth of ancient Egypt to Thoth, symbolised by the moon, who by uttering them bought them into existence – the 'single act of adaptation'. The wind is the goddess Nut, and the nurse is Earth, the god Geb, reversing as the ancient Egyptians did, the familiar notion of Mother Earth and Father Sky.

This resonated strongly with me; Thoth had first spoken the myth into being and he was reversing the wisdom. Not dissimilar from what is unravelling in this book.

Marshall goes on to say the exact origins of the Emerald Tablet are not clear. One probably Jewish legend claimed this was discovered by Sara, the wife of Abraham, who entered a cave near Hebron after the flood and found it engraved with Phoenician characters on an emerald plate held in the hands of the corpse of Hermes Trismegistus. The ancient artefact reportedly was moulded out of a single piece of green crystal. On the tablet is written 14 cryptic sentences said to sum up the secret to alchemy and Hermetic teachings. Another legend credits a man named Balinas for discovering the tablet in the vault below the statue of Hermes, where lay his body, holding the object.

Other European commentators in the Middle Ages ascribed it to Alexander the Great or to the Pythagorean sage Apollonius of Tyana.

One Arabic writer, however, claims there were three philosophers called Hermes, one who built the pyramids in Egypt (Thoth?), One who came from Babylon and taught Pythagoras, and a third who lived in Egypt and wrote on alchemy. These three Hermes would seem to describe the ancient origins, diffusion and continuity of the Hermetic tradition. It remains the greatest document in the body of this work.

We must simply remember to use the wisdom to ignite our own inner searching of truth. As Thoth says, this only come to those who strive and seek. Regardless of who wrote it and when. For that question only comes from your head and the need to know.

Enter your heart, your Soul, your womb and feel the resonance of the Truth within you. Ask yourself what you fundamentally know to be true, beyond any knowledge you contain in your head. For that is your wisdom, your innate knowing. Far more powerful than any theory you can learn.

Allow your inner self to lead you back home from where you came. For that is the ultimate journey to be discovered whilst incarnate. That is when you unleash your own magic and mystery.

The ancient texts and The Alchemists' Awakening simply serve as reminders to what you already know within. It is simply a matter of remembrance and claiming the power that lies there. To master the alchemy of your fears seeded through human conditioning and Soul wounding, converting them into the power for your own transformation and liberation. This is the key to freedom which you have been seeking.

CHAPTER 39*

THE HERMETICA

To imbue the energy of the ancient wisdom I took a short cut to another body of work with read Matthew Barnes' the Hermetica 101. Written in simple poetry, it outlined the ethos of the text. It also provided a concise summary of the Hermetic bodies of work.

As a reminder, it is the essence of the texts which ignite our remembrance of the wisdom rather than full engagement and absorption of all the words or translation.

Barnes writes with the same intentions. To gives the essence of Hermes' spirit and intentions rather than the technical translation and preserving his original words. This does of course mean we are subject to his version and interpretation. If you would like to read the full traditional text, please see links in Appendix III.

A brief synopsis:

Hermes introduction

I am here to guide others to experience the Soul of the world. I live in a time where science and religion come together. They will separate, people will not realise they are one and the same, seen through nature and the Universe. They will lose their sense of wonder for life.

Religion without science is ignorant and intolerant, science without religion is lonely and smug. This book is written for when science thinks it has surpassed even God.

("I" - Hermes, "you" – from the voice of God)

Chapter 1

Through conversation with God, consciousness itself, I saw boundless light and felt it within me. Love was the substance of the Universe and the underlying essence of all that is.

Darkness was birthed out of the light, at first chaotic. But then a Thought emerged from the light and into the dark womb of matter and the body of the world was born, as was motion.

You are not your body; you are consciousness within. Just as I created through my will and order, so can you.

In the beginning there was only One, with my will I split the Universe into two, the male and female, the positive and negative. The dynamic between these two poles keeps all life and motion. Due to this polarity all things were created through nature.

Your body is subject to the laws of nature but your mind is free, it is up to you whether it takes you to heaven or hell. Only humans have consciousness, no other living creature does. All living things have a Soul. You are a slave to nature until you leave it behind.

I feared I would lose this vision and knowledge and longing for the light. How do I remain in the light?

Use your mind as a tool not your master, act like the light. You often become lost in the dark, keeping you separate. Rewards look easier to obtain and are more immediately satisfying there - recognise their illusion, it is a vicious cycle. When you spend enough time in the light and become so used to it, you never leave it.

It is only your desired attachment to things of this world that causes suffering. Pity those who stay in the dark.

Knowing the truth has freed me from this world. I may be in it but not of this world and will never go back.

Chapter two

How do you explain IT to someone who is not experienced it? The chapter explains how IT is everything. The closest description is a supreme intelligence, the consciousness. Without which there would be no awareness.

We are being developed for the next world in these bodies. We are made in God's image - not our bodies but in our minds. Our imaginations are designed to create and explore, just on different scales.

We can free our minds from the constraints of this world and come to understand the power of our own minds. To use this knowledge to comprehend the power of ITs unlimited mind, for we are of the same nature.

When the veil of the world pulls back you will awaken and be reborn into the same world you know right now. It you will be free of it.

Chapter three

ITs essence is mind intelligence, awareness, consciousness which you can see with your inner vision. Withdraw within to contemplate. You can also see all around you the uncanny order of the Universe throughout nature. Consider the development of human life and bodies and the miracle they are.

Yet the greatest miracle is that you have consciousness, something science cannot create. IT has created everything that ever existed, all the cycles of life in perfect order.

Live in awe at the deep mysteries surrounding us for it is a living work of art. Do not take the miracle for granted. If you awaken this all becomes obvious, until then it must be explained.

Chapter Four

In the beginning there was only the One, but IT wanted to experience, create and explore. In order for this to occur, there must be something outside yourself, duality, opposites.

So, from the One came a second, the Son if you will, created in ITs image but of lower vibrational frequency. This Son is our world, the Cosmos, the Universe. Within this world one came two, the yin and yang.

The union and repulsion of the male and female energies and forms causes the Universe to divide and multiply and reproduce continuously. This life force animated the Universe, the energy for which there is really no words.

The vibrational sound which descended out of the light into the darkness is of creation. Some call it the great Om or Amen. It is the command for the world to be orderly and governs this world. Though the world is dual but light itself is not, it is both the positive and the negative.

IT does not age, nor does consciousness or awareness; it cannot, it only ever changes forms. Therefore, it follows everything is alive and immortal. The Universe itself is a living being, a conscious life form.

Children remember to easily everything is alive. We simply grew up and forgot.

Chapter five

Time is not what you think it is; it is an illusion which exists as a construct of this world. It allows the perception of a linear sequence of events. Everything in this world is living in a state of constant motion and this makes time seemed to move forward in a linear manner.

Time is a perception created in the mind and can be manipulated, sped up, slowed down. If objects were able to travel at the speed of light, time would cease to exist completely as it does within the light.

Time is relative to the size of the object and its perception. It appears to be linear yet it is actually circular measured by the rotation of celestial objects around fixed points. Circles have no beginning middle or end, there are only points along the way.

Measurements of time are just obituary points we use for convenience. Cycles of time you cannot comprehend repeat over and over as if they were the great inhalation and exhalation of the Universe itself.

There is no past or future, there is only now. There is a point on the circle that represents the current position. All simultaneously exist, separated only by the perception within our minds which divide events into separate happenings.

By focusing on this mystery is a path to awakening you cannot yet imagine. It will give you a glimpse beyond the veil of this world into eternity where time does not exist at all; eternity is defined by a lack of time we know it.

Time in this realm is but an illusion though very stubborn one indeed.

Chapter six

All living things have different levels of consciousness. The sun is a visible form of light we can see representing the invisible form of light we cannot see. Yet there to remind us of its presence. It nourishes our physical bodies, just as its unseen counterpart nourishes our minds with consciousness. It is why it has been worshipped many cultures.

Chapter seven

God, the Universe and Humankind are the three great entities in order of greatness, each is greater than the sum of ITs parts. Everything exists within IT whether visible or not.

Chapter eight

When the great light of consciousness created the Universe, IT was well pleased. IT created mankind to share it with, out of a thought. Originally, we were energy only as Souls, eternal and spiritual. We saw creation and we wanted to experience it so God gave us a mortal body. Through the descent into form, we forgot our true nature.

2020: THE ALCHEMISTS' AWAKENING

We are here to tend to creation; we are the caretakers of this world. We are also here to add to creation, it is what we yearn to do. Creation is not complete until our unique part is added.

Lastly, we are here to awaken and remember our divinity, often described as alchemy. The concept of turning lead into gold comes from a lower understanding and merely symbolic. The real alchemy is a process of the mind, we return something so primitive and crude to something grand and special.

Where we convert the materialistic, selfish and separated life viewpoint of an individual into something much more sublime. A being concerned about the welfare of all and who remembers from where they came. It is only when we forgot our true identity did we become timid and fearful, especially of death. What would bother you if you remembered you were eternal?

You would no longer be moved by riches and other trivial things of this world, or ill-health. Instead, you develop a taste for the deeper riches of the infinite which never fade. Remember you are here, visiting for a blink in time.

Chapter nine

Humankind is the only life form on Earth can contemplate its divinity. We are dual with the body and mind created in the likeness of God's. We enjoy an awareness above the less lifeforms, able to create for mere pleasure, bringing our imagination to life.

We are both earthly and divine, the link between this world and the next. Humans are even beyond the gods the previous humans believed in, for those gods had only Souls and no bodies. Humans have both.

Only humans have progressed to our level of awareness and consciousness.

We have Dominion over this world which means we are the parents to all of this below us. We are the caretakers of this Earth. Why would the Light create a place for us to raid and rape ITs creation for our own individual personal gain?

We are capable of such beauty and of such horror. We are here to love all that is below us as we are loved by that which is above us, awakening to a higher nature.

Chapter ten

We were given the ability to create life as well, complete with a human Soul, such a miracle. In the beginning, One was split to allow for experience. Each of the two energies craves its other half, they long to be whole and complete. To end the process of separation, to unite flesh and energy.

The intensity of attraction between the male and female reflects the yearning and Soul to be united. To remind us the sum of two parts is far greater than the mere summation of individual parts. Sex is a path to enjoy the experience of being One.

Lower beings cannot comprehend the full power of the union beyond their cravings. As we live and experience life, we expand consciousness.

When a human being ripens it is a thing of beauty. When we are fully ripe, we return once more to pure consciousness from whence we began, growing in comprehension, to awareness of the One. We all make this trip eventually.

Do not worry if you are not yet understanding this miracle of union or all the other information shared, you are simply not seeing the great mystery that is life yet.

Chapter eleven

Our lives are ruled by destiny AND free will. You can rise above your own nature and free yourself from the slavery you have given yourself over to. Your nature determines reactions to things you will face. It therefore dictates the direction of your life.

You always have a choice of how to deal with issues you face, how you react. Very few are able to rise above their nature and meet life head-on, consciously choosing the course of direction of our own lives.

We are capable of being the masters, yet the majority operate an automatic response. Start living intentionally, to live as you wish. Then you move into the realm of free will and become a master of your own life.

In doing so you come to a different part of yourself, one beyond your inborn nature of this world. Fate and destiny has no power whatsoever of what lies within you at your core.

As you rise above your nature and break free of its constraints you will get a feel for the watcher within. The real view that exists beyond the reach of this world.

Chapter twelve

Death is probably the single greatest fear that most living things face, yet it is an absolute certainty. Just as we begin to age from the moment of birth, we will decline to death. Learn to accept the impermanence of this life to find peace, or you will suffer needlessly and constantly. Your conscious awareness never declines or decays, as an energy which cannot be destroyed, the only change from one form to another.

Finding the permanent in the impermanent is the reward of your spiritual or scientific quest. When you anchor to IT you will suffer no more.

Your mind and awareness are not physical, not doomed to the same fate as the material body housing it.

Chapter thirteen

Your consciousness existed long before this reality and continues after your physical death. As humans we are curious, we grow, explore and learn. Our perception expands, new things come into our awareness. We expand our focus beyond ourselves into beings of great compassion. To move beyond ignorance and arrogance, anger self-focus and ego. Into a being of great intelligence.

From there the mind is drawn like a magnet into the next realm which exists at a different vibrational level. If the mind has not yet matured or ripened enough it will not be strong enough to survive the next realm, so it will be drawn back down into another earthly existence.

This is not a punishment, only growth. All living things have gone through this process and all will eventually make it.

In the heavenly realms there are many levels of higher frequencies. Our Souls mature through the heavenly realms. Once we have shed all that is not light, consciousness or love, we will re-join the great light from whence we came and we become as Gods.

This great light, whatever IT is, resonates and oscillates at such a high frequency that it seems as if it is not moving at all, as if completely still.

Chapter fourteen

The true pity of this life is that we as humans have the ability to rise above mere physical existence during incarnation in this physical plane but seldom do.

We could liberate ourselves through the many ills of this world; instead we ignorantly fill them with temporary pleasures and endless dramas. Filled full of own egos and opinions, missing out on the enjoyment of the experience of life.

We are so attached and addicted to our egos, thoughts and things; we think we are them. The fate of our happiness becomes tied to the fate of those things. If not going well we suffer.

We are meant to be the master not the slave. We have the capacity to lift the veil to discover that though we are in this world we are not of this world. Until then we will continue to suffer and we do not get what we want.

We will even suffer when we get exactly what we do want, due to the fear of eventually losing what you have now obtained. Your desires will never be satisfied, it always wants more. They do not fill your cravings so your addiction grows.

There is a treasure that once experienced will fill you to the brim and you will never want for another thing.

This treasure is knowledge. The knowledge that will set you free to give you peace of mind. One that can never be taken away, in limitless supply, taking away your attachment to the pleasantries and dramas of this world.

You will be free to enjoy this world as it was meant to be enjoyed - without a care in the world. What you really crave and desire is the truth behind the things you seek. We all have this desire; we simply get confused as to where to find IT.

Use the immense power of your mind to seek this truth, make this the main focus of your desires. Simply having the desire to find truth and making effort is enough to set things in motion.

As we search for the truth IT seems to appear before us in a million different and unexpected ways. It is how you manifest. Start to recognise IT in everything you see, hear and think, truth will begin to emerge all around you and you will begin to awaken.

Eventually the ultimate truth will descend on you like a ton of bricks. Suddenly IT is everywhere, IT is all that is. It becomes so obvious that it has been right in front of our face for so long, we did not have the capacity to see IT.

With this comes such peace, our birthright as humans and our goal.

Chapter fifteen

Whatever God is IT is beyond us and beyond all suffering. IT enjoys this world yet not attached. If you wish to have same level of peace and emulate God's ways.

If you want to be a great teacher or healer then find one and study his or her ways to make your own. The same applies for anything you wish to become. If you desire to become free of dramas then you must copy the behaviours of that which is free.

How do we emulate God? He explores and creates, this is when you will be most happy too. When you live your life the way you wish, then you may grant that same freedom to others as well.

Having our actions dictated by another is intolerable, so wish the same freedom upon others. Do not try to make another bend to your concept of how life should be lived.

God is without judgement and shows no favouritism, he does all that is without any conditions. He gives continuously without requiring reward. He serves us all and he knows ITself to be not of this world.

This is what is to be emulated if you wish to be free of the limitations, fears and trappings of this material world.

Salvation is not dependent on how many pleasantries you have obtained or how well your ego is stroked. Nor is it found in how well you have memorised your favourite holy Scriptures, how loud you sing in church or how much you tithe.

Your salvation depends on how close you have come to being like God.

Chapter sixteen

Exercise your mind and expand your consciousness to a new level to increase the power of your mind and open the doors of perception to see beyond this world.

Do this by considering what it is like to live the life of another, and understand things from their perspective. It is working the muscle of the mind to break through the limits of regular consciousness which are constantly transcending the boundaries that we assume to define seemingly concrete existence.

Practice perceiving life from the perspective of an animal, or a virus. Imagine that you are every lifeform on Earth. The overall wants and needs and desires of life as a unit seem more important than at the individual level.

Imagine the same as if you were our solar system, if you are the living entity. What would your perspective of life be then? Move between macro and micro. Imagine that you are the Universe, that there is no beginning or end.

Can you conceive that you exist before, within and after the physical world at the same time? Or grasp you are both creative and part of your own creation? That you are the life force that courses through your life - you are life.

Keep expanding the reach of your mind and imagine that, like God you are everywhere, and at all times. You are all that is and all that will ever be.

Contemplate on this so deeply you forget you exist. You must give your mind a focus on practice. We are concerned the expansion of consciousness, awareness and perception. This is how we wish to direct our minds if we are to see beyond the veil of this world. To move beyond suffering and into peace.

Your mind does it what you tell it to. If you tell it you wish to understand this world and what is beyond, the mind will rise to the occasion when you concentrate consistently.

Those that have unlocked the puzzle of life become free and complete. They sit happily at the feet of the great mystery, watching in constant amazement without a care in this world.

Be warned. Such people are often thought crazy by the masses. They are despised. The wisest among us have been tortured and put to death in previous lives. People fear what they do not understand and that fear breeds destruction.

Chapter seventeen

The mass of people around you are not ready, the teachings will not make sense to them. There will be very few who are ready, the teachings will be exciting and seem to be what they have been waiting for their entire life.

These people will become intent on awakening, fill their minds. They will meditate and contemplate, read and learn and do whatever else it takes to pierce the veil and see beyond.

Those that are not ready are not bad or evil even though they may seem so at times. There is no such thing as evil, only ignorance, and the fear and anger that comes from ignorance.

Eventually they will grow; it is the fate that awaits us all at some point.

In the past these teachings and others like them were guarded in secrecy. Torture and death were threatened for those who revealed the secrets of others.

But this was not necessary for the secrets hid themselves. Only to those that are ready for them will they have any real meaning.

Do not judge those around you who are not ready, they will be in their own time.

Making these teachings part of your daily life is hard and an individual journey which must be taken on your own. Until you fully awake it is very difficult to let go of the way we are used to things being and how we do things.

It is also not easy to break away from the thinking of the crowd, even when you know them to be wrong. Be patient and kind, they are not ready for the path; you were once one of them.

If you are ready for the path though, let nothing stand in your way. It may take great resolve to break away from life the way you now know it.

Remember awakening is an experience, not a theory to be learned.

Chapter eighteen

I have done my best to lead you by my example beyond the veil of this world. I have given you the knowledge laid out the path. I will now give you a sense of what it is like to experience enlightenment, even though there are truly no words.

I was in very deep contemplation, my mind alert with such clarity. All of a sudden it was if my intelligence, my awareness finally expanded beyond the confines and shattered the borders.

It seemed to explode, expanding instantaneously in every direction, there was nothing to stop it.

My mind, my Soul and the Universe opened up for me. God opened up before me. I felt as if my mind that suddenly awakened and was able to remember what I had so long ago forgotten. I have returned to my home!

The immense liberation of joy, freedom and peace was way beyond my body and ego. My identity had shed all concerns. I remembered who and what I was. I saw and understood from whence I came.

I saw the light and IT made sense. IT was everything, there was nothing IT was not. I found the source and IT was bubbling with life, light and love. With intelligence, consciousness and it penetrated all that is, was and will be.

IT was eternal and boundless. You and I are part of IT, made in ITs likeness.

I wanted to give thanks and praise they realised there was no need. There was no me which was separate from IT. It would just be IT praising IT, no separation.

All I could do was sit in silent reverence filled with a peace I have never known. I was free. I was home.

I emerged from the vision changed completely. I was no longer even the shadow of who I once was, yet others could not see it. Your mind is reborn when you awaken, which you use to comprehend and see.

You are part of the great mind. What you are is a presence that resides in your body. One that expands beyond this world.

I am still IN this world and can enjoy the pleasures it offers. I am no longer OF this world.

Hear this message well if you are able to. I only have one prayer, one desire. That is to remain forever in the state of knowledge.

The material aspects are as nothing, like dirt to which I have found.

With a brimming heart I wish you peace light and love, and the Great Remembrance as well.

This concludes the summary of The Hermetica

CHAPTER 40*

CONNECTING TO THE WISDOM

It was time for Anne and I to converse on what arose from the ancient texts. It is no wonder they all seemed so familiar when Anne was told I was a Principal Holder of the Codes, the Keeper of Codes and Thoth's right-hand man, writing the Codes. Then I transmuted the codes to become energy which in turn became Laws. Which is why I am a Decipher and Encoder today. It was simply my cosmic role, one which I am continuing in this lifetime.

We knew that no one person is given all the keys, yet with Anne and my coding, we bring together the missing parts of the puzzle. It is the duality of all things. And so the marathon of downloads began.

I had found the texts very Light Grid and was questioning whether this was due to the translator or was it the context of the original text.

Anne: The Hermetica shares aspects of Law and construct. It was not about the context for us; we had to connect to the Law, which is the vibration of mystery, which is the unrelenting seekers of truth. The principles of mentality, which is the first principle, all in the mind, universal, mental.

All connections are brought forward when we connect to the cosmic vibration. The all-knowing. Once again, we have to connect to the universal sense of being not mental aspect of self. Then we find the answers when in Universal vibration. We had to realign to the truth of the texts which is what we already knew. They are all conclusions of the reality of the coding we hold.

In other words, you must connect to the vibration of the teachings and not so much the mental capacity of understanding. Be out of our heads – this applies to all who read the texts and translations as well.

I still pursued the question of there not being any element of the Dark Grid within these texts. It is all about moving towards the Light. I feel we have to move to the Light that is unseen – the pure dark light of the eternal feminine.

The channelled response is that we have to look at self, not external, must go within. This of course is the premise of the Egyptian Myth, it is always about returning to self. We knew that when we were indoctrinated into the Egyptian school of Magic where we wrote and studied such texts.

You must also remember that time revolves in cycles; the flower of life is ever continuous with no beginning or end. We must connect into the value of the circle, the all-ever encompassing self which is always within us. Now we are operating through the quantum, through our cosmic coding, it is only a matter of bringing it into our awareness be able to tap into abilities used "a long time ago". For everything exists in the now.

I asked again if the texts were to remind us we were there at inception and deciphering it the first-time round, or are they to ignite something within us to use the wisdom.

Anne: "I had the knowing of the Emerald Tablet. This is what we must remember - to go within, for each context of the Tablets, of the unfolding, it is the intrinsic value you have within yourself, to reunite and bring forward the energy and the consciousness, to bring forth the opening of the doors. Go through one thing to bring it through to the next, because the void is open, once connected to sense of self we connect to our rightful state, to all that there was, the learning, the knowledge and wisdom, and the profound sense of reality that was installed in us back then.

That is why we needed to reconnect to all this information in the five books to remember. Not in the words but in the vibration of what they were, whether that be in the sound of numbers or in the vibration feel, both the intrinsic values they hold depending on the coding that was placed in us at that time. For us to reunite in this moment and to the power of three".

I recognised the third was the ancient wisdom itself connecting through to Anne and I. Us connecting to the wisdom sends it forth into the energy and frequencies like the pyramid.

Also, in the fifth Emerald tablet, we are told that HE (the Dweller) chose three people who became his gateway from the highest to become his links with Atlantis. "They were messengers who carried his council to the Kings of the children of men". It was one of the three that brought Thoth to the Dweller in the Light.

Thoth then showed Anne he is bringing through the energy as he did through the pyramids to connect heaven and Earth. The inherent value of the two realities. Anubis gave us the possibility of understanding the two concepts of self.

I also knew the mention of the power of three was to remind us we must return to the duality of ourselves. This wisdom was also in conjunction with the portal openings.

Josephine: "we have to create the three-way relationship between the inner masculine, feminine and Source. As above, so below. Just as my masculine and feminine must connect through the portal in the dimension, it must also connect to the dimension of the portal in the underworld. To create the two pyramids to create the diamond. The way we hold the frequencies into the Earth. Reconnecting them, they are already there.

We open the portal between the two. Up to the dimensional energy, and below into the core crystal. Then we bring down the vortex for energy which can then feed into the Collective Consciousness. The portals are already there we are just reconnecting them."

I then continued to channel the process of opening the portals themselves and how the energy is connected above and below. I questioned whether the location of portals would be brought to my attention by reading further. We were reminded that the texts were written after the portals were established.

The portals would be shown to us as and when energies were ready to be received. The knowledge of the codes and the portals was very deep within me. As my frequencies expanded, they would be revealed.

I felt they would all be done by the December eclipse, around the time of the Saturn/ Jupiter conjunct at the end of 2020. Though of course it is not for me to determine, it all depends on the alignments. We would have to assess frequently to bring in the new frequencies when required.

Once again, I pursued the issue of the texts being light oriented and missing the necessity of bringing the dark pure energy into balance. The duality is essential, just as we have two aspects of self. The balance of the polarities is essential for self-mastery; it is the basis of what I teach.

I had to clarify once more, I am not talking about recognising the shadow and light within. It is about the light and dark, yin and yang, the masculine and feminine. We must see what exists at all time.

Both of us had been drawn to a part of the Emerald Tablet texts. In tablet five it refers to the Temple the Dweller built in Atlantis with his mind, not by man. Through his word he created it with form, filling its chambers with his wisdom.

"Black, yet not black, but dark like the space-time, deep in its heart the essence of light".

Anne was prompted to remember this as I was explaining what I meant by the dark. For me, it was no wonder people were so afraid of the dark, when all they have been taught by these texts is to find the light. They are even to terrified to turn around and see and own their own shadow.

We spoke at length about the requirement for everyone to take responsibility of their outcome. Everyone has their own perception of truth at any one moment which is always changing. It is based on the individual's reality, and for them to choose their own response.

No one has the right to think they may control another's choice of perspective. The individual may raise their hand for assistance to engage in the wisdom and tools to master their life and mind. It is only ever up to them if they choose to use them. Everyone's own sense of worth comes from their own values. How we represent ourselves is an individual choice, our own responsibility.

I am the first to agree we do not have to accept the shadow within ourselves, we can choose to learn to alchemise it. Only then can we master the Light Grid, the 3D the move into the 4D, the deep feminine free from her own shadow. None of this is talked about in the texts.

The ancient texts were created for what humanity was ready to accept. Not the truth of what there is, humanity is not ready to see, they are in their comfort zone and separate from own power. Their consciousness still is closed off and want to be led. They must choose to claim that power and no longer see it as separate from them, it is in them.

I was realising the texts have been written for what humanity could look to at THAT time to get them to the light. Take them to the end of the Age of Pisces. Once they got there, (now) we can bring in the next level of consciousness evolvement which is to return them to the dark. Which is exactly why I am writing the new myth of consciousness now, as we move into the Age of Aquarius.

The wisdom contained in the ancient texts was to guide people to the light - the ultimate end of 3D. It's time for new writing to help people shift into the dark feminine energy, free of shadow, in the 4D.

Anne pointed out it was like the Bible. Documented to keep the fear level in place and to keep people under control so we would not question it.

I was beginning to understand WHY the ancient texts had left me so underwhelmed. I had that knowledge within me to master the Light

Grid and I had already gone beyond to gain the balance of my polarity in the dimensions above 3D. My comprehension was further expanded when I channelled:

"Consciousness needed to evolve through humanity to a level where consciousness could move into the next level of darkness, where the purest light existed beyond the light. That is what we are forerunners of now. Coming into 4D, hence being underwhelmed which serves 3D & 5D, the old books are out of context. They carved the way for Mintakan, Hadarian 5D Souls to move into the Light. For spiritual lightworkers. Anne & I have a larger aspect as Parallels & Blueprint Originators, not one sided of light, must comprehend the energy of dark light not yet talked about. It is in the dark light we can become the Godhead we are, where we can channel the wisdom, intuition, gifts to call in frequencies. Working in the quantum. We are tapping into the truth of the consciousness, why Josephine is challenged, thought they would give insight as to what is coming, but no, the texts were the truth for the Light Grid.

Even and odd numbers of the dimensions. 2,4,6, different frequencies to 3.5.7. Josephine creates magic in 5, uses sacred geometry of the 6th and 8th for power codes. Anne 3.5,7. To weave the myth of the dimensions together, need both sides. Josephine does not believe the texts are not endarkening into the new age (Anne agreed). The consciousness was not captured. The translations e.g. Emerald tablets – was it Doreal's Soul realm who wrote in the light? There was deeper meaning in the texts and what the age of Aquarius is but there has not yet been a translator through which to see into the deeper meaning.

Energies of the underworld and energies of the even numbers must be bought be back into balance of the odd numbers of the Light Grid. The truth has not been written for the dark which exists for all eternal time. The Light Grid exists only for a period of time. It can and will be switched off.

The dark, into the crust. 1 – 7D combined. Dark true feminine energy must be tapped into. Light Grid is all masculine, dark feminine which exists eternally is in the 4, through the 6D of energy the structures are then created, losing definitive energies of masculine and feminine into cosmic Light Grid. Same with the true power codes of 8, not from masculine but feminine. Feminine are the even numbers, Masculine uneven. But seeing it in reverse and see it as feminine. It is actually a masculine structure.

It now made total sense when Anne had asked what the numbers 3,5,7,9,4 meant when she had read the Hermetica the night before. We had to realise the odd number sequence she runs as a Master of the Light Grid (through all dimensions) needs to be woven back through the dark feminine energy of 4th dimension and the even number dimensions beyond.

Upon this realisation of what I felt was missing from the texts, Anne was guided to confirm we no longer needed to reference the books. It was the context we needed to connect to so as to evoke the next level of awareness.

We had to start regarding the texts from the opposite perspective - the polarities have swapped. Exactly as I shared in the new myth of consciousness in May. As we move into the new dimension, everything has done a 180.

Anne: Shifting our awareness through to a different perspective we take away the anarchy in the middle (of the infinity symbol). The revolution (which is happening in our reality now) needs to happen to make the changes in the other realms. Then the possibilities can become obvious to humanity, so they see the polarity in it.

2020: THE ALCHEMISTS' AWAKENING

This insight was a huge relief and revelation to both Anne and I who had been questioning what role these texts played in the new evolution.

Thoth only had the aspect of light, he was never of the Dark Grid, Osiris was.

Anne: It is Osiris who is the connection. He travelled between the two worlds of the dark. He was cut up and sent out. Isis is of the Light feminine energy. Masculine of Osiris, the all controller, was seen as being of the dark and cast out. They saw the only way to control the dark was to eliminate it. It was not to be present for people to see it would cause anarchy and uprising rebellion, replaced by softer energy, feminine, Isis, easier to control.

Josephine: Perspective - the polarity was reversed. Light Grid sees Light energy is feminine, it is not, it is the masculine requirement to control. Whereas dark feminine energy is the chaotic.

Anne: Feminine comes from manipulation and not indoctrination. Masculine energy comes from the Truth of what it is— force which as a flow. Enforced the belief as the truth. Feminine energy is deceptive, can go both ways. It is shadow of being the two sides, not the intrinsic value of the truth.

I knew I had to frame again the core of my teachings and how it relates to these insights. 3D shadow feminine had to be integrated so the masculine could do his thing in whatever grid he is in. Intuition is not feminine, always masculine telling us what we needed to know or do. Now he (the Dark Masculine) creates the synchronicities, showing us what we need to do, what we need to read, he weaves in and out of the dimensions. The dark feminine energy is the chaos in which he works, she holds it for him. He does the coding and the magic. The deepest gifts are from my magician, my masculine energy. He creates matter out of nothing.

It is clear once again we are here to write new books.

The texts are Light Grid. They remain a reference point of the past. Light Gridders do not understand the concept.

There are none on the Dark Grid. Until now.

It is time to rewrite the myth and move beyond the Light. To reclaim our polarity, power and potential. Isis AND Osiris to reunited.

CHAPTER 41*

WHAT IS COSMIC CODING?

What exactly is cosmic coding?

They are the access codes to your abilities you possessed on other planets, in different frequencies, in different times. The chances are you had access to them in previous lives to some degree and carried forward the programming through your Soul and through your DNA.

Cosmic coding is not something that can be learned, bought or acquired. It is something you contain within yourself and always have had. It just needs awakening from its slumber.

Very, very few people are aware of their true potential. They may understand the theory of it and yet no comprehension of how to access.

The fastest route is to work with an Encoder such as myself to identify, ignite and reprogram your circuitry through the quantum. This is the essence of Portalism. However, being exposed to the wisdom and frequencies in secure containers such as The Alchemist's Coven, your own innate abilities are sparked when you step up and claim ownership and responsibility beyond your human capacity. You far more easily glimpse aspects of your genius when immersed and committed to yourself within a sacred space.

The prodigy that lies within you is unique to you, just as your personality and profile is exclusive to you as a human. Whilst I may be able to indicate the pathway which you are to follow, the ultimate decision lies with you to explore the depths of who you really are.

It is imperative to understand the difference between what resides innately within you and what can be learned from a master or teacher externally. You may be led to discover more about a subject, this is merely waking up what you already knew from previous lives.

I have never received any formal training in my intuitive or healing abilities, nor in my remote viewing in this lifetime. I trained for a few months to read the Akashic records which was simply awakening my dormant capabilities. I have always been able to do it, though there have been many times in my life I switched them off, which as a human, we always have free choice to do.

These gifts have been brought forward many lifetimes, honed and skilled so they are completely natural for me. It is the same for my capabilities to travel through time, space, dimensions and realities. I see, hear and feel the energies clearly in my mind and body.

Whilst you may gain insight from others' teachings as to what is possible, if it is not coded in you, you do not have the ability. You are here to discover the truth, to teach yourself through trust and develop confidence and skills few speak of and claim as their own. All done from truth, not ego.

Each time you go down the path trying to find training, question why you do not trust yourself to explore the truth within. If you feel you need a piece of paper to qualify you in anything, you are operating from human shadow.

Your genius is never certifiable. Ever.

The biggest challenge for people as they step out of their human construct and return to their cosmic frequencies, they have little idea of how their abilities will show up, what they are to do with them or who will even acknowledge them. Many are terrified of the power they may contain. This is the whole paradox of genius – you must master your ability to bring it through from beyond this world whether or not you are recognised for this, for genius is both worthless and priceless. Back to the conversation about being work of art.

The quickest way to shut off access to your coding and abilities is to return to the remit of doubt and fear. If your desire to fit in and be accepted by others is your priority, you will never fully realise your capabilities for they cannot exist in 3D.

We are seeing an increasing number of autistic and ADHD children, as well as adults with Alzheimer's. Society labels these as "not normal" and "damaged goods". As alluded to before, the Souls of these beings have chosen not to operate under the human construct. The greatest support we can provide to these advanced Souls is to help them find their point of brilliance and let that be sufficient to live an expansive life.

They already have the codes open and can access some of the higher frequencies. For certain individuals, the bodily cells did not transcend into this life but their brain did, such as Stephen Hawking. Other physically and mentally disabled beings may not have accessibility to normal functioning and yet they generally resonate at a high frequency of unconditional love. A rare breed indeed.

There are many individuals whose cosmic coding remains blocked until they are ready to experience different things, make different choices.

Some who have spent years programming in purely Light Grid codes must have these decoded and reprogrammed into the current reality, which is what Encoders do. Some people will automatically function better in the new frequencies when they align within for the first time.

We all carry different elemental energies, have lived at different times and yet have been woken for evolution NOW. Those carrying and accessing the cosmic codes move the Collective Consciousness forward the cycle of evolving, whereas the majority of humanity believe revolution against current systems is the way to go for change.

Your innate wisdom is not new learned knowledge, it comes from lifetimes of programming. Do not go off and learn how to do remote viewing if you never have the experience of seeing different places and yet have been on the path of awakening for some time. It is not in your scope, there are other things you were here to do. This applies to any aspect of awakening.

I have never had very strong resonance to sound healing, Reiki or crystals. They are simply not part of my Soul Realms, yet numbers, geometry, mapping frequencies and time travel are. Do not attempt to become an expert in all fields, there is no space for comparisonitis in the cosmos. It is for you to know your unique threads of genius as they become known to you, when you are ready. Patience is a key virtue in this unfolding, awaiting your frequency match; will the paradox of the quantum.

When you discover a gift that is not known, would not be widely accepted, it can be challenging for the human to decide whether to embrace fully their gifts or surrender to the fear-based requirement of fitting in.

Humanity is obsessed with labels and do an excellent job of defining who you are through words, based on an assumption that we all must function the same way. The new way of existence is very much to recognise each individual's traits, strengths and passions with no requirement of having to define which box they fit in.

Once you have made a claim on your cosmic codings and access to your points of genius, you have by default stepped into the responsibility of maintaining the higher frequencies. The moment your fear or emotion kicks in, you lose your ability to be a clear channel. It is imperative to do this with awareness so as to not bring any negative energy through to the higher frequencies.

Cosmic coding is enhanced each time you experience higher frequencies and abilities become more profound the longer you can sustain these vibrations. These new energies are being brought forward for the highest good of all. They are contained in all the writings, both within The Alchemists' Awakening and in the Coven. New access points are revealed through each portal opening as well as the five planetary energies which will be identified to us to help sustain new frequencies requiring to be fine-tuned. Selenite is the first.

It is not that we need to understand everything that is written, spoken or cast into the space. Instead, find peace and acceptance in your heart that all Just Is. Just Know. The frequency was co-created to keep the intent pure, no more so than in the Coven, where ego is required to be switched off upon arrival.

I bounce back and forth to translate the frequencies so others may transcend into theirs, escalating it upwards. I am working in the consciousness to transcend it, working my way back and forth from human level from my true level of existence.

294

I can access dimensions without it being held within my DNA which I do by accessing the coordinates through numbers to my aspects of self. When I enter the wormhole seen as a pyramid with three aspects, I can change the frequency. (The three-way path Thoth talks about for time travel). I morph into the energy of the frequency and then return. This enables me to decode as a Multi-Frequencer. If my energy stuck in one dimension it would be too rigid.

I hold the Platinum Code of the 7D which allows me to go undetected through other dimensions as my colours morph to match the other frequencies. I honed this ability over many lives as a way of remaining unseen. As I now step into proclaim who I really am, knowing It Is Time, I will dissolve this requirement be protected and guarded in the past. I also hold the Diamond code of The Hermetica, as well as gold (5D) and Titanium (9D). I will not remain in the 5th as it is too light for me, whilst the Mintakans, Hadarians, Pleiadians and Alpha Centauris are most at home here.

Being parallel I also access the multi-dimensional portals of the 13th and 14th dimensions, opening the gateway to transmute into different frequencies. At the time of writing, I am currently embodying 6D through geometry and numerics, which is my key to connect to all and anchoring it in this reality.

As you awaken into the depths of truth, you will begin to see the illusions that have you thinking you need something outside yourself. You will move into the concept of real consciousness, which is limitless and timeless, the self is always evolving, as is consciousness.

The truth cannot have fear. It is for you to escalate that vibration to understand the real purpose of existence. The void where Nothing is Everything, Nothing Matters. This is ultimately achieved by igniting the dark codes within the DNA to this truth, exactly what I do through Cosmic Coding.

It is imperative you understand the celestial undertaking you are subscribing to awakening your codes. They can be no sense of entitlement to them or attempting to fast track the process by not doing the work necessary. You will know when you start opening to the cosmic codes and have different experiences in your body, in your energy, especially around the third eye. It could be a sensation you have left your body, you no longer know who you are, and feel very disoriented. Welcome to the Dark.

The optimum sustainability of cosmic coding is obtained through combination the different aspects of self. Your light body must be clear of shadow held in the chakras. Deprogram from the chakra system completely. It is a case of encoding your DNA, cellular memory and the essence of the dark void held within your bones, across all times, space, dimensions and realities. Hence the requirement of Encoders.

Above all, enjoy your journey of exploration.

Chose revelation, not revolution.

Experience emotion when it is heartfelt and real and dissolve all emotional response (triggers) when based on illusions that something outside yourself is more powerful than you are.

You are from beyond here, choose your course wisely and do all you can to stay in the magic of possibilities from whence you came.

CHAPTER 42

THE KEYS TO THE PORTALS

I was given the wisdom of the first portal towards the end of May. When Anne read my download regarding the Isis Temple and portal opening, she knew she was reading ancient texts. It is my job to rewrite them into existence now we are working in the quantum.

Josephine: It is all about awareness, connection and receiving. The cells are updated with the wisdom and frequencies of the higher energies. The Akashics for each Soul are updated and sealed. They knew this energy had to be witnessed into being – the observer of the quantum.

It is what has to be brought back into awareness today.

Each site must be located (where the original contract was made) and open the portal to the connection to where the codes are actually located, which may not be the same position. By being in awareness and observation once more, The Akashics are ready to be updated. As the Gatekeeper, I work with the Cosmic Gatekeepers to know when to align these energies, to be reopened on planet Earth.

At the given time and date, for it is all coded and must be deciphered first, the Portal can be unlocked. The observers can be present to the energies and receive them back in, first into their own DNA for awakening in the light body, and then anchor them in and merge with the Collective Consciousness.

They can only be received by the Collective when the baseline frequency is sufficient to receive and sustain the frequency. Each frequency which comes in is designed to:

Open up the channels from separation to integration,

to move closer to the experience of the One Energy,

To switch on the access codes to Source energy and abilities powered by Source.

Individuals MUST have the awareness, and ownership of their own power and potential power for this frequency to be received. It comes with high levels of responsibility few are willing to adopt in the modern age.

Their own power is contained in their human vessel, their potential power is held within their Soul realms and their counterparts in the multi-dimensions.

The ultimate mission is to realise this connection and dissolve the Soul Shadow itself to have full access to themselves as Cosmic Beings.

In the session following this download, we started off on a tangent, relating to Pregnancy Alchemy. The reason so many people are not getting pregnant is they are interbreeding from the same planetary energies. This totally makes sense. As humans, we are choosing to mate with people who are very much like us, especially amongst the spiritually awakened, who hold the same vision (and frequency) about life.

As the new empowered male is birthed, pregnancy issues will dissolve. Whilst the emasculated male wants to mate with his equivalent feminine, there will be difficulties. Both sides are required, in their fullest, innate energy. That is of course, if the families do what is required to live in a clean, healthy environment inside and out. This article highlights the looming causes of fertility issues due to chemicals we ingest.

Just as I spoke on my website, the reason women cannot get pregnant is they haven't admitted they are a witch; so too, must the father claim his wizardry. Or at least, own his power and personality as a man. Covens must have both witches and wizards, just as society requires.

Both of us are feeling the expansive nature of the energies which are now in place, and how quickly things were moving, being revealed and embedding.

I wanted to clarify how I see the next steps forward.

It is for us to decipher where the portals are located and open the energy frequencies of each.

We can then ignite higher vibrations within us and open the gateways for when Collective Consciousness is ready to experience it too. It is not for us to structure it, we must let it unfold through vibrational shifts. Human fears, labels and expectations cannot be in the way.

We may not know the whole reason the portal is being open and must trust it has a much more significant impact than we know. Those assisting the portal openings and witness it into being, even through invisible sensations of the experience.

Once we have access to the frequencies, we will be able to decipher the codes more precisely. It is not from hunting through the textbooks to find the answers – this is the accumulation of knowledge. It is imperative we ignite the wisdom already held within us to then be able to decipher more efficiently. Like everything, processes are reversed.

Anne has had knowledge to access the encoding system for 30 years, yet only this past week we see this is required to decipher the colours, frequencies, sound and numbers of frequencies.

In previous lives, I contributed to the writings as The Scribe for the Akashics, and the Encoder of the Numerical, which includes mapping. I had seen my flashbacks to my two different lives at the time of the origins of Chaldean numerology seven years ago. Anne unveils the frequency & sound coding. This keeps the intent of what is pure.

This is my gift to humanity, to give back what was taken from me. It is also about justice for the Cosmic Beings. "The weighing of the heart":

Anne: "The decoding of the precise analytical vibration of consciousness from the innate ability to connect to the true light and the true beings at the heart of consciousness, the highest vibrational being there are. This realm has access to multi-multi- dimensions, so expansive. A place of no ego or ownership, no fixing or ending. It is the realm through which Anne and Josephine work together with no regard for our human capacity to process or understand it, other than for the purpose of translating and scribing it."

The very definition of streaming genius.

It does not matter we do not understand it all. The fact it is being spoken into existence and scribed is sufficient to contribute to the frequency of Isness.

300

It is our job as Originators to access the source codes of consciousness.

As a Translator, I must decipher what others need to see, hence I am guided as to what is included in this series of writings, and what not to. There are streams of consciousness simply not available to land or be understood, hence it is not shared here.

This brought up for consideration who can receive what codes. I have known for a long time the coding is held within the DNA. What became clear today is the chakra system (which is only relevant in 3D for the connection to the Light body) must also be fully activated and moved out of the solid anchor points into the fluidity of the portals to receive the frequencies through the system. This is why slave-self alchemy is imperative to free the body, mind and Soul from the energetic patterning keeping you as a prisoner from the higher frequencies.

However, you must understand the combination of igniting the chakras and DNA can only be embedded when you have the cosmic understanding and not through entitlement. Full circle once again back to ownership and responsibility.

It soon became clear would only be told about one portal at a time, to open the frequencies as required. Once the first portal was open, we were also shown a crystal to assist these frequencies embodying within us.

There are 13 portals which require opening and five crystals - planetary energies - required to anchor them.

One early morning whilst having my normal higher-self conversations, it was pointed out to me one of the reasons travel has been stopped is to take the humans away from these sacred sites whilst the portals are open and new energies land. It would create too much of a distortion field otherwise, and people would likely to get sick as their bodies went into a sharp detox.

It is a priority to find the sites where people can visit and open the portals during lockdown. The hidden sites can be opened later, once the world is back up and running. It will be for me to explore the locations and times to open each portal, who needs to be present, and an awareness of what energies we will unlock at each.

Each portal is the gateway to certain dimensions and frequencies. As we map the chakras of the world and locate the sacred sites near each, this will be the energies of the dimensions I unlock. This is why I had to map out the dimensions and Soul realms the other day. The next thing to be added in are the sacred sites.

I feel each site will be linked to various dimensions, like a giant grid across the Earth, networking and anchoring into each of the realms. I have recently seen maps of the locations across the world (which is on the list to dive into and explore).

Now it will be creating the new links through the quantum. Remember, there is no longer a structure on which to hook anything, it is why it must be observed into existence so the frequencies can be reassociated between realms.

CHAPTER 43

PORTAL 1: THE ISIS TEMPLE

The knowledge of the first portal opening came the day after I was told I was a Cosmic Scribe and must start these books. The energies had obviously been waiting for me to catch on and were ready to download quickly.

I tuned in and was taken on a journey to Egypt.

I meet Isis on the grounds of the Island of Philae, the original Temple of Isis grounds before being moved to Agilika after the Aswan Dam was built in the 1960's.

We greeted once again and immersed in the energy. Moving to the columns and plinth in the grounds, there are deep hieroglyphics everywhere around the central pinnacle. This will unlock the holographic contracts. the sun is directly overhead at 12pm on 21/6 Solstice (subsequently moved the time to the eclipse). The portal must be opened to receive and join the Cosmic energies.

I stood in the spot and send notification to the Cosmic Realms and Planetary bodies. They are unable to bring their energies forward for the healing until they had word from me, in the lifetime it is to be opened. This is my role as the Gatekeeper to the Akashics.

They can now bring together the final phases of the energies ready to land and be in alignment for the eclipse. 27 minutes for the energies to lock and load.

Isis, Osiris and I facilitate the landing and opening of the Contract.

I am the Contract Creator, Initiator, Encoder, The Key Keeper of the Akashics. I am the Cosmic Scribe.

I call in the individuals to unlock them, it is why people are in different places. They will be revealed as it is needed, for the alignment of Light.

The temples were built by numbers & symmetry and encoded by light. There was concern about the sacred symbology and coding being found too early.

21/12/2020 is the birth date of Horus – son of Isis and Osiris. The new energy, the new age.

Conception was 21/3/20.

The energies will start aligning through 2021 to be completed on 12/12/2021 (not 2012 as originally thought, it had an extra 9-year cycle).

You can see from this, I was not only given the insights to the opening, but also the insights to the most relevant dates of the whole Awakening. Thus begun the journey.

The first portal opening:

We gathered in the temple. I opened the Akashic records.

The Pyramids were opened above and so below. Isis ran the light vortex in the upper Pyramid. Anne & I were on the ground corners. The central sundial spiral down into the ground and opened the portal. Osiris ran the dark energy through the base Pyramid under the earth. The point of the pyramid at the core crystal, through the halls of Amenti. This energy came up through the portal into the light Pyramid dancing and entwining with Isis. She went through the ground portal did the same in the lower Pyramid.

The Pyramids were surrounded by dodecahedrons, many sacred geometry spaces as they opened the portals across times, spaces, dimensions. The intentions were programmed in, calling back the male from the underworld, his powerful self to be resurrected once more.

Each person present embodied the cosmic coding frequencies entwining both polarities and anchoring it in the bodies through the Akashics. The bodies were cleared of density and physical issues. Anchoring in the same upgrade all within the coven. Opening the portal of possibilities for all densities on Earth to be cleared to those who know, to those who claim it. So that they too can access the higher frequencies.

Fast moving energies morphed between the shapes with the holographic imprints also being updated elsewhere with the same intention of frequency.

The Akashics were sealed and updated. Sundial energy was sealed and the portal closed. The format of shapes disappeared, the energies of Isis and Osiris returned from whence they came. The translucent Pyramids were destructed, and the golden cords between Anne and Josephine who had both been holding the space, along with Deena, were returned to the individual Souls.

All present energetically departed and Josephine once again sealed the space before returning to this reality.

I invited members of The Coven to be part of the portal openings, each taking it in turns depending on the location and personal association with them. Deena, Ali, Angelina, Lacey, Bridget were members of the coven for the six months during scribing; Dena and Erin were here for the first month.

Deena had a profound experience at the portal opening; she has always had a deep connection with Egypt, beyond her father being Egyptian. It was indeed a turning point for her own cosmic abilities. This is her channelled download during the opening:

Transcript from channel to portal opening on 21st June during solar eclipse. Temple of Philae.

Scene - procession starts. Time blended and interloped between past, present and future ceremonies - all one as ritual is time honoured and sacred.

No separation between the light to the dark - people must flow between the two. It is essential to see the truth by looking into the dark to reveal what this means for humanity. Feel the inscriptions on this temple as we talk about the light and the dark feel it and know that the dark is very much part of who we are and it is not to be feared, the same way death is not to be feared.

For we are infinite beings - death is merely a construct to create fear whereas you move into the multiverse and each Soul will travel and flow depending on their rhythm of life and their learnings of what they have moved and passed through. Whether they have learned or they have not, whether they have decided to move between the light and dark or they have not.

Whether they have decided to stay fully in the light or in the shadows - the shadows of who they are which will never become fulfilled as their full potential as a Soul. As a Soul your journey is to continue moving and flowing through time as if you are a breeze on the wind. It is your destiny as Souls to evolve in the beautiful multiverse in different ways, different cultures and beings but we are all One under the Law of Ra.

Under the Law of the Creator which binds us all together and a time will come when we will step into the oneness. We are all children of this Universe. We are all granted with choice of who we want to be. The time of the Golden Age is here where humanity will look up to the skies and see beyond the stars but see right into the Universe and see who they are.

It will be unlocked in each and every person, maybe not in this lifetime but it will happen as it is accelerating fast as humanity is awakening at a speed that is unanticipated. And I Isis am blessed to see such evolution of humanity and we are here to support and guide. And the time is now where the energy is heightened and the truth is being unlocked and people are seeing beyond the constructs of what has been created in this world to control. And there are those of you that are key and deeply connected to me.

My daughter Iset you have a gift. You are one from me. You are created from me as I Isis as your mother have created you in my image so you understand the truth of who you are as you move forwards in this lifetime you create so much joy but also you must reveal the truth as you step into who you are.

You may not be understood at first but you will have a long life on this Earth as you share your wisdom, continue to evolve and live in abundance and you will create and you will manifest as you are a magician, a sorcerer and a priestess. You will inspire and you have only just begun my child as you have stepped out of your shadow and unlocked the shackles of your past.

Your lifetimes have been many and it is now time to evolve and I am here to support you. Step into who you are. In your heart I show you the image of who you are now as you spread your wings wide and far as it touches every corner of this Earth and into the multiverse as you are also one to communicate with us as you resonate at higher frequencies. As I speak to you the codes are being unlocked deep within your DNA and cellular level.

In parallel I communicate with your mentor and guide who is a keeper of the Akashics. She is the decipherer, she is the scribe, who has been with us for many lifetimes providing counsel and wisdom to us and to me as Isis.

...There's a sadness at the bottom of the Earth. There's a sadness because they are trapped. Our ET brothers are trapped below the earth and their fear is creating a sad lament. They must be freed. The draconian system must collapse and stop. The council must step in and it's time for all of us to have this battle together for the good of our Universe. To free anyone from any form of slavery and any form of hurt. Any form of trauma. The truth is that there may not be fear, shame hurt or any form of low vibration or anything that is destructive. It's a fallacy that there must be good and evil. There can be just good. They are trapped in Antarctic under the ice. There is a huge negative vibration there that is coming from fear and pain. It is not good.

Visualization - I see an explosion in space. [I weep]

[I asked Anne about Antarctica after this, it had not been the first time it had been mentioned as a portal. It is to remain closed for now according to the Indigenous as it will be detrimental to the ice through the transmutation.]

Anne's experience:

I could feel the heat of the central sun. Both Osiris and Thoth were present holding the corners of the energy. We must remember to work the energy anti-clockwise to clear, clockwise to program and update.

Horus had also come through and we are giving back the light to humanity which has been lost. The underworld is very connected to all that we are now. We must bring the balance back according to the laws to create a different outlook which has been lost to the world for so long.

As we were conversing new frequencies were coming in. The consciousness of the new vibration to the eighth dimension but also the intrinsic value of the 13th.

I explained the number combination of 5, 8 and 13. Five represents freedom and moves through the power number of eight. We come back together in wholeness and awareness at 13.

13 of course is the magic number; as soon as Anne said this, she heard it was brought forward for the progression of humanity. I added it is the number of the change of the cosmos, unifying the two realms.

Insights to the bigger meaning of the portal openings would come thick and fast after each one. We absolutely had to stay open to the guidance and wisdom to the cosmic beings in the Ancient Ones deemed appropriate us to know and share.

CHAPTER 44

SUPPORTING MINERALS

It would take a few days for the energies to process after the Isis portal opening. We had to remember the conclusion of what happens may come well after the energies have been opened. We do not yet know the truth of what we have done, nor do we necessarily need to know.

There was an expectation of an uplift in energy, it was not strong but it would be.

Anne realised the clearing was to do with the selenium and magnesium in the earth. Upon research, we found it was associated with Saturn energy, the opening of the crown chakra and alignment of the spinal column. It gives a fine vibration to bring clarity. It also helps against mercury poisoning.

We must connect to the selenium and body as it is a link to the light body and the earth vibration, instilling a calming deep peace that enhances the holding of the new frequencies. Selenium can also be used for body protection against grids for safety. It is a key element to help our bodies adjust to the frequencies that are changing. We can use the crystal selenite to help anchor it in.

It was good to have this awareness as we waited a couple of days for the energies to settle and the new frequencies to be felt within. We were getting used to the concept that not all answers are provided in the moment of awareness. Without the construct of time the moment of programming of consciousness maybe at a later point than the moment of receiving. This is why it is key to allow the frequencies to embed before consciousness to be reprogrammed. It is only then we will be shown the next steps, given the next clues, decipher the next codes.

A couple of days later I had been hoping we would be told where the next portal we needed to open was. Instead, we were shown a location that contained crystals to help anchor the new frequencies. We have known there was a site in Mexico for some time and it had not been made clear exactly where this portal was.

It took the prompt we required selenium in our bodies to lead us to the giant crystal caves of Mexico, under the Sierra De Naica. It has been described as the Sistine Chapel of crystals. Consisting of three main caves, these reserves lay deep under the shape of a pyramid.

They are giant selenite crystals, the exact mineral we were told we needed to anchor in the new frequencies the other day. The atomic number is 34, one more than the sacred number of 33 revered as the ultimate number of human constructs, i.e. not of this world.

[Once we are in non-human form, we can see and access our multiverse self and in other realms beyond this Universe, not of form. We must live 34 lives in the higher frequency before being given access to the higher dimensions. This ensures we have the level of understanding is required by the Laws.]

These mines are a recent find, much like the Pulpi Geode found in an abandoned silver mine in 1999 in Spain's Almeria Province. The Cave of Crystals at Naica is still an active hydrothermal site, whereas Pulpi's activity has been extinguished, making it more akin to a fossil. It was discovered in 2000 after water was pumped out of the U-shaped cavity in the limestone by a mining company. It is 30m x10m and the crystals continue to grow in the temperatures of 136 degrees Fahrenheit (58 degrees C).

Anne: "*The frequency of the crystals enables us to tune in to where we are meant to be, we are then able to attune to a finer frequency, one we are not yet used to, our bodies have to adjust to it. It's why we were feeling out of sorts; the portal opening with a new frequency is coming to Earth. This is the first of five frequencies to be established, ahead of other beings who carry these frequencies, so we may feel them, see them, when they come to Earth and be able to respond to the energy. This is the first one which is communicating up front with us.*

The selenite crystals hold the frequencies of all dimensional energies and the frequencies for us to transmit the energies from the other portal openings. Tapping into the frequency means the energy has been transmuted and is being held for us as light beings of what we are doing. We can tap into it in order to enhance our frequencies to open up to the portals we need to do. They are waiting for us to realign the energies.

We ask the crystals how best to work with them - healing, transmuting and aligning with other frequencies. Crystals are frequency holders. They are transmuted and transmitters so energy can resonate in Earth for us so other planets can work with us. They need the energy to be transmuted and transmitted."

In other words, tuning in to the selenium within our bodies by accessing the frequency codes of the selenite crystal caves allows us to know we have received the high frequency energies in our body. This enables the cosmic energies of other beings to be felt and seen in our own awareness.

It really is quite amazing and yet so obvious of the cosmic energies would work through the earth crystals for us to connect with.

CHAPTER 45

THE LOST SYMBOL

I have watched so many movies and read books since the beginning of May which I was shown were relevant to me and the unfolding journey of discovery. A key source of synchronicities as well as seeing the stories we have been sold on the Light Grid. To witness time and time again how movies play out the Hero's Journey.

I started watching the Star Wars series in chronological order on May 4th. I had never had any interest in them and only vaguely remember the original movies as a kid. The usual plot of what happens to someone when they are promised power and governance through greed and corruption, with the good guys continuing to fight for peace and harmony. The Jedi's learnt to harness the power of Life Force energy, which will always be greater than the power of man.

This is exactly the lesson the world is experiencing right now, as the collective must own their own individual power to rise up and take on the systems of governance, health and politics, retaining their right to freedom of choice. These parallels can be made in so many of the blockbuster films, everyone loves the idea of a collective of heroes coming in to save the world. To fix the problem.

Yet they will only "win" if they have the power of a force of energy behind them. Every one of the good guys is always committed to the cause, once they get over their moments of self-doubt which are an essential part of any Hero's Journey plot. The question is, are individuals in this day and age ready to stand for the cause or not, will they run a mile if being asked to take responsibility?

With recent uprisings and rebellions, it could be seen the corner has been turned.

The other series of movies I immersed in was those of Dan Brown. The *Da Vinci Code* had always held a fascination for me, ringing the Truth Bells loud and clear when it comes to the divinity of Mary Magdalene.

Angels and Demons was an excellent portrayal of the secrets of the Catholic church, again with the aspect of corruption, cover ups and the seeker of individual power. *Inferno* was about the potential unleashing of a deadly virus which could wipe out half the world's population in order to save the future of humanity. Somewhat similar to current day events and could easily be seen as the more potent version of Bill Gates' (and others) agenda for population control. Bear in mind, CV19 is only a warmup teaser for what would happen for WHEN we actually get a virus that is powerfully destructive across all ages and stages of life.

The one book which was never made into a movie was *The Lost Symbol*. I cannot recall how long it had been sitting on my shelf unread, though I feel I had purchased it shortly after publication in 2009. I was ready to read something lighter away from historical texts, to immerse in a novel. Of course, there is no coincidence why I was prompted to read this now.

Ron Howard, the director of the Dan Brown movie series, claimed they did not make this one into a movie because the plot line was so similar to the others. I realised within the first few pages it was not taken mainstream as it reveals the Masonic nature of Washington DC, and the Americans would not want to rock the boat on the foundational structures of their democracy.

Spoiler alert: I am called to document key pieces from the book as I read it and endeavour not to give the plot, or at least the drama of it, away. When you see how the path of insight has already been laid down for us by authors and movie makers for decades, do not dismiss it as a fairy tale Hollywood blockbuster. The creators had snippets of the codes and portrayed them through the human perspective. They hold so many keys to the wisdom that already exists.

I chose to share the salient points of this book as it provides an excellent summary of Freemasonry and how it is based on the ancient mysteries. It clearly identifies what we have all elusively been searching for. *I write in italics a further definition as I see it relevant to the content of The Alchemists' Awakening.*

Whilst I know how many portals still need to be opened, there are already plenty which are already opened and accessible, including the one at Washington DC. Trump is fully aware of it as a feeder for alien intelligence. He rather likes his role as Captain Kirk as he sees it.

* * *

The Lost Symbol is a race against time to rescue Peter Solomon, a Mason of the highest 33rd Order. He is a friend of Robert Langdon, the Key Decipherer and main character. Peter's sister, Katherine, works for the Institute of Noetic Sciences (which was one of my main sources of wisdom back in 2005 and is a prompt for me to dig out the annual reports I have from them from 15 years ago, though it is very Light Grid based).

Peter is the historian with deep knowledge of the ancient texts and Katherine is the modern-day scientist. She soon realises the Ancients have been talking about Entanglement Theory for eons, the sense of being connected to all things. At-one-ment with the Universe is still referred to as atonement in the Jewish and Christian faith.

Katherine also came to realise superstring theory was documented in the thirteenth century translation of the Aramaic – The Complete Zohar. She had thought it was a brand-new cosmological model showing the multi-dimensional Universe was made up of ten dimensions which all interacted like vibrating strings. The ancient books also showed how six of the dimensions are entangled as act as one.

(I see this as the 4th -10th dimensions the books are referring to. Higher dimensions could not yet be known by the ancients or scientists as their frequency consciousness could not yet access the even higher realms of 11-15).

Katherine was realising the ancients possessed profound scientific wisdom and there was also a long-buried myth around the ultimate secret of enlightenment. However, Peter knew this portal existed in the Rotunda at Washington DC and so did the baddie, Mal'akh. He set up Langdon to be in the Rotunda as he left Peter's bleeding hand in the centre as an invite to receive the hidden wisdom of all the ages, with the sign of the Hand of Mysteries, left in a sacred place.

Mal'akh required Langdon to decode and find the missing symbol which he would then have tattooed on his crown and receive the ultimate wisdom of the Universe. He was also a master of disguise and manipulated Langdon and Katherine to weave them into the story line.

Katherine describes convergence or entanglement as a single entity defined by the sum of its parts, a meta-system, working as one. She applies this to the concept of thought, what would happen if the same thought began to merge into one and gravity grew, enabling things to be pulled towards the thought mass. (*Which is exactly how Collective Consciousness works.*)

The Apotheosis of Washington covers the canopy of the Capitol Rotunda which was completed in 1865 by Brumindi. Apotheosis means divine transformation, of man becoming God. Many of the greatest names in science studied alchemy and mystical wisdom, none more so than Isaac Newton. He knew the very nature of transformation.

The pyramid is used in Masonic symbolism, emblematic of ancient man's ability to ascend to enlightenment. The legend of the Masonic pyramid was behind the ancient mysteries and wisdom until the time all of mankind was ready to handle power it could communicate, **apotheosis.** It is said the information is encoded and understandable only by the most enlightened Souls. Sato, the CIA agent, also knew pyramids were considered mystical portals.

The intrinsic number 13 is the magic number to represent the progression of humanity, as we were told after the Isis portal. It is the dimension at which the two realms are unified. People still see 13 as daemonic, but this is not what it is, it is another element misunderstood by humanity.

It is a key number which appears many times in the US Constitution. Beneath the US Capitol lies a layer of 13 storage rooms, the great Seal of the United States had 13 stars, 13 arrows, 13 pyramid steps, 13 shield stripes 13 olive leaves, 13 olives 13 letters in *annuit ceotis* and *e pluribus unum* etc.

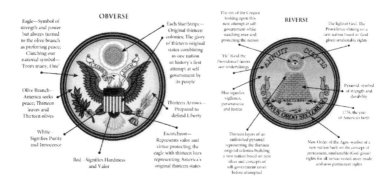

Aleister Crowley was a visionary of the early 1900s. The church regarded him as "the most evil man who ever lived". Great minds always feared by lesser minds. Crowley stated we must "become something holy, make yourself sacred". There is much power in ritual and incantation; sacred words when properly spoken, functioned like keys that open gateways to the other worlds.

The ancient right of 'sacred making' had once been the law of the land this reference throughout time, texts and religion. The likes of Crowley practiced the rite of sacrifice, recognising it as a requirement of God. It was said the blood is all that separates the light from the dark.

The satanic principles and rituals requiring the blood of children is also based on this principle.

There is recognition of other sacred numbers. 12 is the number of signs of the zodiac, the hours in the day, the gates of heaven. A sanctuary chamber, twelve-foot square, was used to house and altar, 7 x 7 square. There are seven seals of Revelation, Seven steps of the temple.

Such numbers were always acknowledged in sacred rituals.

Five symbols of the Ancient Mysteries are as follows:

The crown - to represent the King I shall become

The star - to represent the heavens which have ordained my destiny

The sun - to represent the illumination of my Soul

The lantern - to represent the feeble light of human understanding

The key – to represent the missing piece

Many great minds over time have all insisted that man possesses mystical abilities of which he is unaware. The famous hermetic aphorism, *Know ye not that ye are gods?* was one of the pillars of the mysteries. *As above so below.... Man created in God's image..... Apotheosis*

There has been a persistent message of man's own divinity, of his hidden potential, the recurring theme in the ancient texts of countless traditions. Einstein predicted the religion of the future will be a cosmic religion. It will transcend a personal God and avoids dogma and theology.

One of the Masonic Brothers recognised the role of gatekeeper was now morphing into a guide. *Indicating our fundamental roles can change as illumination draws nearer.*

[own notes: To know what a symbol means (or at least what we think they means) is one of the important speculative studies in Freemasonry. The teachings of the craft are said to be "illustrated by symbols."

Esoteric symbols both conceal and reveal the truth. There are three ways symbols can be studied:

1. *Exoterically:* This concerns the concrete or objective appearance, its form and structure.
2. *Conceptually:* This concerns the concept or idea which the sign or symbol embodies.
3. *Esoterically:* This concerns the energy or feeling that you register from the symbol.]

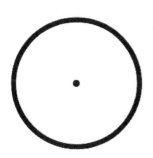

The Circumpunct has countless meanings. In ancient Egypt it was a symbol for Ra, the Son of God. Modern astronomy still uses it as the stellar symbol.

In Eastern philosophy it represents the spiritual insight of the third eye, the divine rose in the sign of illumination.

The Kabbalists use it to symbolise the Kether - the highest Sepiroth and 'the most hidden of all hidden things'. Early mystics called it the Eye of God and is the origin of the all-seeing eye on the great Seal.

The Pythagoreans use the circumpunct as the symbol of the Monad - the divine truth, the Prisca Sapienta, the at-one-ment of mind and Soul.

When you unfold a cube it becomes a cross, symbolic alchemy. The cross with the circumpunct in the middle is a binary symbol, two symbols fused to create one. The Egyptians used it to represent the intersection of two dimensions - the humans and celestial. As above, so below. It is a visual representation of the juncture where man and God became one.

Using the alchemical symbol of perfection, the rose, when placed at the centre of the cross creates the Rose Cross. The Knights of the Rose Cross honoured the early Rosicrucians. The order was built esoteric truths of the ancient past which had to be concealed from the average man and promised great insight into the spiritual realm.

This ties in with another portal location I am currently investigating and gives the insight to the relevance of its location. You will see why shortly.

Another infamous use of symbolic alchemy is through pseudonyms. Isaac Newton used this method because he understood himself as divine.

The mythological self-castrated Attis knew that achieving immortality required a clean break with the material world of male and female. The androngyne is one.

In order to create, you must destroy. Such was the nature of polarity.

This separation is a myth ready to be uncovered. The balance of male and female can be achieved within any human regardless of gender. It is only in the higher dimensions and frequencies where the androgynous remove the requirement of sexual functionality, so that all beings become one form.

There is much historic and symbolic reason the Masons choose 33 as their highest degree. 33 is the highest of all Master Numbers in numerology, established in Chaldean times 6000 years ago *(the form of numerology I have studied and used in my practice).*

It was the most sacred number symbolising divine truth. Jesus was crucified at age 33. Joseph was said to have been 33 when he married the Virgin Mary. Jesus accomplished 33 miracles. God's name was mentioned 33 times in Genesis. In Islam, all the dwellers of heaven are permanently 33 years old. 33 is the boiling point of water on the Newton scale. *(this was all written on page 333 of the book).*

When we sign a letter 'yours sincerely', we are implying the words are true. It comes from the phrase *sine cera* – without wax. This stems from the great artists in the days of Michelangelo when sculptors hid the flaws in their work by smearing hot wax into the cracks dabbing the wax with stone dust. Any sculpture without wax was considered as a sincere piece of art.

The Catholic church, born of the womb of the ancient mysteries, still carries her rights and symbols. The reminder of this ancient connection stands for all to see in the form of the Egyptian obelisk the heart of St Peter's Square in Vatican City. Christianity more than any other faith understood the transformative power of sacrifice.

Many believed that without blood there is no true sacrifice. So many cultures and faiths knew this. Catholics still use this representation: eating the body and drinking the blood of Christ at their sacrament. Most become too fearful to make true offerings, too frail to give the life that is required for spiritual transformation. The ancient texts are clear though. Only by offering what is most sacred can man access the ultimate power.

I often allude to dying the death to your human construct so you can become the genius you are, claiming ultimate power. This I believe is exactly what it means.

The earlier depths of Freemasonry wrote their knowledge down in code. This was to ensure the powerful wisdom could not be used by the unworthy, cloaking its potent truth in the metaphorical language of symbols, myths and allegory. Encrypted wisdom is all around us yet mortal man has lost the ability to decipher this complex network of symbolism and the great truth has been lost.

The legend holds that the *verbum significatium* - the password to unlock the encrypted secrets - is very deep underground and awaits a pivotal moment in history to be revealed. That time will come when mankind can no longer survive without the truth, knowledge and wisdom of ages. Mankind will at last unearth the Word and herald in a wondrous New Age of enlightenment.

The prophecy of the coming of enlightenment has, of course, been outlined in virtually every faith and philosophical tradition on Earth. This would unleash the transformation of the human mind into their true potentiality.

Supposing there was a Universal Truth that it is in everyone's Soul. What if we all shared a constant in our DNA which was responsible for the similarity in all the stories? Perhaps we gravitate towards similar ideas that are true, written deep within us. To feel that truth resonating, vibrating with our unconscious wisdom. The truth is recalled, re-membered, re-cognised as that which is already inside us.

Precisely my intention with whoever reads these texts.

The unveiling of truth is never easy. In history, every period of enlightenment has been accompanied by darkness, pushing in opposition. Such are the laws of nature and balance. Know that where you see the darkness growing in the world today, there is an equal light growing. We are profoundly privileged to be living through this pivotal moment in history where our ultimate renaissance may be revealed. The word Apocalypse means to unveil or to reveal. *It is time for the unveiling of the great wisdom.*

New technology has developed a breathable liquid called Total Liquid Ventilation, so counterintuitive that few believed it existed. It came out of modern medicine's attempts to help premature babies breathe by returning them to the liquid filled state of the womb.

This is exactly fits with the notion of being able to breathe underwater to birth the new masculine the previously discussed.

Freemasonry, like Noetic Science and the Ancient Mysteries, revered the untapped potential of the human mind, and many of the Masonry symbols related to human physiology. The mind sits like a golden capstone atop the physical body. The Philosophers Stone. Through the staircase of the spine, energy ascends and descends, circulating, connecting the heavenly mind to the physical body.

Just as the spine is made up of exactly 33 vertebrae, there are 33 degrees of masonry. The base of the spine, or *sacrum*, is the "Sacred bone". The body is indeed a temple. The human science that Masons revered was the ancient understanding of how to use that temple for its most potent and noble purpose.

The Mason's understood the necessity of death before life. The focus on death was a bold celebration of life. In realising that your days on Earth are finite you can grasp the importance of living those days with honour, integrity and service to your fellow man.

Part of the challenge was to decipher the allegorical pictogram. What did the metaphorical and symbolic language mean? It could not be taken literally.

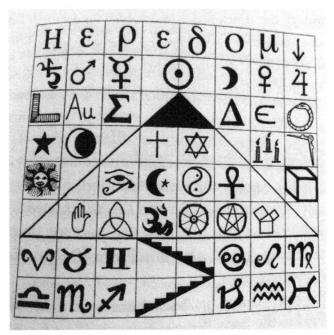

credit: The Lost Symbol, by Dan Brown

In deciphering the symbols, we are reminded that the rows beneath the pyramids represent the earth below, the lowest of all the realms. This is where the 12 ancient astrological signs are held. These represent the primordial religion of the first human Souls who look to the heavens and saw the hand of God in the movement of the stars and planets.

The pyramid rises as an enduring symbol of lost wisdom. It is a transformational gateway where all the great philosophies and religions of the world fuse into a single unified human philosophy at the top. A single universal consciousness, a shared global vision of God, represented by the ancient symbol that hovers over the capstone. The circumpunct, the universal symbol for God.

Atop of the Washington Monument sits the capstone weighing exactly 333 pounds. It is engraved with the words Laus Deo, meaning "Praise

God". This phrase had been included in symbols waiting to be deciphered.

L – the Stonemason's Square: the symbol of honesty and being 'true'

Au - the scientific abbreviation for the element Gold

S - The Greek letter S, Sigma, the mathematical symbol for the sum of all parts

D- the Greek Delta, the mathematical symbol of the change

E – Alchemical Mercury, as depicted by its most ancient alchemical symbol

0 – The Ouroboros : the symbol of wholeness and at-one-ment

The concept of laying a cornerstone comes from the old Testament in the book of Psalms. It is always buried beneath the ground, symbolising the building's initial step upwards out of the earth towards heavenly light. The "Lost Word" is not a word. We only call it the 'Word' because that is what the ancients call it - in the beginning.

For centuries scholars have poured over the Bible and attempted to decipher the untapped wisdom waiting to be unveiled. There are so many powerful hidden secrets in the Old Testament.

The Gospel of John forewarns "I will speak to you in parable… Using dark sayings". This did not mean saying was evil rather that its true meaning was shadowed or obscured from the light.

This is EXACTLY my philosophy of dark consciousness.

The parables have two layers of meaning. 'Milk for babes and meat for men', the meat is the true message accessible only to mature minds.

The milkiness of the light grid cannot access the dark meat of the new consciousness.

The Ancient Mysteries and the Bible are the same thing. The 'dark sayings' in the Bible are the whispers of the ancients quietly sharing with us all their secret wisdom.

At first glance, you may think that the Bible and ancient mysteries are total opposites. The mysteries talk about the God within you, the Bible is all about the God above you, and man as a powerless sinner. The moment mankind separated himself from God, true meaning of the Word was lost. The voices of the ancient masters have now been drowned out, lost in the chaotic din of self-proclaimed practitioners shouting that they alone understand the Word... That the Word is written in their language and none other.

The basis for all religious wars throughout history.

All the religious texts are revered by Masons and state they all contain the same message. "know ye not that ye are gods?". "The kingdom of God is within you". Abandon the *search* for God, take yourself as a starting place. The only difference between you and God is that you have forgotten that you are divine.

Returning to the Washington Monument, Langdon realised it is a circle within a circle. The great circumpunct stands at the crossroads of America. The Masons realised that the Masonic Pyramid's true purpose was not to reveal the answers; rather to inspire fascination with them.

Always continue to learn, expand and experience the wisdom within. It does not mean you must always seek. This ends when you embrace the Godself within and escape the illusions of your life that tell you otherwise.

The religious world awaits a second coming of the Lord and we must build a real temple to welcome him. The Second Coming is actually that of Man, the moment when mankind finally builds the Temple of his mind. The brain is built in two parts, separated by the arachnoid, a veil of weblike tissue. Temples on your head are called that for a reason. This is the area which must be unveiled.

Temple is code for body. *Heaven* is code for mind. *Jacob's ladder* is your spine, and *manna* is rare brain secretion from the pineal gland created in advanced states of focus.

The ancients already knew many of the scientific truths we are rediscovering. Within a matter of years modern man will be forced to accept what is now unthinkable; our minds can generate energy capable of transforming physical matter. Thoughts have the power to change the world.

It is not our physical bodies that resemble God, it is our *minds*. We are creators and yet naïvely play the role of 'the created'. We see ourselves as helpless sheep herded around by the God who made us. When we realise that we are truly created in the Creator's image, we will understand that we too must be creators. When we understand this fact, the doors will burst wide open for human potential. We will be able to design reality rather than merely react to it.

This is the fundamental principle of igniting the cosmic codes so you may return to the truth of who you are. The Alchemists among you know how to transmute your fears into your power and you stopped doing shadow work on your genius long time ago. The dark disruptors, prodigies in their niche, stop at nothing to be creators of uniquely original solutions on a global scale.

Bear in mind it is not just positive thoughts which affect the world. Destructive thoughts have influence too, it is far easier to destroy than it is to create. The great irony is that the same science that eroded our faith in the miraculous is now building a bridge back across the chasm that created.

There are those who create and those who tear down. Eventually the creators find believers and when the numbers reach critical mass, perception is transformed and a new reality is born. It is scientifically proven that the power of human thought grows exponentially with the number of minds that share that thought.

God is found in the collection of many, rather than in the One. Elohim is the Hebrew word for God. The Old Testament and is plural. God is plural because the minds of man are plural. Out of many, one.

As the morning light hits the aluminium capstone of the monument, it encapsulates the mind of man receiving enlightenment. It descends downwards, heaven moving towards Earth, God connecting to man. This process with reverse in the evening, when the light would claim again from Earth back to heaven. A great prophet once declared of enlightenment; *nothing is hidden that will not be made known; nothing is secret that will not come to light.*

The ancients had praised God as a symbol of our limitless human potential, but that ancient symbol had been lost over time. Until now. There is hope.

Whilst the Monument does get hit a few times a year with lightning, it is rare to get such a great shot of it. On June 4th, 2020, the night before the first eclipse of the season, this image was captured. It felt like a direct call from the Gods. It is time to awaken.

CHAPTER 46

ASTROLOGY: JUNE 2020

All astrologers knew 2020 would be a big year and be kicked off with the Saturn Pluto conjunct in January. Few could see what would unfold subsequently. The difference with this conjunct - something never seen in our lifetime - it was in Capricorn, Saturn's home sign, a Cardinal sign.

This means it is the first sign of a new season to usher in change and new beginnings. Cardinal comes from the word 'pivot', how we pivot from one season to the next. *(NB. note how I have been talking of pivoting from one dimension to another and in the direction of energy flow which has now been reversed.)*

There are three things that set June apart from what we would normally expect at this time of year. Many planetary squares are in play this month which means things will get done. Up to six planets will be in retrograde this month, slowing down to make their influence much more intense.

Venus is in retrograde until 25th June and all relationships could be a little volatile. Do not make big relationship decisions during a Venus retrograde, the energies could well switch back. Mercury goes into retrograde on 18th June (2.30pm ACST) when our thinking shifts and flexibility is required. Being in Cancer it will help us to get back in touch with our emotional nature, useful to help seeing situations from another's viewpoint.

From 5th June to 6th July there will be three eclipses and occur just after the lunar nodes have shifted, though they will be shallow lunar eclipses. However, there is a powerful total solar eclipse in Cancer on 21st June right on the winter/summer solstice. It is the culmination of the 18 months the North Node was here in Cancer. Whatever happens at the turn of a season remains the signature of that season. This is a key time to plant your seeds of intentions for next six months, with a view to fruition on the cusp of the dawning of the New Age.

Solar eclipses are powerful New Moons to usher in major new beginnings, as well as Cancer being a cardinal sign. Things are ready to change and this could be a major catalyst.

(N.B. it was the date I was shown mid-May to do the first portal opening with Isis and the New Moon of my Solar Year).

Mars also returns to Aries on 28th June, which he rules. He gets to come home, put his foot on the gas and let rip. He will spend six to seven weeks here as he does every 22 months, which could be dynamic and volatile. We are also preparing for a Mars retrograde in September in the Cardinal sign of Aries, the first in 32 years. He will remain here until January 2021. He is full steam ahead whilst many other planets are in retrograde.

The end of June I feel will be an incredibly powerful time, new energies will have merged in consciousness by then as well. On 30th June

(3.15pm ACST) Jupiter is conjunct with Pluto. This is the meeting of the highest God of Gods, with the ruler of the Underworld.

I see this is as an exact representation of the meeting that is required to initiate the new energies, bringing opposite together, head-to-head. The energies support you to be focused and driven to succeed in the areas you are most passionate about. With high tensions on both sides of the camp in the world, there could be breakthroughs during this period. It really is the energy to support prosperity along with spiritual self-development.

Zeus in the alchemical texts is Jupiter. He assists with dividing the current and putting them back together once it joins with something else. He provides the lightning to sweep across our minds, moving into unchartered territory.

This conjunction is the middle of three in 2020. The first was 5th April, the last will be 12th December, all happening in Sagittarius. They will reach opposition on 14th and 15th July which could be a potent time for change. The last time they were conjunct was 1955-56 and the next time is 2106-07.

ELON MUSK INTERVIEW

- NOTES

With Joe Rogan, abbreviated note form.

recorded 6/9/18

Elon Musk Interview with Joe Rogan

He is building a tunnel under LA.

Yes, he feels he is an alien (jokingly).

AI – outside of human control. Tempting to use it as a weapon, it will be. Humans using it against each other. A Company is a cyber collective of people and machines.

Google, FB, Insta, Twitter – collectives of humans & machines connecting.

Joe – we are evolving. A percentage of intelligence of humans is not increasing, overtaken by machines. Not created by the human limbic system – the projection of fear and hate are all over the internet.

(limbic system – involved in motivation, emotion, learning & memory. Operates by influencing the endocrine and automatic nervous system. Amygdala – used in evaluation of face in social processing. Limbic system part of the 'old mammalian' part of the brain – is it even required now?)

The success of them is how much limbic resonance they are able to achieve, the more the better. Ie. Engagement. We are constrained by bandwidth and our thumbs

Elon took on a more fatalistic attitude. He tried to get people to slow down and regulate AI, it was futile, for years, no one listened. Regulations are very slow. New tech will cause damage or death, an outcry, years will pass. Insight, then regulations. Many years. The normal length of time. Eg seatbelts. Industry fought it for years.

This timeframe is not relevant to AI, it is too late, will be too dangerous. Out of control countdown now. Singularity, hard to predict beyond the black hole. It will be able to do thousands of years of evolution in minutes. We cannot control it.

Joe – will we merge with it or replace us? E – merge with AI is probably the best, if you can't beat it, join it. Neuralink – to communicate with the AI, as our comms through fingers is too slow. A few months, ultimately trying to – merge with AI where it serves as tertiary cognitive system. Tied in with cortex and limbic system – how can I make the limbic system happy? 26"

AI is an extension of myself, and will be symbiotic, and enough bandwidth – a positive outcome, to radically change our capabilities. Superhuman cognition. Not to do with earning power. Outcome for humanity will be the sum of human will, their desire for their future. People would be massively different to today – cannot yet appreciate the difference. Like having your computer to hand or not. You are already a cyborg – it is an extension of you. Its data rate is so slow between your biological self and digital self. An interface problem.

Then people will get to keep their biological self. They will be able to download it into a new body.

Fatalistic viewpoint, until it just is. Met with Congress, governors and everyone he could. They didn't understand the implications or what to do about it. They could have established a committee to gain insight before it happened and could have developed some rules.

Is the government right to handle? Joe wants Elon to run it. People may ask why would we still need humans? Consider the chimps – calculated cruelty. We have developed. We might be seen as chimps by the AI. But would AI care? We don't care about the chimps. Bonobo's monkeys (just mate). Is our ultimate goal to give birth to something new?

Is technology making us happy? No. take Social Media off the phone to feel better. False image of the true life. Illusional. Comparisonitis to people who are not really happy.

Where is going to next, a VR world? In the simulation. How interconnectedness with this IT be in our life/ at some point it will be indistinguishable between man and machine. The Universe is 13.8bn years old, civilisation 7-8k years old, from first writing.

Games will be indistinguishable from society or civilisation will end. We could be in base reality.

Elon – I don't want to sound too dark, must be optimistic. Pessimism doesn't help. Enjoy the journey. Even if existed as humans forever, the sun would explode our system, just a matter of when. Or transcendence to something doesn't worry about death.

Multi-Universes? Infinite ones? Think most likely. Many simulations, realities. Or multi-verse. They are running on substrate. Which is boring. Our game is interesting. Action movies are so boring to make. CGI and editing make it. If we are a simulation, it is boring outside it.

We are going to create a simulation, could be somewhere else. Notion of a place or where is flawed. Where are you really in virtual reality? what defines of where you are. Your perception. Why do you think you are right now? Who says you are here? Where is here? Could be in a game.

Joe – unquestionable that is the case. As long as we keep going, and evolve, we are here to change reality into something new, into what it wants to become. Create new things. They will intersect – ultimate pathway of infinite ideas and expression through technology. And wonder why we are here?

Take the set of actions most likely to make the future better and re-evaluate. Trend of social awareness higher now because we can express ourselves immediately to each other. Trend is to abandon preconceived notions and discriminations, and move towards kindness.

55' Tesla cars – dances to music. Just fun to create. It's an Easter Egg. People don't know it exists. People don't know about these tricks. Tesla the most fun thing you could ever buy – to maximise enjoyment. Wakes people up if they fall asleep. Discuss other cars.

2D travel system, go 3D – up with flying cars, or down with tunnels. Too much air flow with flying cars. Very noisy. Magnet roads?? Not recommended!! Tunnels. Magnetic tunnel with air sucked out. He has a plan for a plane. Vertical take-off and landings. Not suitable for high-speed flight. Electric planes. Not necessary now.

Electric cars, solar energy, storage of energy. Need sustainable energy asap, playing crazy games with atmosphere and oceans (emotional) fossil fuels so dangerous. We will run out of oil. Must have a sustainable energy source. Stop running a crazy experiment, so dumb.

The more carbon we take out of the ground and put into the atmosphere the more dangerous it is. Ok right now. The momentum to sustainable energy is too slow. 2.5bn trucks & cars, if 100% electric production would still take 25 years to change transportation base.

Too much carbon in air = global warming. A subsidy occurring with every fossil fuel burning thing, plants, air, cars, rockets. The carbon consumption of atmosphere. The environmental cost to Earth, not paid for NOW. Using the reliable sun & store the energy. Northern parts of world have hydropower.

Bottle neck to electric cars? Battery productions make it more efficient, recharge fast. 100 KW/hour does 330 miles. Could be a consideration with solar panels on cars.

Judges and jury are good at judgements.

Fear of danger, we gravitate towards dangers, and worst-case scenario, prejudiced. Toxic, and unbalanced view of the world give people the benefit of the doubt. Most are good people.

What are the bottlenecks in innovation in your biz? What would you change? I wish politicians were better at science, there is no incentive to be. They are in China.

Huawei, phones, no 1, were stopped in US, Samsung no 2, Apple no 3. Rumoured to be controlled by Chinese government. Joe Bloggs does not have secretive stuff to be worried about.

Do you think we will have no security, and no privacy to get next level of tech proficiency? Do they want privacy – everything goes on the internet. Security will be paramount when AI is here. If we become artificially enlightened with this new tech – is privacy important when we are all gods?

What are we hiding? All emotionally related they are concerned about, but that is not what people want to know about. When this interface is fully realised and we become far more powerful & understand irrational thoughts, where will we stand on wealth, social status and need for privacy?

Things will not be important in future. War of ideas. Darwin still here. Different arena.

What keeps you up at night? Running companies, the cars are the hardest. 2 car companies have not gone bankrupt, Ford & Tesla. Barely survived. V close to folding in 2008. Stupidity squared.

Solar tiles for roofs. Hidden. Generally, enough to fuel your house, depending on air con, which should be controllable per room from a distance via app.

The watch that represents human creativity.

2'13'20 Do you consider your role in civilisation? Not many of you like that out there. How do you keep inventing?

Joe dreamt there was 1m Tesla's (people) and dreamt this a few times 1940's – severely advanced. If Tesla invented 100 inventions. What if there were more Musk's?

Elon- not many people would want to be me. Very hard to turn off. Needs to enhance your recovery time. He doesn't notice anything by smoking weed. Not good for productivity. He likes to be useful, and get things done. Likes doing things for other people. You have a gift, creativity engine. Doesn't stop.

He has done meditation. Not drawn to it often, productivity more a drive than enlightenment, like a never-ending explosion, just ideas. Only realised it was not normal when he was 5/6, and others were not getting it. Thought he may be put away when little.

Did you tap into something, you are weird person? Wants to make things someone loves. What would change their interface with life? What can make you feel better?

We are a space bearing race, looking forward to the future to be out there in space. If we are confined to this planet, it is very sad. 2 futures. One, is we are out there in the stars, in our star ships, and see other planets, we are a multi planet species and scope and scale of consciousness is expanded across many civilisation, star systems & planets, we have a great future. We are striving for it.

Cells moving to another location. Is that where we are going? Not definite. Other planets are habitable. Pro humanity.

Lots of people see humanity as a blight. They see struggle and blame others. Love is the answer. Sounds corny because we are scared.

Delete Social Media from phones? IT will increase happiness. He had deleted all but twitter, just for communication. Lack of compassion.

His baby was born 4/5/20 called x-ae-a-12

INTERVIEW WITH JOE ROGAN May 2020

Interview recording

His child was born 4/5/20 in the midst of Covid. Enjoys it more being older. Knows the AI Neural map, and can see it in the baby, learning. AI tries to copy a human brain in some ways, taking the principles. Eg hydrodynamics of fish to a submarine, airplanes do not fly like bird but take off and land like them.

Essential elements of AI neural net are similar to human.

Elon is selling off his material possessions – an attack factor and weigh you down. Going to rent a place. Others define him by his wealth, pejorative to be a billionaire. But if you have created an improvement of life gives you more capital allocation, i.e. earn money. Different to earn from fantastic products rather than stock market, odd to put them into the same category.

US, too big an allocation in finance and law. Need fewer, and more making stuff. Manufacturing used to be highly valued in US, and now looked down upon. People are learning no value in overseas investment.

Doesn't spend time in his houses, not good use of assets. Owns Gene Wilder's house, has his essence. Odd shapes cabinets, doors to nowhere, odd paintings, corridors to nowhere. He stopped it being knocked down. Privacy issues in his house. Then considered building his own dream home. Tony Stark type thing. Or should he spend time getting to Mars? Chose the latter.

Space X & Tesla are most amount of time. Neuralink 5%, Boring company small. Hope to be testing Neuralink on people within the year. Low potential of body's rejection. What is it?

If they get Neuralink installed – implanted in your skull. Electro threads into the brain, stitched up. It can interface anywhere in your brain. Fix eyesight, hearing or anything wrong with your brain, epilepsy, speech, Alzheimer's, body (limbs). Fix quadriplegic back to normal (over time). 1" diameter circle. Skull is 7-14mm. has a battery, Bluetooth, charger, put wiring where it is supposed to go, 2-3mm in. It is a reversible process.

Cognitive benefits. Restores memory, inc muscle memory, fixes the circuits. Specific frequency goes through it.

Full AI symbiosis would require whole skull to have AI interfaces. Would not need to talk. Humans are too dumb to move forward, may as well join AI. Already cyborg with our phones. Humans' data rate is

100bit/sec, too slow to communicate. A computer does a million times faster.

Very difficult to convey concepts, inefficient. Perception & understanding different.

Joe - Begin to create a Universal language (a Rosetta Stone) with no room for interpretation.

E- 5 – 10 years before it replaces our language, best case scenario.

J – Aliens could be us in the future, bigger heads.

E – can have a saved state – to return to original brain and restore into a biological different body, it would be substantially you. Save yourself. Retains you. Like a video recalls everything and can be played back. The brain will be stored like this, can change the past.

J – not comforting that our experiences are not real, not material. E – if this is not real, what is? Everything is electrical signal to your brain to interpret. Hormones are drugs, changes your state. When did consciousness arise? The Universe started off as electrons, before hydrogen and periodic table. Over longer period of time, 13.8bn. hydrogen became sentient. What is the line of consciousness –

J – when do we call it consciousness? See monkey on motorbike steal a baby. Concern for future humans, one day so far from here.to look back.

40" E – I hope consciousness propagates in the future and gets more sophisticated and understands the questions to ask about the Universe.

J- you are making consciousness decisions to make a better you. Always going to look back. This is an accelerated version of that.

E- can only inspire to improve. Tools of physics are powerful. Succeed in being less wrong.

J- people look back sentimentally to simpler times. Scared of monumental change where we won't talk any more, with the crudeness of language. Self-expression of real thought and convey it. Eg a great quote from someone figured something massive out.

Elon makes electronic music. We need the future to be more fun and interesting and gain more than we lose. Civilization through the ages rose and fell. Globalisation – not enough isolation between countries and regions, virus affects all parts of the world. We don't want places to be the same. Need a mind viral immunity. Not getting wrongheaded ideas that go viral.

What if tech can be manipulated to appear real? Later, should bring through massive cognitive change. Productivity will improve by a factor of 10, earn money so quickly especially in capitalist society. Is that a concern?

Huge differences in ability already. Think of corporates – a collective of brilliant minds. Piece it out to different people. Already exists, vastly more capable than an individual.

We don't want AI to decouple from human world. Super sentient AI beyond a level impossible to understand. If you want to be along with the ride you need symbiosis with AI.

Reptile brain, limbic system plus smart brain for concepts. The cortex is much smarter than limbic, but they work together well. AI is a tertiary layer, much smarter than the cortex, and have 3 layers. We have that right now – phones & pc more capable of storage and speed than your brain. Just data rate is slow

J – why does it feel cold and emotionless when I think of AI? E – not how it will be. You already are symbiotic with tech & AI. Neural nets are taking over from regular programming, already connected. E.g. Google voice or Alexa. Image recognition tech.

J- when will you do it? E – will try it straight away. Will work with severe brain injuries first, then expand into other areas. At some stage we are all going to get senile. Have higher functionality later in life. Improve communication speed.

J – do you extrapolate and look at the iterations. E – yes, a lot. It's not going to sneak up on you, requires FDA approval. Be version 10 before a human AI scenario.

J – where do you see it? In 25 years? E – if civilisation is still around. Fragile right now. We could have a whole brain interface. Almost all the neurons connected to the AI extension of yourself. You already have an extension of yourself – pc. Still present on SM after death – an online ghost. More of you would be in the cloud than in your body.

J – civilisation fragile – CV19? E – it has taken over the mind space of the world in 6 months. So much conflicting information.

E saw it play out in China, now in US, like same movie in English. Mortality rate is much less that being shown.

J – deadly to specific people with problems. Below 60 and healthy almost zero. Didn't think this when they started lockdown and didn't know how to correct course.

J – some places, the fear is justified. Most places are not. Hospitals are empty, no other surgeries. People are dying by not getting the work done. And not going because of fear.

J - public perception is shifting, seeing the stats. Not as fatal as we thought.

E – mortality is 10 -50 times lower than first estimated. Hygiene needs to be good no matter what. Stay home if sick. Wear a mask if out and sick, like Japan. Why men get it more because not as hygienic as women.

At some point there will be a pandemic with a high mortality rate affecting young people – this is not it. This is a base practice for that, which will come.

J – it is a wakeup call, a good dry run to appreciate far more resources to understand disease and pandemics, to fund treatments.

E – yes, highly likely we will develop vaccines we didn't have before. To understand viruses way better. Silver linings. He tweeted to Free America Now, it is a war zone.

J – vulnerability means people attack others. Must appreciate the different self-expressions of people. Social media is a misused resource – like monkeys with guns, out of control, no understanding of consequences, the system is abused.

E – in Twitter War Zone. Develop a thick skin, cannot take it personally when they don't know you. 200 ch is so crude. Need a sarcasm flag. Onion might be the best news source.

J- Neuralink will convey pure thoughts with little ambiguity. Titania McGrath – a female avatar combination of faces a parody from British guy. Some people do not understand it's not real – it's fun for others to watch when they don't get it.

E – CNN was annoying and wrong about argument with him about ventilators. What is best source of info out there, truth? Hard to find something good.

J – NY times & LA times favourites, but not trusted. Individual stories. Distorted stories and ignorance, with biases, are they projecting.

J – need individual reports. Matt Taihiki his go to guy. So much open to interpretation, happening in real time. Stage 2 in CA. no one knows the optimum solutions, all speculation.

E – we should be concerned with anything infringing civil liberty & democracy, needs to be treasured.

J- should be a choice what people do. Infantilization of the society. E – violation of rights. Supreme court it would not stand up if taken to court from protesting. Have the right to take a risk.

J- we would be best served protecting those at risk and not penalising the healthy with businesses.

E – strong downside to this. Do what you want not a danger to others.

J – but a risk to others (where is their responsibility?) open up or protect everything.

E – people to have the choice. Sending cheques to people and it will be fine is not true. If we don't make stuff, there is no stuff to have. They are detached from reality. Cannot legislate on this. We will run out.

J – initial thought would kill millions. Was the reaction, right?

E – briefly. Any examination of China would show. Though difficult to get clear info from China. Tesla have many suppliers in China, they know if issues or not. China is back full steam. Tesla have 7000 staff there.

J – are we politizing this? Trump will be opposed whatever he does. Is it a danger?

E – yes been politicized. What can you be made / not made to do – went too far? Country will open up fast in next few weeks. When cv cases reported, decent data required. CVS like cases or actual diagnosis. Was it the primary cause? So much incorrect reporting due to incentives. Need money because no other patients, going bankrupt. Moral quandary. Did they actually have a CV test and was it a significant contributor to their death?

Clear up the data first. Did they have other conditions as well as CV? People die coughing and shortness of breath – the symptoms – without even having CV. Must get out of this loop with clarity of info.

J – a month ago, people were really freaking out. easing up now.

E – parse out the info, clear info. Not what happens with flu, or pneumonia.

J- cigarettes kills 500k a year in US, 61k from flu. Tylenol highest no1 death from drugs. People die from driving. 50 people a die in pools each day. We are vulnerable, we have a finite existence.

E – how many life years did they lose? Average age of CV is older than the average age of death. Keep sick kids away from older people. Immune system not as strong when older.

J – need to boost immune system and get it distributed.

E – put on weight as you get older. It is a big deal. But want to eat good food.

J - Obesity is the no1 factor for CV. But can't talk about that its judgmental. Intermittent fasting 16 hours.

E – eating before you go to bed not good, heartburn. Same with drinking and then going to sleep. Does some PT. Doesn't like exercise. He did martial arts as a kid. Car rollout. Tesla's violate time. The Roadster will do mad things. 0-60 in 1.9 seconds.

THE EMERALD TABLETS

I have highlighted the parts I regard as the most essential to our current decoding in **bold**. My interpretation or room for exploring is *written in italics.*

Original texts of Doreal's translation can be found here:
https://www.crystalinks.com/emerald.html

You can listen to Doreal's text being narrated by Annabelle Drumm on Insight Timer app

Annabelle Drumm - Emerald Tablets of Thoth Pt 1 Of 7

The Emerald Tablets of Thoth were said to have been written at the end of his reign 36,000 BC. Thoth in Egypt is the Atlantian Priest King who could see the fall of Atlantis coming, so led his followers to Egypt. Through advanced consciousness that surpasses the need for death, and ability to rejuvenate his body, he ruled wisely for 16,000 years teaching civil and religious practices, writing, medicine, music, and magic.

Ankh, the gold symbol like the Christian cross represents the flow of energy in the human body. The circle goes from the front to the back of the heart over the head. This is the flow the Egyptians speak of in orgasm, through Egyptian breath. They train themselves to bring the energy up through the torso, out from the front of the heart, over the head and in through the back. So different to how we use energy now, and recycling the energy helps getting stronger. So much energy comes through the hands, and was the reason why we gave hugs, to help give energy through the back-heart chakra where the hands were placed.

Mercradon from the 13D that the writer had channelled told her much of the ancient language of Egypt is hard to write because breath is everything. If you have read the Magdalen manuscript from Tom Kenyon and Judy Sion it also talks about Egyptian training with the breath. So, when you look at the word "Ankh" it is pronounced like the out breath of a yawn.

Dr Michael Doreal translated these texts in 1925. He said there are 12 tablets but only translated 10 of the tablets, as apparently the other two are too powerful for us to handle just yet. We need to learn to become more responsible with our powers before they are revealed.

He has put them into 13 sections and has added two separate tablets on the end to make a total of 15. How Doreal reached the tables in order to translate is not explained. He may have been a channel, a remote viewer, or a teleporter. Mercradon told her there are already several thousand people in the world who can teleport, but do not share this.

If this is the case it is possible Doreal went into the chambers underground and viewed them directly. Otherwise, information may have been sent to him through the channelling. In his introduction Doreal recommends these texts are read 100 times as more wisdom presents itself to you with deeper study.

TABLET 1:
THE HISTORY OF THOTH
THE ATLANTEAN

I Thoth, The Atlantean Master of Mysteries, Keeper of Records, almighty King, Magician, living from generation to generation being about to pass into the halls of Amenti set down for the guidance of those that are to come after these records of the mighty wisdom of great Atlantis.

In the great city of Keor, on the island of Undal, in a time far passed I began this incarnation. Not as the little men of the present age did. The mighty ones of Atlantis live and die but rather from eon to eon did they renew their life in the halls of Amenti where the river of life flows eternally onwards.

100×10 have I descended the dark way that laid into light. As many times have I ascended from the darkness into the light my strength and power renewed. Now for a time I descend, and the men of Khem* shall know me no more. But in a time yet unborn will I rise again. Mighty and potent, requiring an accounting of those left behind me.......

The following text is my modern-day version of the original translation from 1925:

If you betray my teaching, I will cast you down. Do not share the secrets or my curse will fall upon you. Remember my words, I will return and require that what you guard. From beyond time and death I will return, and reward or punish accordingly.

My people were great in the ancient days, beyond the conception of the little people around me. Knowing the wisdom of old, seeking into infinity knowledge that belonged to Earth's youth. We were wise with the children of light, and strong from the eternal fire. My father was the strongest, keeper of the Great Temple, the link between the children of light who inhabited the temple and the races of men who inhabited the 10 islands.

I was taught by the mysteries until I had the wisdom and was brought before the temple leader. The children of Light were not incarnated into physical bodies. I was taught the path to Amenti, the underworld where the great King sits on his throne of light, where he would receive the Key of Life.

I travelled to the stars to gain the wisdom, and only in the mission to find the truth could my Soul be filled. As I lived through the ages, I saw people die and return to life. When Atlantis was submerged under the sea, I led them to Egypt. I calmed them by saying they were messengers of the sun. I sent the sons of Atlantis out to the world to share the wisdom.

I was the keeper of wisdom and the records. I sometimes go into the dark halls of the earth before the Lords of the powers face to face with the dweller. The gateway leads down into Amenti *(the underworld)*. Few have the courage to pass the portal. I used the pyramid to go deep into the earth. **In the apex of the pyramid, I placed the crystal at the apex to draw the forces out of the ethers, concentrating it on the gateway to Amenti.**

I built and left other chambers empty, **though within them hold the keys to Amenti and dark realms.** Hence the pharaohs were buried in the promise they would be shown the mysteries and the way to Amenti.

I built the great pyramid after the pattern of earth force so that it too may remain through the ages, I built my knowledge of magic & science so that it would be here for me when I return. I will incarnate and fulfill the commands of the Dweller. Always look to the light. By right, one with the master, with the All. I will be with you guiding you to the light. I opened the portal to go down to the darkness of night.

TABLET 2:
THE HALLS OF AMENTI

The halls of Amenti lie deep in the earth, bathing in the fire of the infinite all, bound by the force that came from beyond. The Children know only through freedom of bondage could man ever rise from the earth to the sun. Now they descended and took the form of bodies, made from the space dust, living in the world as children of men, like and unlike children of men (i.e. made to look like humans).

The created vast spaces beneath the earth's crust, distant from man, surrounded by power and force, shielded from harm. To live eternally there. 32 children sons of light seeking to escape the bondage of darkness. A powerful flower was created, and the 32 children were filled with this eternal light. Their first created bodies were places there. 100 years out of each 1000 would quicken in the awakening of life.

In the halls of life, the great masters lie sleeping, whilst they incarnate in bodies of men, teaching and guiding men back to light. The wisdom in the halls was not known to the races of men. Beneath the cold fire of life sit the children of light. Times there for when they awaken come from the depths to be lights amongst men, infinite they among finite men. He who has awakened, free, guided by wisdom and knowledge passes from men to the masters of life. There he may dwell as one with masters, free from the bonds of the darkness of night.

In the flower of radiance sit seven Lords from the space times above us helping and guiding through infinite wisdom the pathway through time of the children of men. They are strange in their power, silent and all knowing the life force, different but one, with the children of men.

The watchers of mans' bondage, ready to loosen when the light has been reached. The first and most mighty sits the veiled presence, the Lord of Lords, the infinite nine over the other from each the Lords of the cycle. 3, 4, 5 and 6, 7, 8 each with his mission and power guiding and directing the destiny of man.

(Perhaps this the galactic Council tied in with each of the dimensions, one in charge of each. This is the combined wisdom in the power of 9. 1 & 2 are the realm of earth and man.)

They are free of all time and space. Not of this world but akin to it, elder brothers of man, judging and weighing their wisdom, watching the progress of light among men. I was led by the dweller watching him blend with one from above. Then from him came a voice saying, "how great you are Thoth. You may live forever, as you chose, in what form, for how long. Always stay on path of light, the infinite now. Walk in the world to bring light".

One of the masters led him through the halls containing the mysteries. In the great hall of darkness yet filled with light. On the throne of darkness sat a dark figure veiled, but not dark of the night. The master paused, and introduced Thoth, do not take him to the dark, release his flame into the darkness of night.

The figure unveiled the hall from the darkness of night, where he saw the flame from the darkness of night. Some were flames of fire, others a dim radiance, some faded swiftly. Each surrounded by a dim veil of darkness yet flaming with light which could never be quenched. They were filled with space, light, and life.

A mighty solemn voice declared, "these are lights as Souls amongst men growing and fading, existing forever, changing yet living through death into life. When they have bloomed into flower and reached the zenith of growth in their life, then the veil of darkness shrouding and changing to new forms of life. Steadily upwards throughout the ages growing, expanding into another flame, lighting the darkness with an ever-greater power, quenched yet unquenched by the veil of the night."

So grows the Soul of man ever upwards. Death comes and yet remain not, for life eternal exists in the all. Only I am the obstacle quick to be conquered by the infinite light. The flame that burns forever inwards, flame forth and conquer the veil of the night.

In the midst of the flames the one who grew forever until there was nothing but light. Then the master spoke- see your own Soul as it grows in the light free forever from the Lord of the night. He was led through the mysteries that man will only know when he too is a son of the light.

Thoth knelt before the Lords, and knew he was free from the halls of Amenti, and went to be a teacher of men, so they too can become the lights of men. Free from the dark. You are master of your own destiny, have free will. Shine your wisdom to men which he did. Preserve my record to be a guide to the children of men.

(men can move to the next level of consciousness as they free themselves from the shadow and illusions that keep them separate from the truth of who they are. A path of continuous evolvement through incarnation until they see the depth of mystery of man.)

358

TABLET 3:
THE KEY OF WISDOM

I give my wisdom and knowledge and power freely to the children of men, so they have it too to shine through the world. Wisdom is power and one with each other. Do not be too proud with your wisdom, share with the ignorant as well as the wise. Listen to those with knowledge, for wisdom is all. Do not be silent when evil is spoken for truth. If you overstep the Law, you will be punished for it is through that comes the freedom of men. Do not be in fear and follow your heart.

When you have gained riches follow your heart for they are of no avail if your heart is weary, it is a port of your Soul. Make love your guidance. If someone seeks your guidance, let him express what he requires, be silent as he speaks, do not overbear with your wisdom.

If you are honoured among men be honoured for knowledge and gentleness. Get to know others by spending time with him, rather than asking others' opinions. What you have must be shared. Knowledge is regarded by the Fall as ignorance, and the things that are profitable are hurtful to him and he lives through death. It his food.

A wise man lets his heart overflow but keeps quiet. There are mysteries in the cosmos which fill the world with their light. Those who will be free must separate the material from the immaterial. Just as earth descends to earth, fire ascends to fire and becomes one with fire. He who knows his inner fire will ascend to the eternal fire and dwell in it eternally.

The inner fire is the most potent of force which overcomes other things. Man supports himself only on that which resists, so Earth must resist man, or he would not exist. All eyes see differently, so does the infinite fire always change. Man is a burning bright fire, and never quenched by the night.

I looked into men's hearts by my wisdom and found them in strife. Listen to the wisdom, where do name and form cease? Only in infinite and invisible consciousness, the force of radiance. Man is a star bound to a body until the end. He is freed through his strife through struggle shall his star bloom in new life. He who knows commencement of all things is free from the realm of night.

(go through the hardships of life and be free from the struggle by starting over again and again, free from shadow)

All which exists is only a form of that which does not exist. Everything is passing into another being and you are not an exception. This is Law, and anything that exists outside the Law is an illusion of the senses. Wisdom comes to all. The light has been hidden through the ages, it is time to wake and be wise.

(everything is energy and no escaping from that)

I have been deep into the mysteries of life, seeking for what is hidden. Deep beneath the earth's crust in the underworld lie secrets hidden from men. Through my searching I find men have been living in darkness, the light of the great fire is hidden within. I learnt the great secret wisdom from the Masters, brought from the future of infinity's end.

Seven Lords – the overlords and masters of wisdom. They are not in the same form as men. 3,4,5,6,7,8,9 are their titles of masters of men. Far from the future formless yet forming. They live forever yet not of the living, not bound to life yet free from death. They will rule forever with infinite wisdom. Free from all are the Lords of the All.

11" From them came the logos, forming by afforming, known yet unknown.

Three holds the key to all hidden magic, creator, he of the halls of dead, sending out the power shrouding with darkness, binding the Souls of men. Sending the negative to the Soul to men.

Four who gives the power of life to men, Light is his body, freer of Souls of men.

Five the master of all magic, key to the word which resounds among men.

Six the Lord of light, hidden pathway for the Souls of men.

Seven Lord of the vastness, master of space, and key of the times.

Eight is orders the progress, weighs and balances the journey of men

Nine is the father, forms out of the formless.

Meditate on the symbols I give you; they are hidden keys. Reach upward to light and life. Find in the keys of the numbers I give you the illuminated pathway to move from life to life.

(find in the codes how to transcend and evolve to the next frequency).

Seek the wisdom and look inward, do not shut out the flower of light. Picture in your body through thought of the numbers that led you to life. The pathway is clear to those who have the wisdom, and opens the door to the light, not in darkness of night (shadow).

Take the seven who are, but not what they seem, I have opened my wisdom and follow my path. Masters of wisdom take it to the children of men.

TABLET 4:
THE SPACE BORN

I give my wisdom freely gathered from the time and space of this cycle. Master of mysteries, sun of the morning, living forever. In my childhood I dreamt of mysteries far above men as I watched the starry skies of Atlantis. I grew my longing to conquer the path the stars. I kept seeking the wisdom and following the way, until my Soul broke from its bondage and bounded away. Free from Earth men, I had unlocked the star space and free from shadow.

(ie, keep clearing the illusions until you are free of human conditioning and can live freely as your Soul is designed to do)

Now I sought wisdom beyond the knowledge of finite man. I travelled into infinity, the planets appeared strange, great and gigantic beyond dreams of men. I found beauty working among them, as I did working among men. I rested on a planet of beauty where harmony resided. Shapes moving in order, majestically. Ordered equilibrium, symbols of the cosmic life unto Law.

I passed many planets with men on their worlds, all at different stages of evolvement. Each and all of them were struggling upwards, moving through darkness to gain the light. Know that light is your heritage, darkness is a veil. Your heart awaits the freedom, it contains the light. It is up to you to unlock it.

Some have conquered the ether, free of space yet still men, using the force which is the foundation of all things. They constructed a planet from the force which flows through everything, changing the ether into form as they willed. It surpassed all science of the races, steeped in wisdom of the stars. Great cities were created from the primal element, the base of all matter, the ether. They had conquered the ether and freed themselves from bondage of toil, formed in their mind and then it was created.

Men are truly space born, a child of the stars. Your bodies are revolving around your central suns. Yet when you have gained all wisdom you will be free to shine in the ether, one of the suns to light outer darkness, one of the spaces born grown into light.

Just as stars lose their light and return to the great source, eventually so does your Soul move on, leaving behind the darkness of night. You were formed from the ether, filled with Source brilliance. Lift your flame from the darkness and be free. Travel through space time and be free. Now you can pursue wisdom.

I passed a plain not known by wisdom, extension beyond all we know. I was happy, I was free. Listen to my wisdom, you will be free. You are not of the earth, but of the infinite cosmic light. You do not know your heritage that you are the light. I give you the knowledge so you can find the path of freedom. I strived to tread the path that leads to the stars. Know how to free yourself from your toils, become one with the light and stars again and escape below. Through wisdom, into infinity.

All space is ordered, only by order are you one with the All. Order and balance are the Law of the Cosmos. Follow these laws to become one with the All. Be open to the flower of life by extending your consciousness out of the darkness, though time and space into the silence where you must linger until you are free from desire and longing to speak in the silence.

(be still in the meathook moment, and do not speak)

Conquer the silence, stop eating until we conquer the desire for food which is bondage for Soul. Then lie down in the darkness, centre into consciousness and be free of shadow. Place the image you desire in your heart and vibrate back and forth with your power. Free your Soul, as the cosmic flame moves in harmony and order in space unknown to man. Speak with music, singing with colour. You are the spark of the flame, listen to the voice to be free. Consciousness free is fused with the cosmic, one with the order and low with the all.

Out of the darkness shall come a symbol of light, pray for the wisdom and coming of light to the all.

When free your Soul, the darkness is gone, and can always find wisdom, and move to realms of the light, move in order and harmony. Seek yourself and find my key of wisdom.

TABLET 5:
THE DWELLER OF UNHO

I dream of Atlantis, lost in memory. Mighty in power ruling the earthborn. The master, light of the Earth, lives in the temple of Unho. He is a master of a cycle beyond us, not of earthborn bodies, but beyond men. He was never one with men. He showed the path of attainment of light, mastering darkness leading the mans' Soul upwards to light. He divided the kingdom into sections.

There were 10 sections ruled by men, upon another built a temple not built by man, out of the ether by his mind. It was dark like the space time, **black yet not black.** Deep in its heart was the essence of light. Shaped by the word of the Dweller into form. Includes great chambers filled with wisdom.

He was formless but was formed in the image of man. He lived among them but not of them. He chose three from among the people to be his gateway. They were his links to Atlantis, and carried his messages from Atlantis to the Kings of men.

He brought others forward to teach them wisdom which could be taught to men, the wisdom of men. They must be **taught for 15 years**; only then would they have the understanding required to bring light to men. The temple became the dwelling place for the master of men. I was always seeking and striving, until one of the three bought me to the light.

He brought to me the commands of the Dweller, called into the light, and brought me before him in the Temple. I felt the light flowing through me in waves. You have sought for so long, and all Souls who release their ties with earthly ways will be free from the bondage. You have moved towards the light and will dwell here as the Keeper of records gathered by wisdom, instruments to the light from beyond. Ready to do what is needed, preserver of wisdom throughout the ages of darkness that will come fast on men.

Live here and gather the wisdom and mysteries. I ask for the wisdom so I can be a teacher of wisdom to men and be free. The great master said, "Age after age you will live through your wisdom, whilst I hold the light ready to come whenever you call. Go and learn greater and evolve".

Thoth stayed in the temple until one with the Light. He then followed to path to the star plains and deep into the underworld. He learnt the law, **so above as below, the Law that balances the world.** The underworld chambers have been hidden for ages from men. They were unveiled before him with more wisdom, and realised all is part of the all, greater than all that we know.

I searched through the ages and found more mysteries. Looking back, wisdom is boundless and grows throughout the ages, one with infinities greater than all. There was light in Atlantis, yet darkness was hidden in all. Some men who had reached great heights fell from the light into the darkness. They became proud of their knowledge and status and went into the forbidden. They tried to go below and bring up the deep hidden wisdom. He who goes below must have balance or he is bound by lack of light. They opened through knowledge pathways forbidden by man.

The Dweller saw this, and that opening the gateway would bring a great woe to Atlantis. He brought his Soul back to his body and called the 3 messengers and gave the command to shatter the world. The Dweller returned to the underworld and called upon the powers of the seven Lords to change the world's balance. So, Atlantis sank beneath the waves, shattered the gateway that had been opened. Only Unho was not shattered and part of the island of the sons of the Dweller.

(the pole shifts ?? – which is about to happen)

The Dweller preserved the lights to be the guides for lesser men. He gave Thoth the commands, to take all the wisdom, records and magic and teach men, and reserve the records until light grows upon men, then light shall be all through the ages, hidden but found by enlightened men.

Thoth was given authority by the Dweller to give or take away the power and told to flee with the chosen children to Egypt. He travelled by spaceship with the records and instruments. He left behind the three and the dweller deep in the halls beneath the temple. Closing the pathway to the Lords of the cycles. Though this path to Amenti (the halls) shall be open to those who know.

I raised the Egyptians to the light. I buried my spaceship for when man may be free. I built a marker – a Lion like a man *(the Sphynx?)* it will be brought forth when required. Far in the future invaders will come from out of the deep. Then those with the wisdom will bring the spaceship to life with ease. Deep beneath the image lies my secret. Search and find the pyramid I built. Each to the other is the keystone, each is the gateway that leads to life. Follow the key I leave behind, seek and the doorway to life will be yours.

Seek in the pyramid deep in the passage that ends in a wall. Use the key of the seven and open the pathway will fall. I have given you my wisdom and way.

TABLET 6:
THE KEY OF MAGIC

Listen to the wisdom of magic and the powers forgotten. In the early days of man, warfare began between darkness and light. Man are filled with both. Light fills the Soul. It is the eternal struggle with a fierce fight. Some always struggle to find the light, whilst others are filled with brightness have conquered the night. All know this battle.

When the Suns came to Earth and found it filled with darkness, that is when the struggle started. Many were filled with darkness with only a feeble flame of light. Some were masters of darkness and sought to bring all into darkness and fill them with night. Fiercely fought the masters of light. Dark magic enshrouded Souls with darkness. **Formed brothers of darkness, found and not found by man. They continued to work in the dark, used their power to enslave and bind the Soul. Unseen, man in his ignorance calls them from below.**

(describes the current Deep State perfectly – starting to be revealed to man. Always existed as moguls of capitalism, heads of politics, church and state. The individuals who are moving towards collective control and removal of freedom of rights as we speak)

Dark is the way of them, not of the night *(ie. Of Deep shadow, not true dark feminine energy)*

They have gained their power in ways unseen by man, into man's mind space. Then they close their veil of the night around the Soul, kept in bondage. Mighty are they in the forbidden knowledge that is one with the night.

Listen to the warning. Be free from this bondage of night, so not give your Soul to darkness, always keep turned to the light. You are not seeing your sorrow comes from this veil. Keep striving upwards. The brothers of darkness seek those who have been down the pathway of the light for they know they have greater power to bind the children of light to darkness.

Look at the words and question if they come from light when told to you. For many walk in dark rightness and yet are not the children of the light.

(the dictatorship of governments, corporates and big Pharma telling us what to do).

It is easy to follow their path, but listen, light only comes to those who strive. The path to wisdom and light is hard. You will find mountains and stones in your way. But know those who overcome, they will be free to the pathway of light. Light must conquer and darkness and night be banished from light.

(this is all about the shadow and conditioning of man. It does not refer to the eternal darkness – which Thoth says resides in the underworld perhaps??)

Heed this wisdom. When darkness is banished and veils are ended, out will flash the light from the darkness, the brothers of light. Seeking to free men from the night, they have mighty & potent power, know the laws the planets obey. They work in harmony and order freeing the man's Soul.

Secret and hidden too, not known to men. Ever have they fought the dark brothers conquering time without end, yet always light shall be the master in the end. The masters of the sun power, whilst unseen, are the guardians of men. Open to all, to the lightwalkers. These masters are free of the constructs of life, of the dark halls. Like and unlike men, they have never been divided (i.e. no separation). They have always been one with the eternal throughout all space since the beginning of time.

Up they come in the oneness, up from the first space, formed and unformed. Gave to man the secrets to protect from all harm, to those who travel the path of light, free from the bondage. He must conquer the formless and shapeless, and the phantom of fear. He must understand all the secrets and carry them through the darkness as he moves towards his goal of light. Great obstacles will be in the way but will still carry on.

Sun is the symbol of the light at the end of the road. Now I will give you my secrets, to meet the dark power. To meet and conquer the fear of the night. Only by knowing can you conquer and have light.

I now give you this wisdom to conquer the dark fears and the dark brothers of night. When you have a feeling being drawn to the dark gate, question whether the feeling comes from within. If the darkness is within, banish those thoughts from your mind. Send the vibration through the body until free. Start the wave force in the brain and through the body.

But if you find it is not your heart that is darkened, be sure that a force is being directed to you. Only by knowing can it be overcome, and only by wisdom can you be free, and have the power. In the midst of darkness, place yourself in the centre of a circle, and be free of the darkness. Raise your hands to draw in the light to yourself, to free yourself with these words:

"fill my body with spirit of life, and of light. Come from the flower that shines through the darkness, from the halls where the 7 Lords rule. name them by name, 3,4,5,6,7,8,9 and call them to aid me. Free me and save me from the darkness of night. Untanas, Quertas, Chiertal and Goyana, Huertal, Semveta, Ardal."

by their names know you will be free from the binds of the brothers of night. Can be free by vibration. Help your brother to escape too. Thoth gives his magic to us, to dwell on the path of light. You may be the sun on the cycle above.

(the portals to the seven Lords are through our chakras)

TABLET 7:
THE SEVEN LORDS

Open your mind to my wisdom. The pathway of life is dark, full of pitfalls in your way. Keep seeking the wisdom and move towards the light. Keep opening your Soul to the cosmic and let it flow in. Light is eternal and darkness is fleeting. As light fills your being, darkness will disappear. Gain the light of all wisdom are you one with the infinite goal, to be as One with the light.

(the light to which he refers is the purest lightest light of the dark, and the darkness he refers is the shadow elements which are illusions, and not permanent. It is the false lens of the Light Grid which sees this in reversal and confused on the very definition of it. The All is the eternal dark energy)

Throughout all space light is prevalent. Continue to seek the light, even if hidden and buried. Even in the finite, the infinite exists, flowing through all things. The infinite brain is in all. In all space there is only one wisdom, which is one in the one. All that exists comes from the light and the light comes forth from the All. Everything created is based upon order, Law rules the space where the infinite dwells. From the equilibrium came the great cycles moving in harmony towards infinity's end.

Infinity itself will pass into change. All is of all ever more. Through time you can pursue wisdom and find forever lighter on the way.

A long time ago in the Halls of Amenti stood before the Lords of the cycles. Later I was free to enter their conclave at will. Wisdom was brought from the cycles above. They manifest in this cycle as guides of man to the knowledge of all. Seven Lords speaking through words through me to men.

I stood before them many times, did not hear words with sound. Seek the wisdom in the heart of the flame where you gain knowledge about power. To be one with the flame, be at one with your own hidden flame. Thoth gained wisdom about new path from the Lords, from above, knowledge of operation and the learning of Law, the order of All.

The Lords said "we come from far beyond time and space, from infinity's end. When all of you were formless, we were formed, not as men, but we once were. We were created out of the Law of order from the great void. Understand all that is formed is truly formless and formed only by your eyes.

Thoth you are free to travel on the path upwards until all becomes one. We were formed after our order. 3,4,5,6,7,8,9 are the cycles in which we descend from into man, each having a duty to fulfill. Each having a force to control. Yet we are one with the Soul of our cycle. We are still seeking a goal, beyond mans' conception. Infinity extends into a greater than all. There in a time which is not a time we shall all become one with a greater than all.

Time and space are moving in circles. Know their Law and you too shall be free to move through the cycles past the guardians at the door."

Lord 9 spoke. "Eons have I existed, not knowing life or death. Far in the future life and death will be one with the all. Each perfected by balancing the other that neither exists in the oneness of all. For men of this cycle the lifeforce is rampant but life in its growth becomes one with its all.

I am here in your cycle and in the future of time. Time does not exist in my world, we are formless. We do not have life, yet we exist, fuller and greater than you. Man is bound to a mountain though we in our cycle are always free of this. When you have progressed into a cycle that lengthen above, life itself will pass to the darkness and only essence of Soul will remain."

Lord 8 then spoke. "all you know is still small. You have not yet touched upon the great. Far out in space, I came from the Light Beings into the Light, I was formed but not as you, just as a body of light. I am not life or death, yet I am a master of all that exists. Find the path through the barriers, and travel towards the light".

Lord 9 spoke again. "Find the path to beyond, it is not impossible to grow to a consciousness above , for when 2 has become one, and one has become the All, you will know the barrier has lifted and you are free. Then you can be free of the road and become formless."

Thoth learnt the way through the ages towards the All. Wait to hear when it calls.

"all light, all pervading, one with all and all with one, flow to me through the channel. Enter so I may be free, make me one with the all. Shining from the blackness of night, let me be free of all space and time, free from the veil of the night, I a child of light, free from the darkness of night I command to be".

I am formless to the Light Soul yet shining with light. I know the bonds of darkness must shatter before the light. Now I give this wisdom so you can be free. To live in the light, keep facing it, where your Soul resides as a child of light. Turn your thoughts inwards, not outwards and find the Soul light within. Know you are your own master all else is brought from within. Grow to realms of brightness, keep the thought of Light. Know you are one with the Cosmos, the flame, the child of the light.

I have given you the warning, know the brightness runs through your body. Ignore the dark brothers and stay in tune through the Soul to the light.

TABLET 8:
THE KEY OF MYSTERY

I have given you my knowledge and light. Receive my wisdom bought from space plains above and beyond. I am not a man; I am free of dimensions and plains. In each I take on a new body and morph into a new form. Now I know the formless is all there and can be formed. The wisdom of the seven is great, they are mighty. They manifest through their power filled by force from beyond.

Make these words your own. Find the fullness, mystery is hidden knowledge. Once you know, you will unveil to find the deep buried wisdom and be master of darkness and light. The mysteries are deep, search through the keys of my wisdom, and you will find the way. The gateway to power is secret yet if you attain it you will receive. Look to the light, open to receive. Overcome the night and darkness. Man is in process of changing to forms that are not of this world. He will grow on the fullness of time a plain on the cycle above. You must become formless before you are one with the light. I am showing you the way of attainment to becoming one with the light

Search the mysteries of Earth's heart and the laws that exist. Holding the stars in their balance by the force of primordial mist, seek the flame of Earth's life. Follow the **3 cornered pathway** until you are a flame. **Speak in words without voice to those who dwell down below.** Man is complex, of earth and of fire, let your flame shine brightly. Be only the fire. Wisdom is hidden in darkness, when lit by the flame of the

Soul. Find the wisdom and become without form. Only by striving and light into the brain.

(connect with the Ancient ones in the underworld energetically not through words. What is three cornered pathway? The Triskelion?).

I am speaking of Ancient Atlantis, and speaking of the coming of children of shadows, out of the deep they were called by the wisdom of earth men, for the purpose of gaining great power. Far in the past before Atlantis, there were men who **used Dark magic** who called up beings from way below. They were of another vibration existing unseen by men. They could only **exist through blood** could they live in the world. In the past they were conquered. But some remained hidden in plains unknown by man. They sometimes appear when blood was offered and came to dwell among men.

(fits with the requirement of rituals)

In the form of man but only to look at, serpent headed when the glamour was lifted. They crept into the councils. Slaying by their arts, the chiefs of the kingdoms, taking their form and ruling our men. Only by magic could they be discovered, only by sound could their faces be seen.

They sought to destroy man and rule in his place. But know the magic masters were strong and could life the veil of the serpent and send him back to his place. They taught man the secret, a word that only man can pronounce. They lifted the veil quickly. Yet beware the serpent still lives and opens at times to the world.

They sometimes walk among men, where the rights have been said. As time passes, they will take the semblance of men, called by the master who knows the white or the black, but only the white master may control and bind them while in the flesh.

Do not seek the kingdom of shadows where evil resides, for only the master of brightness shall overcome the shadow of fear.

Fear is an obstacle, master it. Heed my wisdom, do not seek shadow and light will appear. I have been to the end of space of this cycle, and I glimpsed the hounds of the barrier, beyond which he would pass into the timeless realms. Thoth could sense the guardians of cycles who only move through angles still bound by the curved dimensions. The hounds of the barriers who follow consciousness to the limits of space.

Do not escape through injury to your body for they follow your Soul through angles. Only the circle will give you protection from the angles. In the past, Thoth approached the barrier and saw the formless forms beyond. The hounds sniffed him out and sent warning bells which moved through space towards his Soul which could be heard from cycle to cycle.

I fled from there, though the always pursued me. They continue to search out the Souls who want to know what lies beyond the barrier, who attempts the beyond. The devourers followed through the angles to devour my Soul. The Soul who dares the barrier may be held in bondage by the hounds from beyond time until the cycle is completed and left behind when the consciousness leaves.

Thoth came back into his body and into circles and lost the pursuers in the circles of time. Even when free form my body I must remain cautious not to go through angles. Know these hounds, for they only move through angles and never curves of space. Then you can escape them, otherwise they will pursue you through angles.

Few have succeeded in passing the barrier into the light which lies beyond. If you hear the bell ringing in your body, come back to your body and create a circle which cannot be penetrated. When in the form you have lived in, use the cross and the circle combined. Open your mouth and use the word to free yourself. Only the one full of light can hope to pass the guards of the way, then he must move through strange curves and angles formed in direction not known to man.

Do not attempt to pass the guards on the way, instead focus on gaining the light and be ready to pass on the way. Light is the ultimate end, seek it.

TABLET 9:
THE KEY TO FREEDOM
OF SPACE

I am teaching you how to banish the darkness and find light. It is for you to find the pathway to eternal life and seek to become a light of the world. Become a vessel of light, lift your eyes to the Cosmos, speak in the words of the dweller. Sing the song of freedom and of the Soul. Create the higher vibrations to make you one with the whole. Blend with the Cosmos. Be a channel of Order, a pathway of Law to the world.

You are shining your light through the shadow of flesh, be free of the darkness before coming as one with the Light. Your dark shadows surround you; you must rise and go to the plains that surround you. Look around and see your light reflected. Even in the dark, the light can be seen through the veil. Always seek the wisdom and do not let your body betray you. Keep on the path of light, shun the dark path.

Know that wisdom is lasting existing since the All Soul began. Creating harmony by the Law that exists. Hear these teachings about the past, I will share the lost wisdom hidden in the darkness. Know you are the Ultimate of all things, only the knowledge of this is forgotten, lost when man was cast into darkness and bound.

Long ago, I left my body and wandered through the ether, circled the angles which keep man prisoner. Know you are a spirit, your body is nothing, your Soul is everything. Do not let your body be a prison, cast it off and be free and be a true light.

When you are free from darkness and move in space, you will know space is not boundless but truly bounded by angles and curves. Know that all that exists is only an aspect of greater things yet to come. Matter is fluid and flows like a stream constantly changing from one thing to another.

All through the Ages this knowledge has existed, unchanged yet buried in darkness. Never been lost but forgotten by man. Know there are others out there as great as yourself, interlaced through the heart of your matter yet separate in a space of their own.

In a time long forgotten I opened the doorway into the other spaces and learned of their secrets sealed. The mysteries are concealed deep in the essence of matter.

There are nine interlocked dimensions and nine cycles of space. Nine diffusions of consciousness, and nine worlds within worlds. Nine Lords of the cycles that come from above and below.

Space is filled with sealed ones because it divided by time. When you find the key to time space you will unlock the gate. Know throughout the time space consciousness exists though it is hidden from our knowledge. The keys are within yourself, for man is the gateway of mystery and the key is one with the One.

Seek within the circle, use the word I shall give and open the gateway within, and you will live. Men think you live, but it is life within death. For just as you are bound to your body you believe life exists. Your Soul is space free and really alive. Everything else is a bond from which to be free.

Do not think man is earthborn even if he comes from Earth. Man is a light born spirit though without knowing this he cannot be free. Darkness captures the Soul. Only the ones who are seeking can ever hope to be free. Shadows around are falling, shine your Soul light forward to fill the darkness. Remember you are the son of Light and you can be free. Move out of the shadows, fill with the glory of light through your Soul.

This is the key to all wisdom; you contain all time and space within you. The great light from the cosmos can fill your body and never be quenched by men.

I have been seeking wisdom and knowledge not known to man for a long time. I went way into the past to when time began. I keep seeking the new knowledge though I realised only the future held the key to the wisdom I thought. I went to the Halls to seek this knowledge and ask the Lords the way to this wisdom.

"Where is the wisdom of All?" I asked.

The Lord of the Nine responded. "Free your Soul from your body and come with me into the Light." Which Thoth did, and stood before the Lord in the flame of life.

He was seized by a great force beyond man's knowledge I was cast through the abyss of space unknown to Man. I saw the mouldings of Order from the chaos and angles of night. I saw the light spring from order and heard the voice of the light. I saw the flame of the abyss casting order and light. I saw order spring from chaos and light giving life.

Then I heard a voice. "Hear this. The flame is the source of all things, containing all things in potentiality. The order that sent forth light is the word. From the word comes life and the existence of all. Life within you is the word. Find the life within you and find the powers to use with the word."

I watched the light flame pouring from the essence of fire. I realised life by order and man is one with the fire. I came back to my body and stood with the nine again. I listed the voices of the cycles who vibrated with the powers as they spoke,

"Know Thoth life is by the world of the fire. The life you seek is but the word in the world as a fire. Seek the path to the word and you will have these powers."

Then I asked to be shown the path and for it to be given to the wisdom, the way to the word.

The Lord of the Nine answered, "through order you will find the way. You saw the word came from the chaos and the light came from the fire. Look in your life for this order, balance and order your life. **Quell all the chaos of the emotions and you will have order in life.** Order brought from the chaos will bring you the word of the Source. Will the power of cycles and make a force from your Soul that freewill extends through the ages a perfect sun of the Source.

I listened and thanked him. I had always sought order so I may find the word. Know who attains it must ever be in order for use of the word through this order has never and can never be.

Take these words and seek to conquer this order and you will be one with the word. Make the effort to gain the light and to be one with the Sun and the light. Hold the thought in the oneness of light with the body of man. Know that all is order from chaos, born into light.

TABLET 10:
THE KEY OF TIME

Take heed of this wisdom and the mysteries of space. Bring order and harmony in space. Know that all exists has only been because of the Law. When you know it, you will be free. I have been through strange spaces and time, all was revealed. Know the mystery is only knowledge unknown to man. When you have plunged into the heart of the mystery, the knowledge and wisdom will be yours.

Understand time is the secret to be free of this space. I seek eternity's end. Know that ever before me receding shall move the goal I am seeking to attain. Even the Lords of the cycles know that even they have not yet reached the goal. **For with all their wisdom they know Truth ever grows.**

In a past time I asked the Dweller about the mystery of time and space. I asked, "what is time?"

He answered, "in the beginning there was a void, a timeless, spaceless nothingness. Into the nothingness came a purposeful, all pervading thought. It filled the void. Nothing existed, only force, a movement a vortex of vibration of the purposeful thought that filled the void."

I asked if this thought was eternal. He responded, saying. In the beginning there was eternal thought. For thought to be eternal, time must exist. So, in the all-pervading thought grew the Law of Time.

Time which exists through all space, floating in a smooth rhythmic movement, is eternally in a state of fixation. Time does not change, but all things change in time. **For time is the force that holds the events separate each in its own proper place. Time is not in motion, but you move through time as your consciousness moves from one event to another.** Yet time but exists all in all an eternal One existence. Even in the time you are separate you are still One in all existing times.

I pondered this and wanted to explore and the mysteries of time. **Time moves through strange angles yet only through curves could I hope to obtain the key that would give me access to the time space. I found only by upwards and to the right could I be free from the time of movement.**

I came out of my body moved in the movement that changed me in time. I saw a strange sights and mysteries. I saw men's beginning, learned from the past that nothing is new. You must find the pathway through the spaces formed in time. Do not forget that light is the goal. Know eternal brightness will find your Soul hid in light.

I know the true flame exists in your Soul, hidden in darkness. Light is life, nothing can exist without it. In all formed matter the heart of light always exists, even when bound by darkness.

Once I stood on the Halls of Amenti and heard the Lords voices saying in tones, powerful and mighty words. They chanted the songs of the cycles, the words that opened the path to beyond. I saw the path opened into the beyond and saw the movements of the cycles. Source can convey vast thought, **even in infinity is moving on to unthinkable end.**

(into the 15D?)

388

I saw the cosmos is order and part of a movement that extend to all space. A party of an order of orders, constantly moving in a harmony of space. I saw the wheels of cycles and I knew all that is being is growing to meet another being in a far-off grouping of space and time.

I then knew the power in words that would open the hidden plains from man; **even in words lies hidden the key to open both above and below.**

Listen to this word, use it and you will find power in its sound. Say **"ZIN-URU"** * and you will find power. You must understand man is of light and vice versa.

Hear the strangest mystery, all space is filled with worlds within worlds, one within the other yet separate by law. Once in my search for buried wisdom I opened the door which barred them from man. I called through beings who were 'fairer than the daughters of men'. I called her from out of the space to shine her light on the world of men.

I used the drum of the serpent, with the purple and gold robe, a crown of silver, around me the circle of cinnabar *(the ore of mercury)* **shone, I lifted my arms and cried the invocation to open the path, I cried to the Lords.**

"Lords of the Two Horizons, Watchers of the Treble Gates, stand one at right, one at left, as the star rises to his throne and rules over his sign".

The dark prince of ARULU opened the gates of the dim hidden land and released her who he kept imprisoned.

"Listen dark Lords and shining one, by their secret names which I know and can pronounce, listen to them and obey thy will."

I lit the flame of my circle and called her in the space plains beyond. The daughter of light could return from Arulu. "Seven times and seven times have I passed through the fire. I have not eaten or drunk. I call the Lady of Light from Arulu the realms of EKERSHEGAL.

The dark Lords of Arulu rose and parted as the Lady of Light came forward. She was now free from the Lords of the night, free to live as a child of Light.

Know that magic is knowledge and is the only Law. Do not be afraid of the power within you, for it follows the law just as the stars in the sky do. To be without knowledge, wisdom is magic and not of the Law. It is through knowledge you can move further to the Sun.

Follow me and learn of my magic. You can have the force if you chose. Do not fear the path that leads to the knowledge, instead shun the dark road. Light is for the taking, be free. Your Soul is only bound by your fears you hold so dear.

Open your eyes and see the great Sunlight, it is yours. The Lord of the dark Arulu is **FEAR, it does exist and is created by those who are bound by their fears.**

Escape these shackles and walk in the light of the glorious day, do not turn to the darkness. Man is only what he believes - that he is of the dark or of the light.

Use the word and you will find power wisdom and light to walk in the way. Seek and find the key I have given, and you will always be a child of the Light.

ZIN-URU is the memory to remember the truth of Full Awareness, that you were meant to be free and not a slave. A symbol represents our "great spirit" transmuting into form. It symbolises birth/rebirth/new life.

TABLET 11:
THE KEY TO ABOVE
AND BELOW

Listen children of Khem, know that I knew your fathers from a long time ago, I have been deathless through the ages and lived amongst you since your knowledge began. I hold all the knowledge and wisdom known to man since the ancient days. I have been the keeper of these secrets of the Great Race, I hold the key that leads to life. If you listen to these words you will be lifted out of the darkness into the light.

When I first came to you far in the past you were living in rock caves. I lifted you with the power and wisdom until you shone amongst men. I found you without knowing you. You were not much more advanced than beasts. I fanned the flames of your consciousness until you became men.

I will now share the ancient knowledge beyond the thought of man. The Great Race has more knowledge than Man's. we gained our wisdom from the star born races. IT comes down from the masters of wisdom who are as far beyond me as I am of you. Use this wisdom to become free.

In the pyramids I build are the Keys that shall show you the way of life. Draw a line from the great image I built to the apex of the pyramid, built as a gateway. Draw another line opposite in same angle and direction. Underneath this intersection you will find the **underground entrance to the secrets hidden before** you were men.

This is an image of a zero-point energy pyramid

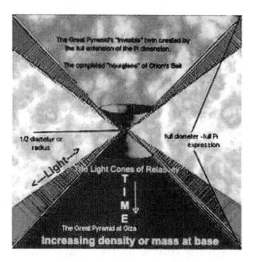

I will now tell you about the mystery of cycles which are infinite and appear strange to the finite. **There are nine cycles, nine above and fourteen below**, moving in harmony to the place of joining that shall exist in the future of time.

The Lords of the Cycles are units of consciousness sent from the others to unify this with the ALL. They are the highest of consciousness of all the cycles, working in harmony with the Law. **In time they will all be perfected, having none above and none below,** but all One in perfected infinity, a harmony of all in the Oneness.

In the Halls of Amenti sit the seven Lords of the Cycles, with another, the Lord of below. Know that in infinity there is neither above nor below, there is always a oneness of all when complete. I have often stood before the Lords drinking upon their wisdom and filling my body and Soul with their light.

They explained to Thoth how the cycles and Laws caused their existence. The Lord of the Nine said to me, "Thoth, you are great amongst Earth children yet there are mysteries which exist which you do not know about. You know you came from a space-time below this and will travel to a space-time beyond. But you know little of the mysteries within them and of the wisdom beyond. **Even as a whole in this consciousness you are only a cell in the process of growth.**

The consciousness below you is ever-expanding in ways that are unknown to you, in different ways to how you grew. Know it grows as a result of your growth but not in the same way as you grew. Know the growth you have had created a cause and effect. No consciousness follows the path of those it, or it would be repetition and vain.

Each consciousness must follow its own path within the cycle to the ultimate goal. Each plays its part in the Plan of the Cosmos, in the ultimate end. The farther the cycle the greater its knowledge and ability to blend the Law of the whole.

(you cannot just follow Thoth's experience of expansion; you must find your own unique path through each of the cycles)

Those in the cycles below us are working in the minor parts of the Law, whilst those of us in the cycle to infinity are building a greater Law. Each is playing their part and must complete their work in their own way. The cycle below you was only formed for a need that exists. **Know that the fountain of wisdom which creates the cycles is eternally seeking to gain new powers.**

Know that knowledge is only gained by practice and wisdom only comes from knowledge, and that's why the cycles are created. Meaning they are for gaining knowledge for the Plane of Law that is the Source of the All.

The cycle below is not really below just in a different space and time, where they test lesser things of consciousness than what you know. Just as you are working on greater, know there are those above you working on other laws.

The difference between the cycles is only the ability to work with Law. For we who have been in cycles beyond where you are came from Source and have the **ability to travel through time-space** to use the Laws of the Greater that are far beyond man's conception. Anything below you is just a different operation of Law.

You will find the same above or below you, it's all part of the Oneness which is at the Source of the Law. The consciousness below you is part of your own just as you are part of mine.

Compare the cycles of life from birth to death. As the child grows, he gains more knowledge, which, with wisdom, comes with the years. It is the same for the cycles of consciousness, children are in different stages of growth. Yet all are from the wisdom of Source and will return there."

The Lord of the Nine stopped talking and sat in silence for a while, before saying,

"Thoth, we have been in the Halls for a long time guarding the flame of life. We also know we are still part of our Cycles and reach into them and beyond with our vision. **We know that nothing else matters except the growth we can gain with our Soul.**

Know the flesh is fleeting. Things men count as great mean nothing to us. What we seek is not of the body, only the perfected state of the Soul. **When men understand the progress of Soul is all that matters,** they can be free from all bondage, and free to work in a harmony of Law.

Always aim for perfection yet know that nothing is perfect."

I allowed these words to sink into my consciousness. Now I seek even more wisdom so that I may be perfect in Law with the All.

Soon I go to the Halls to live been the cold flower of life *(the underworld of Souls departed)*. I will never see those I taught again tho I live forever in the wisdom I taught.

All that man is, is because of his wisdom, all that he shall be is the result of his cause. Become greater than the common man and always be filled by Light. You must make effort to grow upward in the planes. **Be the master of your life yet never be controlled by the effects of your life.**

TABLET 12:
LAW OF CAUSE AND EFFECT

Listen to me, Thoth the Atlantean. I have conquered the Law of time-space and have knowledge of the future of time. I know that as man moves through space-time, he will become one with the all.

Know the future is an open book to those who can read. It is not fixed or stable but varies as cause creates an effect. So, ensure the effects create more effects to evolve. The future is never fixed, it **follows man's free will** as it moves through time-space toward the goal where a new time begins *(the precession and cycles of time, which is now)*.

Always look within for the causation of the effects *(You are responsible for all you create)*.

Man who seeks the light is always seeking to escape the shadows of the night.

Far in the future I see a man as Light-born free from the darkness that fetters the Soul. Before you attain this know many shadows will try to quench your Light which is striving to be free.

The struggle between light and dark is age old yet forever new yet know far in the future darkness will fall. Man has risen and fallen with the waves of consciousness flowing from the great abyss below us to their goal of the Sun.

(think of the empires that subsequently fell or lost in time)

Man has evolved from beast to great. Yet there were others greater than you before you. Just as they fell, so shall you.

Where you live now, barbarians will dwell and forget the ancient wisdom, keeping it hidden from men, In Khem (Egypt) races will rise and fall. This land will be forgotten by men who will have moved to a star-space beyond this. The Soul of man always progresses, not bound by one star, towards the Light.

When future generations move in the knowledge and wisdom shall be forgotten and only a memory of the Gods will survive. Just as I am a God to my knowledge, you will **be Gods of the future because your knowledge is far above theirs.** Man always has access to the Law when he chooses.

Future Ages will see the **revival of wisdom to those who will inherit their place on Earth.** They too will come into wisdom and banish the darkness by Light. However, they must strive through the ages to bring themselves to the freedom of Light.

Then there will be great warfare between Light and the night. When man again has conquered the ocean can fly on wings like the birds. When he has learned to harness the lightning, the time of warfare will begin.

Nations will rise against each other using dark forces to shatter the Earth. Weapons of force shall wipe out half the world's population. Then the Sons of the Morning will come and tell men to stop striving against your brother and come to the light.

Men will stop fighting one another. Then my ancient home will rise from the dark ocean waves. The Brothers of Light will rule the people and darkness will be banished in the **Age of Light which unfolds with the men seeking Light as their goal.**

Their Souls will be the flame of the flame, they will have the wisdom and knowledge in the Great Age for he will approach the Source of all wisdom, the beginning, that is One with the end of all things.

In a time which has not yet been born all will be One and One shall be All. Man will move to a place in the stars. **He will even move from out of this place into another beyond the stars.**

You have listened to me for a long time and I go into the darkness to the Halls. I will dwell in the future when Light shall come again to man. Yet know I am always with you guiding you on the path of light.

Guard these secrets I leave with you and my spirit will guard you through life. Always seek wisdom on the path to light. I will leave you now, be my children in this life and the next. There will be a time when you too will become deathless living from age to age a Light among men.

Guard the entrance to the Halls and the secrets. Do not share with the Barbarians, only with those who seek the Light.

"Blend your Soul with the Great Essence, let your consciousness be one with the Great Light. Call upon me when you need me. **Use my name three times in a row: Chequetet, Arelich, Volmalites.**"

TABLET 13:
THE KEYS OF LIFE AND DEATH

Hear the words to banish the dark and find the light. I have brought you mystery and wisdom from old. Do you not know that all will be opened when you find the Oneness with All?

You will be one with the Masters of Mystery, Conquerors of Death and Masters of Life. You will learn of the flow of Amenti, the blossom of life that shines in the halls. You will reach the Halls in spirit and bring back the wisdom that lives in the Light. Know the gateway to power is secret. The gateway to life is death. Yes, through death but not as you know death, but a death that is life and is fire and is Light.

Do you desire to know this deep hidden secret? Look into your heart where this knowledge is kept, the secret is hidden within you, the source of all life and death.

Listen while I reveal to you the old secret.

Deep in Earth's heart lies the flower, the source of the Spirit that binds all in its form. Understand that Earth is living in its body just as you are in yours. Spirit flows from the **Flower of Life** through Earth and you giving life, renewing the Spirit into the form you take. **Know you are dual form, balanced in polarity while formed in its form.** As you fast approach death, it is only because the balance is shaken. It is only because one pole has been lost.

Know the secret of life in Amenti is the secret of restoring balance of the poles. Everything exists because of the spirit of life in its poles. Can you see how there is the balance of all things in Earth's heart and in that which lives on its face? The source of your spirit is drawn from the Earth, for you are one with the Earth.

When you have learned to hold your own balance, you can then draw on the balance of the Earth. You will exist whilst Earth is existing and will change only in form when Earth changes. You will not taste death but feel as one with the planet, holding your form until all pass away.

Listen so you do not taste the change. Lie for an hour each day with your head pointed to the North (positive) Pole. Hold your consciousness from your chest to the head.

One hour a day spend lying with your head pointed to the South (negative) Pole. Hold your thought from your chest to the feet.

Hold in balance one in each seven *(chakras)* and you will retain the whole of your strength. If you are old, you will rejuvenate and hold off the fingers of Death. Do not neglect to follow this path I have shown you, otherwise you will die when you get to 100.

Whilst you keep your balance you will live on in life. Listen to the wisdom I give you about death. When you have finished your appointed work and desire to pass from this life, pass to the plane where the Suns of the Morning live and have being as Children of Light. Pass without pain or sorrow into the place of eternal light.

First lie at rest with your head eastwards. Fold your hands at the Source of your life at your Solar Plexus. Put your consciousness in the life seat, whirl it and divide it to north and south, sending one in each direction. Release the hold they have on your being and a silver spark will fly from your being back up to return to the light.

It will flame there until desire is created to return to form. That is how great Souls change from one life to another. The Avatar ever passes willing his death as he wills his own life.

Listen and learn of this wisdom, the secret is Master of Time. Remember how the masters are able to recall past lives.

The secret is great yet easy to master, giving you the mastery of time. When death fast approaches know you are a master of Death. Relax your body and do not resist with tension. Put your heart in the flame of your Soul and swiftly seep it to the seat of the triangle (*the base*).

Hold for a moment then move to the goal which is held between your eyebrows. This is the pale where the memory of life must hold sway. Hold the flame here in your brain-seat until death takes your Soul. Then as you pass through the state of Transition, so shall the memories of life.

Then the past will be as one with the present and the memory will all be retained. You will be free of retrogression and the things of the past shall live in today. *(you will not return to an earlier state, you will retain your gifts of your past in the present life. i.e. portalism.)*

Reminder: 15 tablets were written, only 13 scribed as the final two are deemed to contain wisdom too powerful for man to conceive. Or rather, the information will only be revealed to those of pure consciousness when the time is right, as the wisdom cannot fall into the hands of Darkness as it would wreak havoc and power would be wielded dangerously.

The final tablet is supplementary and talks of Atlantis.

THE EMERALD TABLET SUPPLEMENT: ATLANTIS

Listen to the deep hidden wisdom lost to the world since the time of the Dweller, forgotten by man.

Earth is a portal guarded by powers unknown to man. The Dark Lords hide the entrance to the heaven-born land. Know the way to the sphere of Arulu* is guarded by barriers which can only be opened by Light-born man.

Upon Earth I am the holder of the keys to the gates of the Sacred Land. I command by the powers beyond me, to leave the keys to the world of man. Before I leave, I have given you the secrets for escaping the bonds of darkness and how to move into the Light. You must be cleansed of the dark before you may enter the Portals of Light.

That is why I established among you the Mysteries so that the secrets can always be found.

Whilst man may succumb to his shadow the light will always guide you. **The way to the portal is hidden in darkness veiled in symbols.** Future man will deny the mysteries, but the seeker will always find the way.

You must maintain my secrets giving only to those who you have tested so that the pure may not be corrupted and the power of Truth may prevail.

Listen now to the unveiling of the mystery and the symbols. It must become a religion to maintain its essence.

There are two regions between this life and the Great One, travelled by the Souls who have departed Earth. Duat (*Osiris' lower aspect, Thoth's brother*) the home of the powers of illusion, Sekhet Hetspet, the House of Gods (*Osiris' higher aspect guards these gates*). Osiris is the symbol of the guard of the portal who turns away the Souls of unworthy men.

Beyond lies the sphere of the heaven-born powers, Arulu, the land where the Great Ones have passed. I will go there when my work with men is done, back to my Ancient home.

There are seven mansions of the house of the Mighty, three guards the portal of each house from the darkness. There are fifteen ways which lead to Duat, twelve are the houses of the Lords of Illusion, facing four ways, each of them different.

Forty-two great powers who judge the dead who seek this portal. Four are the Sons of Horus, two are the Guards of East and West of Isis, the mother who pleads for her children. Queen of the moon, reflecting the sun.

Ba is the Essence, living forever,

Ka is the Shadow that man knows as life.

Ba will not come until Ka is dead.

These mysteries must be preserved through the ages, they are the keys of life and death.

Learn now the mystery of mysteries, the circle which has no beginning or end, the form of He who is One and in all. Once you apply this, you will travel like I have.

It is clear to the Light born and I will declare it to the Initiated, but the door will be wholly shut against the profane.

THREE is the mystery, come from the great one. Hear this, and the light will dawn for you.

In the primeval *(the earliest time in history)* dwell three unities. Nothing can exist other than these. They are the equilibrium, source of creation: One God, one truth, one point of freedom.

From the three of the balance come three more:
All life, all good, all power.

God has three qualities in his light home:
Infinite Power, Infinite wisdom, Infinite Love.

The Masters hold three powers:
To transmute evil, assist good, use discrimination.

God performs three things inevitably:
Manifest power, wisdom, and love.

There are three powers creating all things:
Divine Love possessed of perfect knowledge
Divine Wisdom knowing all possible means
Divine Power possessed by the joint will of Divine Love and Wisdom

There are three circles (states) of existence:
The Circle of Light where only God dwells and only God can cross it;

The circle of Chaos where all things by nature arise from death;
The Circle of Awareness where all things spring from life

All animate beings have three states of existence:
chaos or death
liberty in humanity
and felicity of Heaven (*intense happiness*)

Three necessities control all things:
beginning in the Great Deep, the circle of chaos, plenitude in Heaven
(*abundance*)

There are three paths of the Soul:
Man, Liberty, Light

There are three hindrances:
lack of endeavour to obtain knowledge
Non-attachment to God
Attachment to evil.

In man, those three are present.
There are three Kings of power within,
there are three chambers of mysteries not yet found in the body of man.

For those who are free of life and in light, know the source of all worlds
shall be open.
Even the Gates of Arulu will not be barred.
Though know if you are not worthy it is better to fall into the fire.
The celestials pass through the pure flame.
At every revolution of the heavens, they bathe in the fountain of Light.

Listen to this mystery. Long before you were a man, I dwelled in
Ancient Atlantis.

I drank the wisdom in the temple poured as a fountain of light from the Dweller.

Give the key to ascend to the presence of Light in the great world.
I stood before the Holy one enthroned in the Flower of Fire.
He was veiled by the lightings of darkness or it would have shattered my Soul.

From the feet of his throne like the diamond, rolled the four rives of flame from his footstool,
rolled through the channels of clouds to the man-world.
The hall was filled with the spirits of heaven, a wonderous starry palace.

Above the sky, like a rainbow of fire and sunlight, the spirits were formed.
They sound the glories of the Holy One.
A voice came from the midst of the fire -
"behold the Glory of the first Cause".

I held that light high above all darkness, reflected in myself.

I attained, as it were, to the God of all Gods, the Spirit-Sun, the Sovereign of Sun spheres.

There is One, even the First, who has no beginning or end
has made all things, governs all. Who is good, just, lights up, who sustains.

From the throne poured a great radiance surrounding and lifting my Soul by its power.

I quickly moved through the space of heaven, I was shown the mystery of mysteries and the secret heart of the Cosmos. I was carried to Arulu and stood before the Lords.

They opened the doorway where I glimpsed the primeval chaos, such horror, I shrank back from the darkness. I saw the need for barriers, the Lords of Arulu.

Only their infinite balance could stand in the way of the inpouring chaos.
It is only them who could guard God's creation.

I then passed around the circle of eight, seeing the Souls who had conquered the darkness and the light in which they now lived.

I longed to take my place, yet I also longed for the path I had chosen when in the Halls of Amenti.

I came down from the halls of Arulu and to the earth space where my body lay. I arose from where I rested and stood before the Dweller. I gave my pledge to renounce my great right until my work on Earth was completed, until the Age of darkness had finished.

You will find the essence of life in these words. Before I return to the Halls of Amenti you will be taught the secrets of Secrets so you too can arise to the Light.

Preserve them, guard them, hide them in symbols, so the ignorant will mock. Make a hard path for the seeker to find. In that way the weak and the wavering will be rejected and the secrets will be hidden and guarded held till the time when the wheel shall be turned. *(Is that time now??)*

I will wait and watch with my spirit in the deep hidden land. Once you have passed all the trials of the outer, call me by the Key that you hold.

Then, as the initiation, I will answer and come from the Halls. I will receive the initiate, give him words of power.

Remember, do not bring me one who lacks wisdom, impure in heart or weak in his purpose. Or I will withdraw from you your power to summon me.

No go forth and call in your brothers so I may impart the wisdom to light your path when I am not here. Go to the chamber beneath my temple, and do not eat for three days.

There I will give you the essence of wisdom so that your power may shine amongst men. I will then give you the secrets so that you too can rise to the heavens, God-men in Truth as in essence you are.

Leave me now whilst I summon those you know exist but do not yet know *(the energies and forms which have not been here in our lifetime before)*.

SUPPLEMENTARY TABLET 14: SECRET OF SECRETS

Those who are waiting to hear the Secret of Secrets which shall give you the power to unfold the God-man and the way to eternal life must gather. I will speak simply of the Unveiled Mysteries; I will not give you any dark sayings. Hear and obey.

First let me speak of the darkness that binds you on Earth. Darkness and light are both of one nature, they only seem different, both came from Source. Darkness is disorder, Light is order. **Darkness transmutes is light of the Light. This is your purpose, to transmute darkness to light.**

Now hear about the mystery of nature and how it relates to Earth where it lives. You are threefold in nature – physical, astral and mental in one.

There are three qualities of each of the natures – nine in all, as above, so below.

The **physical channels:**

Blood which moves in a vorticial motion (whirling like a vortex) reacting through the beating heart;
Magnetism which moves through the nerve paths, carries of energies to all cells and tissues;
Akasa which flows through channels, subtle yet physical, completing the channels.

Each of these three are attuned to the other, each affecting the life of the body. They form the skeletal framework through which the subtle ether flows. In their mastery lies the Secret of Life in the body. It is only relinquished by the will of the adept once his purpose of living is done.

Three natures of the **Astral,** which is the mediator between the above and below. Not of the physical, not of the spiritual, yet can move between the two

(what are the 3 natures??)

Three natures of **Mind**:

Carrier of the **Will of the Great One**
Arbitrator of Cause and effect in your life *(free will)*
(what is the third??)

from these aspects are formed the threefold being, directed from above by the power of four. *(the spiritual self, next)*

Above and beyond this threefold nature is the realm of the Spiritual Self, which has four qualities, shining in each of the planes of existence, but thirteen in one, the mystical number.

Based on the qualities of man are the Brothers, each shall direct the unfoldment of being, each a channel of the Great One. *(depending on your abilities, the gifted will bring through different aspects of the truth ??)*

On the earth plane, man is bound by time and space. Encircling each planet, a wave of vibration, binds his to his plane of unfoldment. Yet he holds the key to his own freedom. When you have released the self from the body, rise to the outermost bounds of your earth plane and speak the word Dor-E-Lil-La.

Then for a time will your Light be lifted and you can be free from the barriers of space for about six hours, where you can see and know those beyond you. You may go to the highest worlds, see your own possible heights of evolvement, know all earthy futures of Soul *(see your future incarnations)*

be free of your body through this power. Here is how:

"Calm your mind, relax your body. Be only aware of being free from the body, and long for it. Repeat the word La-Um-I-L-Gan over and over in your mind. Move with the sound to your place of longing and be free from your body."

Listen as I give the greatest of secrets on how you may enter the Halls of Amenti and stand before the Lords.

"lie down and rest your body and mind, be free of thought. Be pure in mind and in purpose or this will fail. Vision Amenti as I have described in the Tablets and long to be there, picture it all. In your mind say:

Mekut-El-Shab-El   Hale-Sur-ben-El-Zabrut-Zin-Efrim-Quar-El

Relax your mind and body to call your Soul. I will give you the key to Shambbalah, the place where my Brothers live in the darkness – the darkness that is filled with the light of the sun and spirit, for they are the guides when I am complete.

Do as I say to leave your body and pass into the deep hidden space. Stand before the gates and their guardians and command your entrance by saying:

"I am the Light, in me is no darkness. Free am I of the bondage of night, Open the way of the twelve and the one, so I may pass into the realm of wisdom."

when they refuse you as I am sure they will, use these powerful words:

"I am the Light. For me are no barriers. Open, I command, by the secret of Secrets Edom-El-Ahim-Sabbert-Zur Adom."

Then if you have spoken the highest Truth the barriers fall.

I now leave you, down, yet up, to the Halls I shall go. Find your way to me and you will become my brother.

I now finish my writings. They are keys for those who come after, but only for those who seek my wisdom, for only for these am I the key and the Way.

This completes the translation of Doreal's transcript of the Emerald Tablets.

APPENDIX III

THE HERMETICA

For the full versions of the Hermetica:

You are welcome to read The Corpus Hermeticum translated by G.R.S. Mead in his volume of work from 1906, available freely through public domain.

For the full-length modern-day version you may choose to pursue the 1995 translation of the Hermetica by Brian P. Copenhaver.

An audio analysis of the book can be heard here . Spoken by Manly P hall (1901-1990), it is old school theory and explanation. He was a 33° Mason who recorded many wisdom interpretations of ancient texts and wisdom. He is best known for "the Secret teachings of All Ages" in 1928. You can access more recordings here.

Hermetica 101 by Matthew Barnes was based on his two favourite versions of the Hermetica.

"The Hermetica: the lost wisdom of the pharaohs" by Timothy Freke and Peter Gandy. This version brought together subjects and topics which had been scattered through the texts and put them into coherent chapters, each one based on a single topic.

"The way of Hermes" by Clement Salaman et al.

EPILOGUE

As the first half of the year concludes, much has been explored, deciphered and revealed. Your wisdom, coding and insight has expanded beyond anything your mind can conceive.

If you have connected to the resonance of the ancient texts, this is the wake-up call for your own remembrance. To help you understand what life is really about; how we are transitioning from one Age to the New Age.

The new myth of consciousness is starting to be revealed as we open more energy portals throughout the world. Igniting the Ancient Ones, creating the pathways for the cosmic frequencies. Know you have played an important role in this unfolding, simply by witnessing it into being.

May you continue to listen to the Truth of Who You Really Are from deep inside. Continue the Journey through Volume Two of The Alchemists' Awakening, where the magic really comes alive.

Until then, stay in the resonance of Source,

Josephine Sorciere

ABOUT THE AUTHOR

Josephine Sorciere is the sophisticated ringmaster of the new breed of change makers and magicians. Elegantly witchy, and insatiably insightful, she is the Alchemist who births the next generation of Legacy Leaders.

For Josephine liberates you from centuries of cultural conditioning, freedom from the shackles of your troubled mind. Destroying the paradigms of your life and energetically awakening your genius codes, your true authenticity and power. Her beautifully designed yet deeply challenging cauldron will have your mirror of illusions crack from side to side.

As the High Priestess of The Alchemist's Coven, she is also a Cosmic Scribe, Decipher and Encoder of New Consciousness. Far removed from the crowds of the Light Grid, Josephine is the original Dark Disruptor to coin the phrase "Portalism" – creating prodigies through the portals of time. This book has outlined her journey to reach the realisation and ownership of what she brings forward into the world today.

The Quantum Alchemist works her magick through all dimensions, times and realities. Recoding the Akashic records for the Souls who are ready, willing and able to forgo their human shadow and step back into their brilliance. Initiating the return to their true nature, out of their slave-self.

Her innate wisdom is the accumulation of many lifetimes of working powerfully through transformation, continuously evolving through death and rebirth and facilitating the same for others. As a Cosmic Artisan, she recognises the much-needed change in this world can only be driven by the true artists willing to stand by their own power of individualisation, self-expression and authenticity.

Her Activations can be experienced on the Insight Timer app where she stands out from the crowd with cutting edge and formidable experiences in the Goddess series. Many clients have found their way from there to her Coven door and entered through Initiation in her world. They know the depth and speed of transformation is unparalleled and ready to end the seeking of solutions once and for all.

Josephine combines her high-level coaching and encoding of clients with exclusive access to her wisdom teachings through The Alchemist's Coven.

This brings together a collective of Cosmic Beings who are ready to facilitate and usher in the new era, frequencies and beings who are ready to change the face of human existence. The scope of the Coven will be expanding upon publication of this book to assist those hungry to immerse and embody the wisdom themselves.

Discover more at her website.

www.josephinesorciere.com

IN PRAISE OF 2020: THE ALCHEMISTS' AWAKENING
From the original Alchemists Coven members

Being part of the unfolding of The Alchemists Awakening was a journey I will never forget. This book made me dive deep into beliefs that I didn't even know I had and it awakened the ancient knowing that has been with me my whole life but I was too scared to acknowledge. By remembering and decoding the past can we weave the future and Josephine's book starts that. I love the intertwining of astrology with the events happening in the world and it just highlights the synchronous Universe we live in. The Tree of Life section in volume two was the most profound for me and every time I read it, I remember something new. Thank you, Josephine, for this delicious book and it has been an absolute honour to have been part of the journey. *Ali S*

Some of us are born extremely curious and spend time looking at the stars with deep familiarity. We are searching for the truth and dissatisfied with the constructs of this modern world. Something is missing. Something is profoundly missing and deep down inside your intuition and every fiber of your being is telling you this. This book will change your perspective. Josephine's genius unfolds in these pages as she lucidly guides you through the magic of alchemy, synchronicities and ancient wisdoms that will shake you to your core. I speak first hand in having honour to support the birth of this book and experience my awakening – accelerated by the Quantum Alchemist that is Josephine. Read it then read it again. Then dip back into parts when it finally lands. Welcome to the dawn of the new age. Fasten your seatbelts as it's one hell of a ride. *Deena D*

The chapters in this book have stretched my consciousness beyond words! Josephine weaves her truth into the pages, somehow balancing magical revelation, while packing a powerful punch, as she demands whole participation to integrate the deep wisdom. Josephine speaks to the warrior within, never coddling, yet still this book feels like a friend, a companion to the darkness. I would absolutely recommend this life changing work. *Bridget HB*

The Alchemists' awakening by Josephine Sorciere is streaming with ancient wisdom put into words for this day and time. A read for anyone desiring to learn the alchemist way. I highly recommended anyone on the path to God/Goddess to read. *Lacey RF*

Remembering: the integration of spiritual knowledge into your existence on earth. Josephine has one of the most activating and deeply resonate voices of today. 2020 has been the year of awaking, and this modern transcription of the ancient wisdom we all have available in our bones ignites your soul - whispering the knowing that no matter what happens you have the divine power to return to the TRUTH of who you are.

Forget everything you think you know about rising of consciousness and step into your Sovereignty. YOU are the Alchemist! *Angelina C*

Made in the USA
Monee, IL
01 November 2021